Fundamentals of Investment Appraisal

Fundamentals of Investment Appraisal

Steve Lumby and
Chris Jones

THOMSON

™

LEARNING   Australia • Canada • Mexico • Singapore • Spain • United Kingdom • United States

For more information, contact Thomson Learning, High Holborn House, 50-51 Bedford Row, London WC1R 4LR or visit us on the World Wide Web at:
http://www.thomsonlearning.co.uk

British Library Cataloguing-in-Publication Data
A catalogue record for this book is available from the British Library

ISBN: 978-1-86152-607-6

Reprinted 2006 by Thomson Learning

Printed and bound by CPI Antony Rowe, Eastbourne

Contents

To: the Chelsea people – Vanessa and the Gang
the Osset Folk – Janet, Harriet, Emily and Edward
and everyone at Anfield

Preface

It is Enterprise which builds and improves the world's possessions
.... If Enterprise is afoot, wealth accumulates whatever may be
happening to Thrift; and if Enterprise is asleep, Wealth decays,
whatever Thrift may be doing.

John Maynard Keynes, *Treatise on Money*

This book is concerned with corporate investment decision making, in
particular the evaluation of long term capital expenditure decisions. In
many ways this represents a return to the purpose of the first edition of
our related text, *Investment Appraisal and Financial Decisions*, published in
1981. Over the years, that text has expanded to cover a broader area of
financial management and includes topics such as cost of capital, dividend decisions and the management of risk through the use of financial
derivatives. However, we feel that there is a need for a shorter text that
concentrates on investment decisions.

We aim to build an understanding of practice through the development
of theory. Most of the theoretical approaches covered are relatively non-
problematical, such as the theoretical strength of net present value as a
decision criterion. However, the practical applications of techniques often
cause significant difficulties and it is necessary to keep in mind that some
of the assumptions underlying the theory may sometimes be questioned. In
particular, the most fundamental assumption of all – that of maximization
of shareholder wealth as the prime objective of management – may well be
compromised by the personal objectives of managers themselves.

The book has been written to provide a comprehensive introduction to
the subject of investment decision making that is appropriate for students at
an introductory level of either academic and professional study. It will be
particularly appropriate for MBA students.

We have omitted any significant coverage of issues such as capital structure, dividend policy and financial derivatives such as options. We have
also omitted detailed coverage of some aspects of risk management but we
have included a chapter that describes a number of approaches to risk
along with an appendix that provides some coverage of the mathematics
involved.

The authors of the book have experience of teaching financial management at a wide range of institutions (London School of Economics, Leeds Polytechnic, University of Sheffield, Sheffield Hallam University, and private sector professional centres, amongst others) and to a wide range of students both academic (HND, BA, BSc in business studies, accounting and finance, and also MBA of full time, part time and executive types) and professional (ACCA, ICAEW, CIMA)

We have probably learned more from these experiences than our students and we have certainly found it necessary to look for new ways to present this fascinating subject so that it is made more real for them. The introduction contains more detailed coverage of our approach along with an explanation of the book's structure.

As with *Investment Appraisal and Financial Decisions*, our more comprehensive text, there are both 'quickie' and full scale, exam type questions at the end of each chapter, along with a brief summary of what has been covered. The reading lists are designed to be reasonably accessible and, in general, articles based on advanced mathematical applications have been omitted. The 'quickie' questions are designed to emphasize the more significant areas of each chapter and also provide an opportunity to test understanding and give some feedback on that (answers to 'quickie' questions are in the back of the book). The exam style questions have been selected to cover the most important areas of each chapter and provide practice for both the real world and examinations. These questions have been written by the authors or taken from the examinations of professional bodies and we are very grateful for the permission of those bodies to use their questions. Tutors can obtain a solutions manual for these questions from the publisher.

This book expresses a normative theory of investment decision making. It is about developing a general understanding of the way investment decisions are made and, perhaps, how these processes could be improved. Thus, whilst the book may well provide solutions to practical problems, this is not its primary objective. The authors accept no responsibility for losses incurred as the result of applying the theories discussed to real world decisions! So far as possible we have adopted a descriptive and graphical approach in this book. We believe that this makes the material accessible to far more readers and also that the adoption of a mathematically based approach can often obscure the reality and significance of important conclusions. We believe that the level of understanding provided by this book is a prerequisite for the use of more sophisticated mathematical approaches and that these should really be covered in a more advanced course.

Financial management is a fascinating and rewarding area for study. We hope that you enjoy the course for which you use this book and that it will encourage you to go further in your studies of this subject

Finally we would like to express our thanks to the people at Thomson including Alan Nelson, Jennifer Pegg, Jenny Clapham and Penny Grose.

Introduction

The nature of investment decisions

An overview

This book covers a particular area of managerial economics: the theory of investment decision making by business corporations. It is concerned with how management within companies[1] *should* make[2] investment decisions,[3] and so it can be said to adopt a normative approach because it sets out to establish a standard, or norm. But such a theory cannot hope to succeed in its task if it is developed in isolation from what actually does happen in practice, and so we shall also examine how investment decisions *are* made, in order to guide and enrich the development of our normative approach.

The value base

Investment decisions by companies are no different in their fundamental aspects from other decisions of a non-financial nature, be they in industry or commerce (such as marketing decisions) or elsewhere (such as decisions to transfer footballers, or even international diplomacy decisions). In essence, *all* decisions are based on the concept of the comparison of alternatives, and it is in this sense that the theory of investment decisions really has its roots in valuation theory, because all the alternatives in any decision-making situation have to be valued in order to be compared. Therefore, although we can say that all types of decisions involve the same fundamental process, each is given its own unique characteristics by the valuation base which it employs.

The investment decision theory developed in this book is founded on the valuation bases that come from capitalism[4] and the idea of the free market economy. It is important that this is specified from the outset, as a different valuation base would be likely to produce a different overall theory of investment decisions. However, many parts of our financial theory will be applicable to other types of economic organization, and you may wish to consider and reflect upon the implications of our theory for more social value bases, such as those which might be appropriate to the public sector and, in particular state-owned public enterprises. This is particularly interesting since the past fifteen years has seen an apparent change in value bases in those particular areas and a transfer of many public sector enterprises into the private sector.

The 'model' approach and the structure of the text

We have stuctured this text in four sections:

1. Introduction to the context of financial decisions – Introduction and Chapters 1 and 2.
2. The capital investment decision – Chapters 3 to 8.
3. The impact of uncertainty on the capital investment decision – Chapters 9 and 10.
4. Investment decisions in an international context – Chapter 11.

In the course of our development of a normative approach to financial decisions, a considerable number of abstractions from and simplifications of the 'real world' will be made, in order to distil the difficulties and focus attention on areas of major importance.

Adopting this type of a 'modelling' approach is normal in the study of economics and related areas. However it brings with it a danger that it is seen as fully describing a 'real' world and providing simple solutions to real world problems. It is important to remember that we are developing a normative theory and are therefore attempting to give advice on how financial decisions *should* be taken. In general we will work with simplified models and if the theory were to be followed in practice, without recognising the full range of possible complicating factors the quality of financial decisions made in business might deteriorate rather than improve.

The difficulties caused by taxation, inflation and capital scarcity will all be taken into account, as will the concept of risk and the fact that the future is uncertain.[5] All these real world complexities will be added layer by layer to the simplified model with which we start. Even though that model might be a poor reflection of the real world, it provides a logically sound framework upon which to build.

A warning

As a final point, the reader should be constantly aware that the theory of investment decisions which is presented here is neither in a state of general detailed agreement, nor does it yet provide complete solutions to many of the important problems of financial decision making. In order to reflect this state of affairs, we shall examine the causes and evidence of these controversies and point out the irrationalities, ambiguities and inconsistencies that necessarily accompany the development of any theory that aspires to real world application.

The decision process

In order to examine the decision process and to answer the question: 'How do we make a decision?', we have first to discuss the circumstances in which a decision needs to be made. We can specify two necessary conditions for a decision situation: the existence of alternatives and the existence of an objective or goal.

The first necessary condition

The existence of alternatives is necessary because, if there are no alternatives from which to choose, then there is no need for a decision. This condition can be specified further in that not only must alternatives exist, but they must be seen to exist by the potential decision maker. There are two points of interest here.

First, notice that we talk of a decision *situation* and of a *potential* decision maker. This is because the mere existence of perceived alternatives does not necessarily mean that a decision will be made. For instance, the potential decision maker may well procrastinate, and therefore the passage of time takes him (or her) out of a decision situation and into a situation where there is only one possible course of action and no alternatives are available. (Death is the ultimate example of the passage of time removing a decision situation from an individual.)

The second point of interest is that we are *not* specifying that all possible alternatives are perceived, if they were, we could call this an optimal decision situation. We are, rather, examining how decisions are made, given that a particular decision situation exists. Whether the decision is truely optimal or non-optimal is of no concern at present.

The second necessary condition

The second necessary condition for a decision situation arises from the fact that the actual process of 'making a decision' is liable to cause the decision maker to expend both time and effort. Rationally he will be unwilling to do so unless he expects that some of the perceived alternatives will be preferred to others in relation to attaining the desired objective. Thus the existence of an objective is the second necessary condition: without it, there will be no purpose in making a decision.[6]

Valuation of alternatives

Together, these two necessary conditions provide the rationale for making decisions: if the decision maker does not perceive alternatives, or sees no reason to choose between the alternatives if they are perceived, then no decision will be made (excect one of a totally arbitrary kind, as in note 6). But once these conditions do exist, a decision cannot actually be made until values are placed upon the alternatives. In fact, we can assert that the only reason why any alternative course of action is ever evaluated is in order to make a decision about it; therefore, the valuation method used must be related to the objective involved in making the decision and the way in which that objective is expressed.

For example, if our objective were to drive from A to B in the shortest possible time, then we should value the alternative routes from A to B by a common value criterion which was related to our objective of time, and choose whichever route took the shortest time. Suppose there were three alternative routes and one we valued by time, one by distance and one by scenic beauty. We obviously could not make a decision because the alternatives have different measures or yardsticks of value and so cannot be compared. Alternatively, if all three routes were measured in terms of scenic beauty, we should again be unable to make a decision, even though we could compare the routes – because the basis of the comparison is not the one which gives the rationale for the decision: the value base of the objective, which in this example is 'time'.[7]

Therefore, any decision-making process consists of these three components: a series of perceived alternatives, an expectation that these alternatives are not all equally desirable in terms of attaining an objective held by the decision maker, and a common value base related to the decision objective. So it is with all financial decisions made in business.

Investment decision making

This book focuses attention on only two of the three components that we have identified in the decision process and examines how they relate to the making of investment decisions: the expectation that the perceived alternatives are not all equally desirable in terms of attaining a specific objective, and the common value base that is related to this objective and is used to compare the alternatives.

The remaining component of the decision process is the series of perceived alternatives. We shall not be examining it in the main body of the text as it is primarily a condition for the decision *situation*, and we are concentrating on the decision-making process, assuming that the decision situation already exists. However, this omission does not mean that the 'search process' (as it is called) for alternatives is unimportant. It is in fact extremely important. If this search process is not efficient in seeking out alternatives, then there is a grave danger that the decision itself will not be optimal because the 'most preferred' alternative may go unperceived.

The decision objective

Turning to the two decision process components that we shall examine in detail, we immediately become involved in value judgements, because the objective we use for investment decision making, and the consequent value base, will determine the decision reached as to which alternative is selected. Therefore, what objective are we going to use and what valuation base are we going to set up for our theory of financial decisions?

We stated earlier that the fundamental value judgement upon which our approach is based is capitalism. The approach is thus most appropriate for largely unregulated, competitive economies. In such economies, it is reasonable to assume that companies exist for one overriding purpose: in order to benefit their owners.[8] Whilst companies provide income for their employees and the wider local community, supply the needs of a particular market, and provide other benefits such as technological advance, the fact remains that the fundamental rationale for their existence must be to bring benefit to their owners.

This rationale for existence undoubtedly holds true for the great majority of privately owned[9] companies (and also, to some extent, for state-owned industries although their rationale for existence can be more complex[10]). Therefore, management's objective in making investment decisions *should be* to further the very reason for the company's existence, of benefiting the owners, i.e., the shareholders. We shall see that there might be other managerial objectives but, in essence, we will treat those as deviating from what they should be (this is consistent with the idea of adopting a normative approach) So if decision objective is to benefit the owners, what is the value base to be used for the comparison of alternatives?

To answer this question, we have to examine the decision objective more closely. It is obvious from what we have already said that not only should company managements make financial decisions so as to benefit the shareholders but they should also strive to maximize that benefit, otherwise shareholders will be interested in replacing them with a set of decision makers who will do this. Therefore, what is meant by the term 'maximizing owners' or shareholders' benefit'?

Maximizing shareholder wealth

We are going to assume that maximizing benefit means maximizing wealth. Although there is nothing surprising about this, we have to be careful here because we are going to assume that maximizing the increase in the owners' wealth is the *only* way in which management decisions can benefit owners.

This is a simplification of the real world, because it is quite possible for shareholders to gain benefit from a company other than by increases in wealth. For example, shareholders of a company such as Body Shop may gain benefit from ownership in terms of pride in the fact that the company has a proactive stance towards protecting the environment and this is reflected in broader terms by the existence of various investment vehicles such as *ethical* unit trusts. However, this is a comparatively minor point and we shall proceed on the relatively sound assumption that increase in wealth is the main, if not the sole source of benefit from company ownership.

What about firms selling military arms to countries whose policies are repugnant, or firms causing pollution to land, air or water resources? Do these types of activity enter into consideration of our decision objective? On the basis of our underlying assumption about the nature of the economy, our answer must be that they should not, because if these activities were thought to be truly undesirable, governments would legislate to constrain companies' decision-choice alternatives so as to exclude them (as in many cases they do). Company decision makers should only need to perceive and analyse the decision alternatives in terms of maximizing the owners' wealth. From this viewpoint we can treat financial decisions as not being anything to do with morality. Morality, the law and other things might act as constraints on what a company does but they are entirely different issues and are generally assessed using different criteria.

In market economies, we can develop a theory of financial decisions for privately owned firms in this way because of the workings of the market system for company capital. Ordinary share capital, the substance of ownership, is normally provided through supply and demand markets (e.g., stock exchanges), which means that potential shareholders can buy shares in companies that they expect will provide them with the greatest possible increase in wealth (i.e., shareholders have to make financial decisions in much the same way as management, choosing between alternative ownership opportunities), and existing shareholders can sell their shares if they see other companies providing greater increases to their owners' wealth than they are receiving. (An important concept here, and one we have yet to deal with, is that the future is uncertain and so any decision amongst alternatives usually has a risk attached to it: the risk that the alternative chosen may not turn out as expected. Some alternatives are riskier than others and so shareholders will really want to own companies that they expect will give them the greatest possible increase in wealth, for a given level of risk. This concept we shall consider much more fully later.)

Therefore, if a company were to make its decisions on bases other than that of maximizing shareholder wealth, the whole rationale for the company's existence – so far as shareholders are concerned – would be in doubt and they would be likely to take their investment funds elsewhere. In the extreme case, company law provides the opportunity for shareholders to replace a company's decision makers if enough of them believe that decisions are not being taken in their best interests.

Defining wealth

However, we still cannot determine the value base for financial decision making until we have defined 'wealth', because the purpose of the value base is to act as a common denominator with which to make the alternative courses of action directly comparable and to see which one leads furthest towards the decision objective. As the objective of financial decisions is assumed to be to 'maximize the increase in owners' wealth', let us define 'wealth' and so determine the value base.

Wealth can be defined as the capacity to consume or, to put it in more straightforward terms, money, cash, or other assets.[11] Thus the objective of management becomes the maximization of shareholders' purchasing power, which can be achieved by maximizing the amount of cash paid out to shareholders in the form of dividends. But which dividends should a company's management try to maximize: this year's, next year's or what?

The point here is that it would be a relatively easy task for a company to maximize a single year's dividend, simply by selling up all the assets and paying a final liquidation dividend! (We are ignoring the niceties of company law here, but the point still remains.) Obviously this is not what is meant by our decision objective of maximizing dividends, and the trouble arises through the omission of the time dimension. When fully defined, including the time dimension, the objective of a company's financial decision makers becomes the maximizing of the *flow* of dividends to shareholders *over or through time*. It is beyond the scope of this book to discuss the dividend decisions taken by companies and we will work on the assumption that the generation of cash flows by companies, dividend payments over time and shareholder wealth all amount to the same thing.

The role of accounting profit

There are two points of fundamental importance that arise from the development of this decision objective. First, the word 'profit' has not been mentioned and the emphasis has been laid on wealth defined as cash. Second, the introduction of time means that decisions must be analysed not only in terms of immediate cash gains and losses, but also in terms of *future* gains and losses.

These two points are interlinked. Profit, when used in a business sense, is a concept developed by financial accountants in order to assist them with their auditing and reporting functions, performed on behalf of shareholders.

Accounting has developed over hundreds of years from a base called *stewardship*. It was really designed to provide evidence that people holding responsibility for other people's assets could account for them (i.e. demonstrate where the resources went). In many ways this is still lies at the heart of financial accounting. Although financial reports are produced each year and contain the figure *profit* it should not be interpreted as being the same thing as the increase in the value of the company during the year. Annual reports are produced using a number of conventions and rules, the most important of which is that the figures are expressed in terms of historic cost (with one or two possible exceptions). There is also a certain amount of judgement exercised in the production of the statement and it has been said that profit is the invention rather than the discovery of the accountant . The Accounting Standards Board (the body that defines many of the rules used by accountants) has expressed the view that accounting should not be seen as being concerned with value or worth. As we will see, wealth, worth and value are all concepts related to the future (and cash flows in the future) but profit is related to the past.

Investment decisions are basically economic or resource allocation decisions. Management have to decide whether they should allocate the firm's scarce resources (land, labour, machinery, etc.) to a particular project. The economic 'unit of account' is cash, not accounting profit, because it is cash which gives power to command resources (i.e. resources are purchased with cash, not profit). Thus to use the accounting profit concept in financial decision making would be to use an entirely inappropriate concept – a concept specially developed for reporting the outcome of decisions and not developed for helping to take the actual decision itself.

However, we cannot discard the accounting profit concept completely. To do so would be rather like a sports team whose policy is that they do not mind whether they win or lose, so long as in playing they give maximum entertainment to their supporters. This is fine, and it is probably the correct attitude; but generally speaking it is on winning and losing that the success of the team is ultimately judged and therefore that part of the game cannot be ignored. So it is with accounting profit. The company's financial decision makers should have as their major concern the maximization of the flow of cash through time to the shareholders, but they should always do so with an eye to reported profit. Profitability, as expressed in annual published accounts, forms a major criterion by which shareholders and prospective shareholders judge a company's success and, as we shall see later, it is important that people do form correct judgements about a company's performance.

A further reason why the effects of financial decisions on reported profits cannot be completely ignored is provided by the fact that the level of retained profit, in company law, can form a very substantial maximum barrier to an annual dividend payment. Thus a company that wishes to maximize its dividend flow must ensure that its dividend payout intentions are legally within the confines of company law.

Therefore, with the exception of these two provisos, we can say that the financial decision theory developed here is built on an analytical framework that is largely devoid of the accounting profit concept, although it would be correct to assume that, in the longer run, good company cash flows will result in good reported profits.

The time dimension

Turning to the second point of importance in our decision objective, the introduction of the time dimension, we have already noted that the arbitrary time segmentation of a continuous flow process has been the cause of major problems for the accounting profit concept, but to see the true significance of the introduction of this factor we have to return to our discussion on value.

An asset (such as a machine or a share in a company) is valued on the basis of the gains, or losses, that the owner receives. Furthermore, these gains and losses do not refer to just a single time period, but to the whole period of future time for which the asset will exist. (This concept is sometimes referred to as the asset's earning power.)

Let us consider an asset of company ownership: an ordinary share. Ordinary shares are traded (i.e., bought and sold) in supply and demand markets and so its market valuation represents an equilibrium value, a value at which demand for the share by people who wish to buy it equates with the supply of the share by people who wish to sell it. But what process actually gives a share its equilibrium price, what makes prospective purchasers wish to buy it at that price and what makes prospective sellers willing to sell it at that price? Let us examine the prospective purchaser's reasons.

Suppose an ordinary share of XYZ plc has a stock market price of 150p.[12] A prospective owner of that share would only be willing to buy it if he thought it was worth at least 150p. In other words, he would expect that the gains to be received from ownership would have a value of 150p or more.

These gains of ownership consist of two elements: the stream of dividends received for as long as he owns the share, and the selling price received when the share is sold (and so ownership relinquished) at some future point in time. However, it is important to note that this future selling price of the XYZ share is itself based on the value the succeeding owner puts on the benefits that he in turn expects to receive from ownership – the dividend flow received and the selling price that he will receive upon selling the share at some future point in time. So the process goes on *ad infinitum*. Therefore, although there are two benefits of ownership, the dividends received and the future selling price, this latter benefit is itself determined by the flow of dividends expected to be generated by the share subsequent to its sale. (We can treat the cash flow received if the company were to be wound up or *liquidated* as a final dividend.)

Given this argument, our theory will assume that shares derive their (equilibrium) stock market price on the basis of the sum of the dividend flow that they will produce through time. (As the future is uncertain, it is more correct to talk of valuation based on the *expected* dividend flow, but we shall return to this later.) Thus the greater the future dividend flow, the more highly are the shares valued. Therefore if our financial decision makers are taking decisions so as to maximize dividend flow through time, then via the direct link between dividend flow and a share's market price, this action will result in the *maximization of the market value of the company's shares*. It is this that we shall take as being the operational objective of financial management decision making.[13]

The objective hierarchy

So let us summarize our assumed hierarchy of decision objectives:

1. Decisions are taken by companies so as to maximize owners' wealth.
2. Owners' wealth can be maximized through maximizing owners' purchasing power.
3. Purchasing power can be maximized through maximizing the amount of cash the company pays out to shareholders in the form of dividends.
4. With the introduction of the time dimension the objective becomes the maximizing of the value of the dividend flow through time to the shareholders.
5. The maximization of the value of the dividend flow through time maximizes the stock market's valuation of the company's ordinary share capital.

However, it is important to realize that although it is this 'fifth level' of objective we shall use in developing the theory of financial decision making, it is really only a surrogate objective for the fundamental, underlying objective of maximizing shareholders' wealth.

A fundamental assumption

As a final point, let us state the assumptions about the shareholder which have been implied in the analysis. It was earlier argued that the maximization of shareholders' wealth had to be the fundamental decision objective, because of the nature of the capital markets. However, the validity of this assertion depends entirely upon the assumption that shareholders perceive wealth in the way we have postulated and that in this perception they are rational. In essence this means that we have assumed that shareholders see wealth as the receipt of cash flows through time and that they will always prefer a greater to lesser cash flow. These appear reasonably safe assumptions, but we shall consider situations where they may not hold, when we look later at dividend policies.

Technology and investment decision making

The past fifteen years have seen what amounts to a technological revolution. This has been described as an information revolution on a par with the industrial revolution of the 18th and 19th centuries. It is now most unlikely that decision makers will not have access to computer facilities and the power of the typical desk top machine is now such that sophisticated software can be used to aid their decisions. In most cases the type of software used will be based on spreadsheets such as Microsoft Excel or Lotus 123 and you are encouraged to use the software available to you when answering the problems set throughout the text. However, it is important that you understand the underlying principles so it is not advisable to rely solely on the financial functions embedded in the software. It is also worth mentioning that some of the functions can be somewhat problematical as we will see.

Summary

- The decision process consists of three elements:

    — a series of perceived alternatives;

    — an expectation that these alternatives are not all equally desirable in terms of attaining an objective held by the decision maker;

    — a common value base, related to the objective, by which the alternatives may be compared.

- As far as financial management is concerned, it is assumed that the objective of investment decision making is the maximization of shareholder wealth. This is normally translated to mean maximizing the current worth of the company's shares.

- Given that shareholder wealth is seen in terms of an ability to consume goods and services and that it is cash which provides consumption power, so share value can be maximized by maximizing the sum of the expected stream of dividends through time generated by the share.

- Accounting profit is essentially an inappropriate concept within the context of financial management decision making because it is a *reporting* device, not a decision-making device. Finance decisions are economic or resource allocation decisions and the economic unit of account is cash; hence decisions are evaluated in terms of their cash flow impact. However, the reported profit impact of financial decisions remains an important consideration in terms of the correct communication of management's actions to shareholders and others.

Notes

1. Be these either large stock exchange quoted companies such as ICI or Unilever, or small unquoted companies such as a local printing company or car rental company.

2. The terms decision 'making' and decision 'taking' can be used synonymously. However, the term decision 'making' will be used in this book because of its more positive emphasis on deliberate creative action.

3. We will carefully define just what investment decisions are, but for now this can be taken as meaning such things as a decision to invest in a new machine.

4. There are many variants of capitalism (which in itself is just one type of economic system; for example, alternatives could include socialist, feudal and primitive communal economies) but its two general features are the private ownership of property and the allocation of the economy's resources (land, labour and machinery) through a supply and demand price mechanism.

5. Indeed, we shall also occasionally allude to the psychological processes behind firms' financial decisions, where conflicts of interest arise.

6. In a way, in specifying this second necessary condition, we are ignoring the situation where a decision *has* to be made, even though this second condition does not exist. For instance, if you are out for a walk with no particular destination in mind and you come to a crossroads, a decision *has* to be taken on what direction to go, even though the second necessary condition is really unfulfilled. Such situations are of little interest as far as the decision *process* is concerned; we could call them indifference decisions.

7. For the present, we shall ignore the possibility of multiple objectives, although we shall touch upon it later. However we may observe that where multiple objectives exist in real life, one objective is often regarded (either implicitly or explicitly) as being of overriding importance, with the other objectives acting as constraining factors or considerations.

8. In abstract terms we can define a company as a collection of assets. The owners of the company have therefore pooled their funds to assemble such a collection and are logically only likely to do so in order to bring benefit (either directly or indirectly) to themselves.

9. The term 'privately owned companies' can be a source of confusion. It refers to all companies which are owned by individuals, either singly or collectively, whether or not they are 'publicly quoted' (plc) on a stock exchange or otherwise. Thus both public and private companies (in financial nomenclature) are privately owned companies.

10. See, for instance, Ivy Papps, *Government and Enterprise*, Hobart Paper No. 61, Institute of Economic Affairs, 1975.

11. We shall be ignoring the effects of inflation until later.

12. This is obviously a simplification, as in practice each share has two equilibrium prices, a buying price and a selling price. The former will be the higher of the two, and the difference constitutes the market maker's 'turn'. However, for simplicity, we will ignore this complication and use a 'middle' value.

13. Of course, if the company's shares are not quoted on a stock exchange, then the objective simply reduces to the maximization of the value of the company's shares. This, however, still leaves the problem of how the shares are to be valued. In fact they should be valued on exactly the same basis as quoted shares: the future expected dividend flow. It is one of the great advantages of a stock market quotation that this value is 'automatically' and continuously provided for use both by management and by investors.

Quickie questions

1. What is the search process?
2. What is the fundamental objective of investment decision making?
3. Why is accounting profit an inappropriate criterion for investment decision making?
4. How are shares valued?

1 Corporate objectives, management objectives and corporate governance

Wealth maximization and the company

In the introduction we pointed out that we will assume, for the purposes of analysis and the development of our normative theory of financial decisions, that maximization of shareholder wealth is the objective of financial decisions.

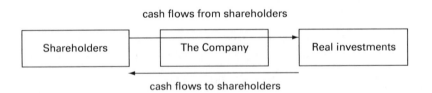

If we accept this assumption, the company becomes a transparent vehicle for the transmission of resources from the shareholder into investments (investment) and back to the shareholder (return). This will generally take the form of cash. In a sense, the company only exists to allow for these cash flows and it is necessary because the individual shareholder is not otherwise in the position to make the (relatively small) investment in, say, a factory that they might wish to. However, the reality of the situation is somewhat different. The company is not a neutral vehicle because it contains decision makers (managers) who have their own interests to look after as well as those of the shareholders. In the situation where the shareholders are not the same people as the managers, this is likely to result in conflicts of interests and may well mean that decisions are not made in order to maximize shareholder wealth.

Maximizing versus Satisficing

A company's management (or, more strictly speaking, its directors) are in what is termed a 'principal–agent' relationship with the shareholders. The shareholders are the principals – the owners of the company's assets – and the managers are employed as their agents to manage those assets on their behalf.

The major problem facing any principal (owner) is that of control: how to control the agent (manager) to ensure that the agent always acts in the best interests of the principal. The problem arises out of the fact that there may well be a conflict between the personal objectives of the agents and the objectives that their principal wishes them to pursue.

Shareholders will want their managers to take decisions so as to maximize the worth of the company's shares. However, management will have their own personal objectives. These objectives will be mainly concerned with three things: their pay, their perks (non-monetary rewards such as holiday entitlements, working conditions, company cars, etc.) and their job security.[1] The past few years have provided many examples of company bosses who appear to have paid themselves much more than would seem to be necessary especially in the area of privatized utilities. Remember that every million pounds taken out of the company by its managers is a million pounds less for its shareholders, no matter how it is presented (salary, bonus, share options etc.) However, top managers might argue that, like footballers, they are vital for the success of the company and that in the same way that it is worth Manchester United paying Roy Keane over £50 000 a week, it is worth paying top performing managers large sums to obtain their services.

In such circumstances, it is sometimes argued that managers will become shareholder wealth satisficers rather than maximizers. This implies that managers will do just enough to keep shareholders reasonably satisfied in terms of increasing their wealth and, at the same time, put their remaining efforts into the pursuit of their own personal objectives.

Thus a satisficing management may be thought more likely to pursue a specific target which – if achieved – would be felt to be sufficient to keep shareholders satisfied, rather to pursue a more general target of maximization. For example, management might pursue a target of increasing the value of the company's shares by, say, 10% per year, rather than having as their objective trying to achieve the maximum possible annual growth rate in the share price.

In addition, satisficing behaviour implies that the management team will not organize the search process of alternative courses of action so as to seek out the very best, maximizing course of action. Instead, they will terminate the search process as soon as a satisfactory (but not necessarily the best) course of action is identified.

Agency theory postulates that principals respond to the problem they face in two ways. First, they develop monitoring devices to try to ensure that managers are attempting to maximize the company's share price. Second, they create incentive schemes for management so that it is in the manager's own best interest to pursue share price maximization. In practice it is very difficult to devise either monitoring or incentive schemes that can be relied upon to produce the required results for shareholders.

Ownership and control

There are many ways in which the actions of a company's managers are monitored and controlled so as to try and ensure that they act in their shareholders' best interests rather than their own.

However, before we briefly examine these, it is important to make one clarifying observation. This is that a principal–agent problem only really arises when there is a significant divorce between ownership and control.

For example, in an owner-managed business there is no such problem whatsoever, as the owners are the managers, and so the objectives of one group are also the objectives of the other. If we move on to a larger, family-owned business, where the owners are not necessarily the managers, there is still likely to be very little problem. This is because, in these circumstances, the owners will still be able to exercise close personal control over their managers. Even though the shareholders may not be the managers, the shareholders in such a company are likely to know who the senior managers are, and are likely to be able to monitor their actions directly.

It is only when a company's development reaches the point where there is a clear-cut division between owners and managers, when the company is too large and the owners are too widespread for them to be able to exercise effective personal control, that the principal–agent problem of control starts to manifest itself. For many companies, this point is reached when they decide to stop being a private company and instead become a public company, quoted on a stock exchange.

For the vast majority of private companies – especially, small private companies – the principal–agent problem does not exist in any meaningful sense. Thus, in discussing the problem, we must view it in relation to the larger company and, in particular, to the stock exchange quoted company.

Regulation of the relationship between directors and shareholders

The main vehicles for the regulation of the actions of directors are as follows:

1. The fiduciary responsibility that is imposed on directors by company law.
2. The legal requirement for an annual independent external audit of the company.
3. The 'listing rules' of the Stock Exchange.
4. Stock Exchange 'Principles of Good Governance and Code of Best Practice' – The Combined Code
5. Stock Exchange and Companies Act regulations on directors' transactions.
6. The 'City Code' on Take-Overs and Mergers.

Fiduciary responsibilities

A fiduciary responsibility arises whenever assets (either tangible or intangible) are entrusted by one party to the care of another party. Thus it can be said that fiduciary responsibilities arise directly out of principal–agent relationships.

In essence, the directors of companies have a fiduciary responsibility to their shareholders to act in their best interests. Furthermore, they must be prepared to demonstrate that they have discharged their responsibilities correctly, if challenged to do so in the law courts.

The scope of these responsibilities is not clear-cut; nor are the responsibilities unchanging. However, they are underpinned by three basic principles which have the force of law behind them:[2]

1. Directors should not place themselves in a position where their own personal interests conflict with the interests of shareholders.
2. They should not profit from their position at the expense of shareholders.
3. They cannot use information that is obtained in confidence from the company for their own benefit, or for the benefit of any other persons except the shareholders.

Annual reports and independent external audit

Another important element in the array of devices set up to monitor and control the actions of boards of directors is the annual audit requirement.

The Companies Act 1985 requires all limited companies to have an annual audit of their financial affairs, conducted by independent, external auditors. The prime purpose of this audit is to report to the shareholders on the conduct of the management's stewardship of the company's assets.

As such, this independent external audit can be seen as the bedrock control mechanism of the principal–agent relationship between shareholders and their managers. Indeed, it is interesting to note that whilst such an audit is now a legal requirement, independent external audits existed long before they were enforced by law. The audit not only certifies the annual report of the company but also examines the company's financial systems to ensure that proper control is being exercised.

However, as mentioned earlier, the financial statements produced by companies are based on a system known as historic cost accounting which is not really designed to disclose the economic performance of the company. A good example of this is the research carried out by companies. The standard treatment for research (and much development work) is to treat it as an expense rather than an investment. This has the effect of reducing the reported profits of the company (despite the fact that it may contribute significantly to cash flows in the future). It has been suggested that this might have the effect of reducing the amount of R&D undertaken, particularly when the bonuses of managers are linked to company profits.

Stock Exchange rules

The London Stock Exchange is authorized by the 1986 Financial Service Act to regulate the UK Stock Exchange, in line with a series of European Community directives. These regulations are contained in what is referred to as the 'Yellow Book'.

The Yellow Book rules stipulate that the directors of a quoted company have both an individual and collective responsibility to ensure that the company complies with obligations under the regulations.

For purposes of the current discussion, the principal obligation of directors imposed by the Yellow Book rules is to release price-sensitive information to the market as a whole, so as to avoid a 'false market' in the valuation of a company's securities.

The implications of this in terms of the principal–agent problem is fairly obvious. If directors should fail to disclose information to the stock market, such that the share price is kept artificially high or low, then this could prompt action by the shareholders which would be damaging to their wealth. Shareholders might find themselves buying shares which, in reality, were over-valued; or they might sell their shares when they were under-valued.

Stock Exchange 'Codes of Best Practice'

Over recent years concern has been expressed about a number of aspects of corporate governance including:

1. an increasing use of 'creative accounting';
2. a number of high profile business failures;
3. high levels of pay for directors, especially in privatized utilities;
4. short termism (i.e. actions by managers driven by personal, short term objectives such as bonuses rather than long term shareholder value)

Concerns about creative accounting (i.e. manipulating financial statements so that they look the way that managers want them to look) have been with us for decades and were a major reason for the development of the system of accounting standards (rules) we have today. These concerns were further emphasized by Griffiths who published a book called *Creative Accounting* which exposed a number of ploys used by accountants to massage financial statements.

A number of well publicized and spectacular corporate bankruptcies in the late 1980s and early 1990s – most notable amongst which were those of Maxwell Communication Corporation and Polly Peck – led to more general concern about the standard and quality of the stewardship function of directors of large public companies.

Numerous cases were highlighted in the financial press and in the law courts concerning ill-advised decisions on acquisitions and financing; instances of massive corporate fraud; excessive increases in directors' remuneration (particularly when corporate performance was poor); and 'one-way' incentive schemes which resulted in large financial rewards for directors when things went right, but had no adverse impact on remuneration if things went wrong.

All of these things were taken very seriously by the stock exchange and led to the development of a series of 'Codes of Best Practice'.

In June 1998, the London Stock Exchange published its *Principles of Good Governance and Code of Best Practice* – more generally known as *The Combined Code* – which followed work by the Cadbury, Greenbury and Hampel committees. This sets out general principles of good governance which are as follows:

- There should be an effective board.
- There should be a chairman and a separate CEO (chief executive officer).
- There should be non-executive directors such that the board cannot be dominated by a small group.
- Good quality information should be produced on a timely basis.
- There should be a formal transparent procedure for board appointments.
- Directors should be required to submit themselves for re-election at least once every three years.
- Remuneration should be adequate to attract and retain directors but should avoid excessive payments. Also, part of the remuneration should be linked to performance.
- There should be a formal and transparent procedure for setting remuneration packages.
- The level of and policy relating to remuneration should be disclosed in the annual report.
- The board should enter into dialogue with institutional investors where practicable.
- The board should encourage participation at the AGM.
- Apart from the traditional reporting and financial control requirements, the board should ensure that there is an appropriate relationship with the company's auditors.

It also requires institutional investors to take an active role in assessing the performance of directors and at the AGM. The Code provides details of how the principles should be achieved.

Directors' transactions

Closely related to the foregoing is the Stock Exchange's 'model code' on directors' share dealings and the Companies Act regulations on directors' transactions.

To buy or sell shares on the basis of information which has not been publicly disclosed is known as 'insider dealing' and is illegal under the Company Securities (Insider Dealing) Act 1985. This ruling applies to directors as well as all other potential investors. However, it causes particular problems for directors for they will, almost inevitably, be in possession of some price-sensitive information concerning the company which has not yet been disclosed to the stock market, but which would alter the market's valuation of the company's shares.

Therefore, at certain times in particular (for example, just before the company announces its annual results), the directors may have information which indicates that the shares are currently being over- or under-valued by the stock market. If directors were to deal in the shares at such times, it would clearly not be in the interests of their shareholders.

As a result, the Stock Exchange specifically requires companies to stipulate a code of practice for their directors based on the Exchange's own 'model code'. Although the provisions of the code are quite lengthy, the principal elements are:

1. Directors must not deal in their company's shares on a short-term basis.
2. Directors are not allowed to deal in the shares of their company prior to the disclosure of regularly recurring information (such as the annual results), or an announcement of an exceptional nature (such as a take-over bid).

Company law also regulates transactions between directors and their companies. The Companies Act 1985 stipulates that where a director has either a direct or indirect interest in a proposed contract with the company (for example, a director may own an asset which he intends to sell to the company), then that interest must be declared at a board meeting, and there may also be a duty to disclose the information in the company's accounts. These transactions are referred to as 'Class 4' transactions in the Yellow Book. Subject to some exceptions, the Yellow Book rules require such transactions:

1. to have the prior approval of shareholders;
2. to be fully disclosed in a circular to shareholders.

In addition, they cannot be voted on by the class 4 party.

The City Code on Take-Overs and Mergers

Although this is a specialized area which is not dealt with in this book, it is worth noting, within the context of the present discussion, that directors' actions are particularly constrained when the company is subject to a take-over bid.

It is easy to conceive of a situation in which a take-over bid for a company may be unwelcome to its directors, who might fear that they will lose their jobs and/or independence as a result – but which may be in the best interests of shareholders, in that the price offered values the shares at a premium to their current market value. (Or, alternatively, the directors may wish the bid to succeed although it is not in the best interests of the shareholders.) Under such circumstances, the directors may be in a position to defeat the bid through the actions that they take. In such a situation, the directors are subject to a code of best practice – known as the 'City Code' – as a Yellow Book requirement

The aim of all of these measures is to reduce the imbalance of power between directors and shareholders and to ensure that directors really do act in the best interests of their investors. However it seems unlikely that rules and codes will ever be able fully to protect shareholders. The business failures have continued (e.g. BCCI and Barings) as have the high profile salary increases of certain directors. For example, the *Financial Times* reported on August 19th 1997 that the chief executive of British Biotech took a 59% pay increase for the year to April 1997, despite a fall in the share price of the company during the year from 288p to 242p and a reported loss of £28.5 million. It also reported that four directors who resigned during the year made £9 million by exercising share options.

Incentive schemes

Early in our general discussion about principal–agent relationships we stated that principals have two responses to the problem that they face. One response is the development of regulatory devices, as we have just seen. The second response is the creation of management incentive schemes, to try to ensure that there is much greater congruence between management's own personal objectives and the shareholders' objective of wealth (or share price) maximization. Indeed, the Combined Code specifies that 'The performance-related elements of remuneration should form a significant proportion of the total remuneration package of executive directors and should be designed to align their interests with those of the shareholders' (Combined Code p 17)

To be successful, an incentive scheme must fulfil a number of criteria:

1. It should reward management effort and ability, not luck.
2. Its rewards should be potentially large enough to have a significant impact on management total remuneration.
3. The incentive reward system must work each way – rewarding good performance and penalizing poor performance.
4. The incentive scheme must take the concept of risk into account.
5. Reward should be related to performance over a time horizon which matches that of the shareholders.
6. It should be simple and inexpensive to operate and be difficult to manipulate or exploit.

Let us expand a little on each of these points in turn. Shareholders are interested in wealth maximization which, as we know, translates through into the maximization of the value of the company's shares. The first criterion in the list given above relates to the fact that the performance of all companies is, to a greater or lesser extent, dependent on general economic conditions within both the domestic and international economy. Therefore management should not be rewarded for a rise in the company's share price which has simply occurred through an improvement in general economic conditions. Nor should they be penalized for a share price fall resulting from depressed economic conditions.

What the foregoing implies is the need for an incentive scheme based on relative share price performance. In other words, management should be rewarded when the movement in the company's shares (either up or down) is more favourable than their competitors' share price movements – they should be rewarded for a greater rise in the share price, or a smaller fall.

The second criterion is required because, rationally, a manager will always have in mind the trade-off that exists between his incentive scheme gain from trying to maximize the worth of the shares and the likely gain from directly pursuing personal objectives through satisficing activities. Therefore if the incentive reward is relatively small, it is unlikely that the scheme will result in the desired modification of managerial behaviour.

The third criterion is necessary if the incentive scheme is to be proactive in affecting managerial behaviour. In other words, satisficing activity must be seen to have a negative rather than just a neutral impact on managerial rewards. A one-way incentive scheme rewards good performance, but does not penalize poor performance.

The danger with a 'one-way' scheme is that it encourages management to take risk, without them suffering as a result from a potential adverse outcome: management might be tempted to undertake a risky venture on the basis that if it turns out to be successful there will be a favourable impact on their remuneration. However, if the outcome is unsuccessful only the shareholders – and not management – bear the resulting costs.

This is therefore the reasoning that lies behind the fourth criterion. Any incentive scheme must force management to look at both possible outcomes (i.e. good and bad) of a risky investment.

The fifth criterion relates to the problem that shareholders wish management to maximize the value of their shares over the time period that they intend to hold them. Therefore it becomes necessary to avoid any incentive scheme that might encourage management to make decisions which have a favourable short-term impact on the share price, but an adverse longer-term impact.

Finally, the need for the last criterion is fairly self-evident. If the incentive scheme is complex and expensive to operate, it may well be that the benefits that it brings are outweighed by the monitoring costs. Furthermore, if the incentive scheme is capable of being manipulated, then shareholders may find themselves rewarding management for illusionary gains to themselves.

Types of scheme

Fundamentally, there are two types of managerial incentive schemes, with many potential variations. One is based on accounting numbers – typically profitability (although it may be on sales growth). The other is based directly on share price performance.

A typical incentive scheme based on accounting numbers would reward management with a bonus based on either the growth rate of profitability or the absolute level of profitability (usually in excess of some minimum level), where 'profitability' may be defined either pre- or post-tax and interest charges.

Out of our six specified criteria, such a scheme is likely to be satisfactory on only one count: it is likely to be simple and cheap to operate. In all other respects (with the possible exception of criterion 2) such a scheme is unlikely to bring about the desired effects from the shareholders' point of view.

Incentive schemes based on share price performance are usually *option-based*. In such a system key decision-makers in the senior management team are allocated share options. These give the individual the right, (but not the obligation), to buy a specific number of the company's shares at a fixed price per share at any time over a specific future time period (typically, between three and ten years).

Having stated earlier that there are basically two types of managerial incentive schemes, they do of course both have the same objective of trying to ensure that managers take decisions which are in their shareholders' best interests. The great advantage of this second type of scheme is that it is directly related to shareholder wealth through the market value of the company's shares. Incentive schemes based on accounting profit only have, at best, an indirect relationship to shareholder wealth.

The key point about share option schemes is that management have the right to buy shares in the company at a *fixed* price. Therefore, the higher the actual share price, the greater is the worth or value of the option. Consequently, management have a very direct interest in maximizing the value of the company's shares.

Share option incentive schemes are likely to be more effective than profit-related bonus schemes, in that they will satisfy more of the criteria that we specified. However, they are likely to be far from ideal. The main problems with share option schemes are:

1. They represent a type of 'one-way' incentive.
2. They can reward management for share price movements which arise out of general economic conditions, rather than superior managerial performance.
3. They fail to deal adequately with the question of risk in decision making.

Can a 'perfect' incentive scheme be devised that satisfies our six criteria and results in a congruence of managers' and shareholders' objectives? The answer is: probably not.

There are two main reasons for this assertion. The first is that a really effective scheme is likely to be complex and expensive to administer. Therefore, the sixth criterion is unlikely to be satisfied. The second reason relates to the fact that – particularly with respect to the first criterion specified – what is really required is a scheme that rewards *relative* share price performance. The problem here is one of being able to identify a genuinely similar company for comparison purposes.

We mentioned earlier that although the performance of all companies is affected, to some extent, by general economic conditions, all companies are not affected to the same extent. For share price performance comparability purposes, we need to identify companies whose performance is affected by general economic condition in a very similar way to that in which our company is affected. Such a genuinely comparable company may be extremely difficult to identify in many cases.

It is generally recognized that executive incentive schemes have not been particularly successful (except, of course for the executives concerned) A review of 103 companies by the corporate governance consultancy Pirc found that 72% of the new share option schemes in 1997 paid out awards for annual earnings growth of 2% above inflation and that this had been achieved in seven of the last ten years

Conclusion

What conclusion can be drawn from this discussion? We began by assuming that the objective behind financial management decision making was the maximization of the shareholder wealth, which is 'operationalized' in terms of maximizing the value of the company's shares.

We then asked the question: are managers really maximizers, or are they more likely to be shareholder wealth satisficers? This point is important because, as was mentioned earlier, if management really have as their objective the satisficing rather than the maximizing of shareholders' wealth, then our normative theory of financial decision making would change. It is clear from the discussion above that some managers have be criticised for taking more out of companies than would seem appropriate. However, it is very difficult to judge the value of top managers to companies, in the same way as it is difficult to place a financial value on the contribution a top footballer makes to his team. We are of the view that although satisficing behaviour may well exist in the short term, it is unlikely to do so in the medium to long term – particularly in stock exchange quoted companies.

There are two principal reasons for this argument:

1. the competitive market for the shareholders' funds;

2. the competitive market for management jobs.

In a stock exchange quoted company, shareholders can monitor their management's performance through their company's share-price performance, relative to that of similar companies. If one set of management is only satisficing, whilst the management of a similar company is striving to maximize shareholder wealth, then this fact can be expected to be reflected in the respective share price performance of the two companies (because of the resulting lower flow of dividends). Under such circumstances the satisficing company's management are likely to suffer adverse criticism in the financial press and their shareholders are likely to 'vote with their feet' – selling their shares and buying into the maximizing company. The resulting selling pressure on the company's shares is likely to depress their market price and, unless the situation is corrected fairly rapidly, market forces – perhaps in the form of an 'unwelcome' take-over bid – will lead to a change in management.[3] Thus the competitive market for shareholders' funds can help to ensure adherence to the maximizing objective. So, a manager might be paid a very large amount of money but the shareholders of the company can make up their own minds as to whether or not she is worth it.

In addition, one way for a manager to pursue his own objectives in terms of pay and perks is through job promotion. Given that most managers perceive that promotion can be gained through doing a job well, then it follows that in a competitive market for managerial jobs – as exists within a company – individual maximizing managers will look to advance their own personal objectives by replacing satisficing managers. Thus a satisficing manager runs the risk of being displaced by an ambitious maximizing manager.

It is never going to be possible to ensure that all actions by the executives of companies are in the best interests of their shareholders. It is thus not possible to argue that all decisions made in companies will necessarily follow the theories and 'good practices' we will be describing throughout this book. However, this does not mean that we should simply throw up our hands and surrender to management self interest. Indeed, one measure of management performance that might be used by shareholders is how far decisions do follow the good practices we describe.

Summary

This chapter has covered the following major points:

- Shareholders and managers are in a principal–agent relationship where the principal is faced with the problem of controlling the agent's actions to ensure that the agent works in the best interests of the principal.

- The principal's response to the problem is to develop monitoring devices and create incentive schemes.

- Managerial, (and especially directors') performance is monitored and controlled by a range of different legal and quasi-legal devices, which include fiduciary responsibilities, external audits, Yellow Book rules, the 'model code' on directors' share dealings, Companies Act regulations on directors' transactions and codes of best corporate governance practice.

- Incentive schemes are desirable to bring about goal congruence between directors and shareholders. However the design of such schemes is fraught with problems and they are, in reality, unlikely to provide really effective control.

- Financial managers are unlikely to be able to sustain satisficing rather than maximizing behaviour for more than the short run. This is because of the competitive market for shareholders' funds causing the shareholders of satisficing companies to switch to maximizing companies; and because of the competitive market for management jobs both with the firm and between firms.

Notes

1. Job security refers here to the risky nature of a company's business. The more risky the company, the more likely it is to go bankrupt, so causing the management to lose their jobs. Hence management may be concerned to reduce the company's exposure to risk and such action may not be in the shareholders' best interests. This point will be explored further at a later stage.

2. The seriousness of these fiduciary responsibilities should not be under-estimated. A director was subject to a claim of £406m by the liquidators of a company called Bishopsgate Investment Management for alleged breaches in fiduciary duties.

3. Changes in management, and hence changes in objectives, may come about in several ways. Shareholders, either behind the scenes or in the open at the company's annual general meeting, might force a change or, alternatively, a company's non-executive directors may be the catalyst responsible for action to be taken.

Further reading

1. Three articles which given an interesting overview of finance are: J.F. Weston, 'Developments in Finance Theory', *Financial Management*, Spring 1981, S.C. Myers, 'Finance Theory and Financial Strategy', *Midland Corporate Finance Journal*, Spring 1987, and W. Beranek, Research Directions in Finance', *Quarterly Review of Economics and Business*, Spring 1981.

2. Pike reports survey data on managers' perceived objectives (amongst other things) in R.H. Pike, 'An Empirical Study of the Adoption of Sophisticated Capital Budgeting Practices and Decision-Making Effectiveness', *Accounting and Business Research*, Autumn 1988, and R.H. Pike, *Capital Budgeting Survey: An Update*, Bradford University Discussion Paper, 1992. In addition, two interesting earlier articles on objectives are R.N. Anthony. 'The Trouble with Profit Maximization', *Havard Business Review*, November–December 1960 and B. Branch, 'Corporate Objectives and Market Performance', *Financial Management*, Summer 1973.

3. For a discussion on conflicts between managers' and shareholders' objectives, see: G. Donaldson, 'Financial Goals: Management vs. Stockholders', *Harvard Business Review*, May–June 1963; C.M. Findley and G.A. Whitmore, 'Beyond Shareholder Wealth Maximization', *Financial Management*, Winter 1974; N. Seitz, 'Shareholders' Goals, Firm Goals and Firm Financing Decisions', *Financial Management*, Autumn 1982; and J.R. Grinyer, 'Alternatives to Maximization of Shareholder Wealth', *Accounting and Business Research*, Autumn 1986.

4. The ideas of satisficing and of the principal–agent problem can be found in: H.A. Simon, 'Theories of Decision Making in Economics and Behavioural Science', *American Economic Review*, June 1959; M.C. Jensen and W.H. Meckling, 'Theory of the Firm: Managerial Behaviour, Agency Costs and Ownership Structure', *Journal of Financial Economics*, October 1976; and E.F. Fama, 'Agency Problems and the Theory of the Firm', *Journal of Political Economy*, Spring 1980.

5. For a lengthy discussion of the search process (among other things) see: J. Grieve Smith, *Business Strategy*, Blackwell 1985.

6. For a more extended discussion on the control and monitoring of directors' activities see: R.R. Montgomerie, 'Responsibilities of Directors and Advisors' in *Handbook of UK Corporate Finance* second edn, editors J. Rutterford and R.R. Montgomerie, Butterworths 1992. See also *Corporate Governance: Responsibilities, Risks and Remuneration* eds K. Keasey and M. Wright, John Wiley and Sons and ICAEW 1997

7. The Combined Code is essential reading. This spells out the relationship between the directors and the company (and shareholders). *Committee on Corporate Governance, The Combined Code*, Gee 1998.

8. In addition, two good books on corporate ethical responsibilities are W. Shaw and V. Barry, *Moral Issues in Business*, Wadsworth 1992, and N.E. Bowle and R.F. Duska, *Business Ethics*, Prentice Hall 1990.

9. For a really different view of the relationship of managers to their company and shareholders which is fun to read see *Barbarians at the Gate* B. Burough and J. Helyar, Arrow Books 1990 (there is also a film based on this book but the portayal of the central character, Ross Johnson, as some sort of innocent is somewhat misleading).

10. Finally, for two thought-provoking articles, see: F.A. Hayek, 'The Corporation in a Democratic Society: in whose interests ought it and will it be run?' reprinted in H.I. Ansoff, *Business Strategy*, Penguin 1978; and J.J. Chrisman and A.B. Carroll, 'Corporate Responsibility – Reconciling Economic and Social Goals', *Sloan Management Review*, Winter 1984.

Quickie questions

1. What is the principal–agent problem?
2. List the main ways in which directors actions are monitored and controlled.
3. What are the main criteria for an effective managerial incentive scheme?

Problems

1. How might you go about devising an incentive scheme for top management?
2. What is meant by the term 'a risky investment'? What makes some investments more or less risky than others?
3. What might be the financial management objectives of state-owned industries?
4. Discuss the means by which management's actions are monitored and controlled by shareholders.

2 Strategic planning and the finance function

Introduction

In the introduction, we discussed the concept of financial decision making and the need for an objective in order to make a choice amongst alternative courses of action. Then in Chapter 1 we put forward the generally accepted assumed objective that managers take decisions so as to 'maximize shareholder wealth', (or 'value', as it is sometimes termed). We saw that this implied that they were effectively trying to maximize the value of a company's shares.

We then posed the question about whether such an objective was realistic – given human nature – and that led us to consider the nature of the principal–agent relationship that exists between shareholders and their managers. In doing so, we examined the various control mechanisms that are imposed on managements and the way in which management incentive schemes might be designed to provide agreement between the shareholders' objective (that of wealth maximization) and management's own personal objectives.

Finally, we concluded that because of the potential threat of an unwelcome take-over bid and the competitive market for management jobs, the objective approximating to shareholder wealth/share price maximization was probably a reasonably reliable representation of reality. It was also pointed out that even if managers do have agendas other than the creation of shareholder value, we can still put forward a framework for 'good' decision making.

However, before we turn to look at the area of financial management decision making in more detail, we need to set out the context within which these decisions are taken.

First we need to consider the strategic business planning process out of which are developed the company's financial plans. Secondly we need to look at the broad role of financial management generally in order to highlight the specific aspects which are focused upon in this book. We then need to review how the finance function is organized within the firm and finally we need to look at the place of the firm within the general economy and, in particular, the role of the financial markets which supply the finance that enables companies to undertake their activities.

Strategic business planning

Although the idea of maximizing shareholder wealth is the fundamental objective underlying business activity, it is insufficient as an objective on its own in order to guide decision making. What is required is the addition of some substance to the objective, to explain how it is to be achieved. This is the area of strategic business planning.

The key planning questions

The strategic planning process for a business begins with trying to obtain answers to three simple questions (in the order stated):

1. Where are we now?
2. Where do we want to be?
3. How are we going to get there?

Just how the company should obtain answers to these three question is not something that is universally agreed upon. Strategic planning has more theories – and more fashionable 'flavours of the month' – than does financial management (which has its fair share!).

Strategic planning is not the focus of this book's attention and so we will not dwell too long on the area. But what we will do here is try to provide fairly straightforward answers to these questions and so avoid much of the controversy.

SWOT analysis

The first question – 'Where are we now?' – is normally answered through the use of SWOT analysis. SWOT is an acronym standing for Strengths, Weaknesses, Opportunities and Threats. It provides a useful framework for analysing a company's existing situation, both in terms of its own strengths and weaknesses and in terms of the opportunities and threats posed by the external environment within which it operates.

To undertake SWOT analysis, the company first undergoes a self-critical review of its existing strengths and weaknesses. In doing so it looks at its existing product range; its fixed asset base; its human resources and its managerial capability. This 'inward look' is then followed by an 'outward look' at its operating environment.

In looking at both the opportunities and the threats that it may face, the company would examine such issues as changes in consumer demand for the company's products and services; the range of competitors that the company faces in the market-place and the way in which technological change is affecting the company, its products and its organization.

Matrix analysis

Once the company feels it has a clear response to the first question, it can then turn to the second, related question: 'Where do we want to be in three to five years' time?'[1] Attempts to answer this question cause the greatest controversy in terms of management (as opposed to financial management) theorists.

In the 1970s and early 1980s the 'portfolio grid matrix' approach was fashionable. This is, essentially, a very simplistic approach to try and attempt to identify those business areas which hold greatest promise. The most famous, and original, of these was the Boston Consulting Group's so-called 'Boston Box'. This consisted of a two-dimensional grid, with 'market growth rate' on one axis and 'market share' on the other. Out of this came four different types of business definition: Stars, Dogs, Cash Cows and Question Marks. Fig. 2.1 illustrates the concept.

The idea is that the company should invest in the 'star areas' of its business operations, where there is strong growth potential and the company has a high market share. Conversely, the company should divest itself of operations in 'dog' areas, where growth prospects are low and the company has low market share. In business areas where the company has a high market share but low prospects for future growth, further investment should not be pursued. Instead the company should simply concentrate on trying to maximize the cash flow that can be generated from the existing investment. Finally, in 'question mark' areas of the company's operations, a strategic decision has to be taken: whether to increase investment in the hope of gaining market share or to maintain the company's existing limited presence in the market and await further developments and opportunities.

Although the ideas behind the Boston Box approach generated many more sophisticated variations, they all suffered from the need for a great deal of qualitative data which could not easily be transformed into a quantitative – that is, financial – analysis.

Furthermore, it is not at all clear whether the basic advice of the Boston Box would turn out to be correct. Cash Cows may well be worth further investment, as might Dogs, as long as they were profitable.

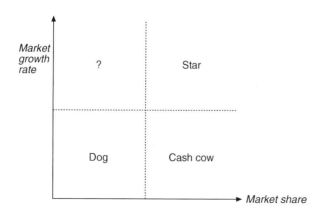

Fig. 2.1 *The 'Boston Box' matrix grid*

Competitive analysis

These rather simplistic approaches to the company's attempt to answer the question 'Where do we want to be?' gave way in the 1980s to the 'Competitive Analysis', developed by Michael Porter at the Harvard Business School.

Porter believed that the objective of businesses is to create 'competitive advantage', which he defined as the difference between the worth of the company's output to its customer and the cost to the company of producing the output. From a financial standpoint therefore, competitive advantage is really gross profit: the difference between revenues and cost of sales.

Companies go about maximizing their competitive advantage by utilizing competitive strategy – that is, they move into those areas of business that hold out the potential of creating the greatest competitive advantage for the company. These areas will be where the company can create 'superior value' for its customers, either by charging a lower price than its competitors (because its cost of sales is lower), or by offering customers unique benefits that are not available from its competitors.

The value drivers

According to Porter, there are five key factors which determine how attractive an area of business will be to a company:

1. buyer power;
2. supplier power;
3. entry opportunities;
4. substitute possibilities;
5. competitor rivalry.

These 'competitive forces' are termed 'profit' or 'value' drivers, and it is these that the company must take into account in answering the question 'Where do we want to be?' in terms of:

1. What business areas should we expand into?
2. What business areas should we withdraw from?
3. How can we improve a business area's level of profitability?

'Buyer power' relates to the industry's fundamental level of competitiveness. The greater the scope of the customer to play one supplier off against another, the less profitable the industry is likely to be.

'Supplier power' relates to the company's ability within an industry to keep down its cost of sales. The scarcer the alternative sources of supply of the company's inputs, the less profitable will be the industry.

'Entry opportunities' refer to the ease with which competitors can gain access to the market-place. The lower the barriers to entry, the lower will be the industry's profitability.

'Substitute possibilities' concern the degree of competition from other industries in related areas. For example, if you were to manufacture sausages, not only would you be concerned about other sausage manufacturers, but you might also be concerned about hamburger manufacturers, as your customers could switch from eating sausages to eating hamburgers. The greater the threat of substitutability, the less profitable the industry.

Finally, there is the degree of rivalry between existing competitors. Rivalry will tend to be more intense the more equally matched are the competitors, the lower is the growth rate of the industry and the greater is the proportion of fixed operating costs within the industry. In such circumstances, intense rivalry brings lower profitability.

The strategic approaches

Going through this detailed analysis helps the company to understand the competitive setting within which it exists and, on this basis, reach decisions as to the direction in which it wants to go in the future. Porter believes that the choice about which business areas the firm should position itself in and how it should compete in those areas to successfully generate competitive advantage relates to the ideas of creating 'superior value' for the customer.

Porter suggests that there are four strategic approaches available to the company, of which just one should be focused upon. If not, there is a danger that by focusing on multiple strategies, the company loses clarity of purpose. These strategic approaches are:

1. Broad product differentiation where the company tries to specifically differentiate all its products across the complete range from those of its competitors, looking to add unique benefits (such as better quality or greater convenience).
2. Narrow product differentiation where the company aims for product differentiation in a very narrow, specialized product range.
3. Broad-based cost leadership where the company drives towards creating superior value by concentrating on minimizing operating costs over its complete product range.
4. Focused cost leadership where the company looks to specialize in a very narrow product range and go for maximum scale economies and production cost efficiency.

Investment and financing strategy

Having made these crucial, strategic decisions, the company is then faced with the third question: 'How do we get to where we want to go?'

In many cases there is a blurring between the process of answering the second and the third questions. In answering the second question the company is setting up its strategic objectives; whilst in answering the third question it is required to appraise the financial and operational viability of the different strategic approaches suggested above. This is the subject matter of much of the remainder of this book.

The planning objective of financial management is to maximize shareholder wealth through the maximization of the value of the company's shares. In order to do this, the management must first of all identify a suitable business strategy. The choice of this strategy is through understanding the competitive environment, specifically in relation to those five key value drivers. It is characteristics of these five factors which are going to determine the firm's net cash flow generated over time in terms of the rate of sales growth and the level of profit margins.

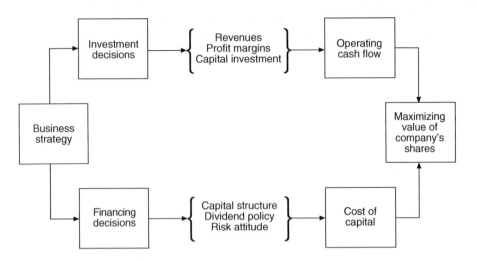

Fig. 2.2 *The strategic planning process*

Therefore it is at this stage that the company formulates its investment strategy in terms of the capital (fixed asset) expenditure decision.

The other factor involved with shareholder wealth maximization is the cost of capital to the company. Maximizing shareholder wealth is achieved not only through maximizing revenues and revenue growth and minimizing cost of sales through the investment strategy; it is also achieved through minimizing the cost of the finance put into these investments. Thus the firm will need to develop a financial strategy covering such elements as the company's capital structure (i.e. its debt–equity capital mix), its dividend policy and its attitude towards risk (and hence its credit rating).

It should be stressed that the company's overall financial strategy is crucial. It is very easy to concentrate too much on investment decisions and by doing this neglect other areas of the total picture. If the company's cost of capital is higher than that of its competitors it will be at a serious competitve disadvantage. Not only will the competitor company be more profitable overall but the company might find that certain projects are not worth pursuing whilst this is not the case for its competitors.

Suppose the cost of capital for company A is 20% but that company B's cost of capital is only 15% (because of a different capital structure for instance). If both companies take on projects yielding 25%, company A will enjoy a margin of 25%−20% = 5% whilst company B enjoys a margin of 10%. Also, an investment yielding 18% will be worthwhile for company B but not for company A. Company A is at a considerable disadvantage compared to company B when it comes to creating wealth for its shareholders.

The overall planning process is shown in Fig 2.2.

The role of financial management

Before moving on to look more closely at the theory and practice of financial decision making, it is important to see the place of financial decision making within the overall financial management function. This book is not concerned about the whole spectrum of financial management, but it is concerned with what are probably the most fundamental elements within that spectrum and, as such, it has important implications for the other elements.

Essentially, the financial management function can be divided up into five principal areas:

1. Translating the company's business plan into a financial plan.
2. Evaluating the financial plan to ensure its validity, given the company's objective as far as shareholder wealth maximization is concerned.
3. Ensuring that sufficient finance is made available in order to undertake the planned activities.
4. Controlling the plan's implementation.
5. Reporting the outcome of the business plan's implementation to all interested parties.

Therefore, the starting point is where the company – either formally or informally – draws up a business plan. This would normally be done in non-financial terms: sales targets, percentage market shares, capacity levels and manpower levels, etc. These plans would then have to be examined and analysed (and modified, if need be), to ensure that their financial implications are satisfactory and that they will help to increase shareholder wealth.

In addition to evaluating the financial feasibility of the business plan, financial management has also to ensure that the company has adequate financial resources at its command to enable it to undertake the plan. If those resources do not already exist within the company, then arrangements have to be made to raise additional finance from the financial markets.

The business plan is then implemented and controlled, typically through standard costing, budget-setting and variance analysis. Finally, the outcome of all this activity has to be reported to the company's own management in the form of management accounts, and to its shareholders in the form of financial accounts (i.e. the profit and loss account, balance sheet and cash flow statement). In addition, financial reports to other interested parties such as the employees, the company's bankers and the tax authorities may also be required.

Organization of the finance function

Fig. 2.3 is a typical organizational chart for the finance function of a large company. From it can be seen how these different elements of financial management are normally split up between the three major participants: the Finance Director, the Chief Accountant and the Treasurer. The main responsibilities of the Finance Director are as follows:

1. the setting of the company's broad financial strategy;
2. decisions on major capital expenditure on new assets and the acquisition of other companies;
3. interpretation and implications of macro- and micro-economic financial developments for the company;
4. implications for the company of government economic and fiscal (tax) legislation and proposals;
5. the dividend decision.

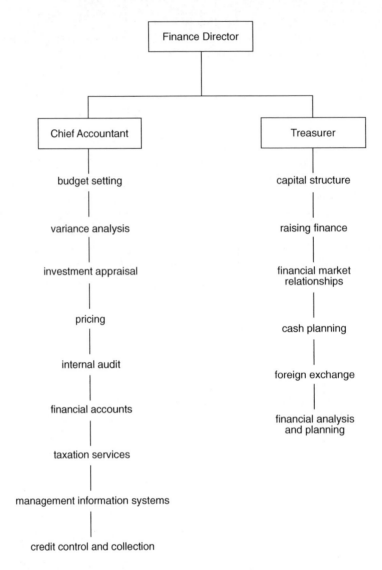

Fig. 2.3 *The finance functions*

Finance Director

Chief Accountant

- budget setting
- variance analysis
- investment appraisal
- pricing
- internal audit
- financial accounts
- taxation services
- management information systems
- credit control and collection

Treasurer

- capital structure
- raising finance
- financial market relationships
- cash planning
- foreign exchange
- financial analysis and planning

The Chief Accountant is responsible for the following tasks:

1. preparation of financial reports to all internal and external user groups including: management, employees, shareholders, bankers, other creditors and tax authorities;
2. installation, maintenance, updating and review of the company's management information systems;
3. preparation and control of budgets;
4. pricing policies (in conjunction with marketing);
5. capital investment appraisals;
6. management of working capital.

The Treasurer's main responsibilities concern the following seven areas:

1. the establishment and maintenance of good relationships with shareholders and financial institutions;
2. ensuring that sufficient finance, and credit facilities, are available to meet all foreseeable contingencies;
3. the issue of securities and investment of surplus cash;

4. cashier and payroll activities;
5. management of the company's exposure to foreign exchange risk;
6. corporate financial planning;
7. interest rate planning.

The firm in the economy

The are basically two major groupings within a simple economic system: households and firms. 'Households' is the term used by economists to refer to individuals within the economy (like you, the reader) who own the physical resources such as land, property, machinery, raw materials or labour. Households then transfer these resources to firms who use them to produce outputs (which can be anything from cornflakes to theatre tickets) that people want. This process is shown by the innermost pair of arrows in Fig. 2.4. It is known as the 'real' sub-system in the economy's flow of funds, as it deals with the flow of real or physical inputs (resources) and outputs (goods and services) in the economy.

Firms pay households for their resources with money in the form of wages, rents and prices. In turn, households pay for the outputs of firms also by using money. Thus there is a secondary pair of arrows in Fig. 2.4 which is referred to as the monetary sub-system, as it relates to the flow of cash between households and firms.

The money that households receive from firms in payment for their resources is known as their income. The money households pay to firms in order to buy the outputs of firms is their expenditure. Households generally have an excess of income over expenditure, known as savings. Similarly, the households' income represents the firms' costs and the households' expenditure represents the firms' revenues.

In aggregate, within an economy, the household sector usually has a surplus (of income over expenditure), while the firm sector is in deficit (i.e. it

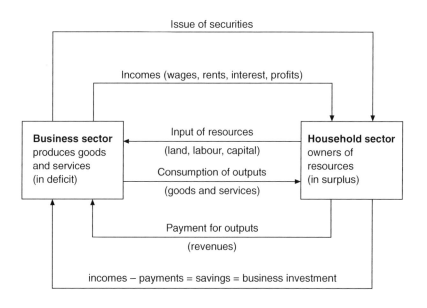

Fig. 2.4 *Simple two-sector economy*

requires additional cash). Therefore households lend their savings to firms and, in return, firms pay out interest and dividends to households. This flow is represented by the outermost pair of arrows on Fig. 2.4 – the financial sub-system.

Obviously, what has been described here is a very simplistic analysis; a more complete picture of the flow of funds within the economy would involve at least three other sectors: the government, the financial intermediaries (of which more later) and overseas economies. However, our purpose for the moment is sufficiently served by this very simple illustration.

The problem of liquidity

Within this simple illustration of the flow of funds in an economy, there lies a problem. Generally speaking, households dislike lending their savings to firms unless they have the ability to get their money back again quickly and easily, if they so wish (because some unforeseen need to spend their savings on goods and services has arisen). In other words, households only like to invest their savings if they have a considerable degree of liquidity.

On the other hand, firms want to be able to keep the money that they borrow from households for lengthy periods of time, because they will often want to invest it in long-term or permanent assets such as machinery or buildings. It would be no good a firm borrowing £1 million from households one week, and then the households asking for their money back the next week (because some unforeseen circumstances have arisen) if, in the meantime, the firm has bought a new factory with the money. Thus the problem is that there is a mis-match between firms and households in their liquidity requirements. Because of their liquidity preference, households generally only want to lend short term, but firms want to borrow medium to long term.

Within the economy, this problem is overcome in two ways: by the existence of financial intermediaries (such as banks), and financial markets (such as the stock market). Both financial intermediaries and financial markets stand between the firms and the households in order to solve the mis-match in liquidity requirements.

Taking a bank as the best-known example of a financial intermediary, the role they play can be simply illustrated as follows. Suppose a household has £1000 of savings. They want to invest those savings, but they also require to be able to recall their money (liquidate their investment) if an unforeseen need for it arises. Instead of lending the money directly to a firm, which is likely to want to keep the money medium to long term, and will not want (or be able) to offer the household the facility of returning the money at short notice, the household lends the £1000 to a bank. In other words, the money is placed on bank deposit. The bank undertakes to repay the contents of the deposit account to the household at any time, but then promptly lends £900 of the £1000 to a firm. The loan to the firm may be for, say, a five-year term. The result of this is that the household has the required liquidity for its savings and the firm has got its required illiquidity.

But what happens if, shortly after the loan is made to the firm, the household demands their money back? The bank has only got £100 of the original £1000. It is here that the bank takes advantage of being able to pool the savings of many households. Knowing that it is unlikely that *all* the households who have placed money on deposit will simultaneously want their money back, the bank tries to keep sufficient liquid resources (the £100 kept back would be part of these) available to be able to satisfy those households who do actually want to liquidate the investment of their savings.

This mis-match of liquidity requirements between households and firms is also reconciled through the existence of capital markets like the stock exchange. Basically the stock exchange provides a market-place where medium- to long-term securities (loans and shares) issued by firms to households can be sold (or liquidated).

For example, the household which wanted to invest £1000 of its savings could, instead of going through a financial intermediary, invest the money in the firm directly. In return the firm might issue £1000 worth of share certificates. If a stock market did not exist, a household would be extremely reluctant to take this course of action because ordinary shares form part of the firm's permanent capital and are unlikely ever to be repaid unless the firm is itself wound-up. Thus the household's investment would be completely illiquid.

However, the problem is overcome through the existence of stock markets. If the firm's shares are quoted on the stock market, it means that there are institutions known as market makers whose function is always to be prepared to buy (and sell) shares in the firms from households. Thus if our household which has invested £1000 in the shares of the firm wishes to liquidate the investment because unforeseen circumstances have arisen and the money is needed, they can simply sell their shares – not back to the company, but on the stock market (to the market maker) – and so liquidate their investment.

Risk and return

There is, of course, an important difference between the two examples used of the household with £1000 of savings. When the bank deposit account is liquidated, the household will recover the precise amount placed on deposit – £1000 (plus any interest that has accrued). However, when the £1000 investment in the company's shares is liquidated, just how much money will be recovered – it could be more or less than £1000 – is uncertain, because the market maker sets a price according to the levels of supply and demand for the shares. This is in turn a function of expectations at the time of the future performance of the company. Thus the household suffers a degree of uncertainty in the latter case which is avoided in the former.

This problem of risk – that is, uncertainty of outcome – will play a major role in the development of the theory of financial decision making. In many ways it is what financial decision making is all about. Householders (i.e. investors) dislike risk – they are risk averse – and will only be willing to take on risk if they can be expected to be rewarded for so doing. This reward comes in the form of the expected level of return. Thus much of financial decision making is concerned with the risk and return trade-off – is the expected return worth the risk involved?

In fact we can identify two factors that determine the rate of return we expect to receive. The first is that we receive a reward for forgoing consumption now in exchange for consumption later. It is a reward for forgoing the convenience of access to resources now and it is called the *liquidity premium*. At the time of writing this stands at around 6% (although there is a significant range of returns available from the market). The second is that we receive a reward for taking risks (or at least on average we do, because the whole thing about risk is that sometimes we come out ahead whilst at other times we do not). This is called the *risk premium* and it will vary according to the perceived risk of the investment.

For this reason, the householder in our example would expect to get a higher return on savings invested in shares (coming in the form of dividends plus a possible capital gain on subsequent sale) than when they were placed on bank deposit (coming in the form of interest). In fact, the capital markets provide a whole spectrum of different risk (and expected return) investments in which households can place their savings. The nature of this risk and the determinants of the reward structure will be returned to at a later point.

Summary

This chapter has covered the following major points:

- There are three key planning questions: where are we now?; where do we want to be?; and how are we going to get there?

- The 'where are we now' question is usually answered using SWOT analysis, which looks at the business's strengths, weaknesses, opportunities and threats.

- There are many approaches to tackling the second question. In the 1970s and early 1980s, matrix analysis such as the Boston Box, was fashionable.

- This simplistic approach has given way to Porter's 'competitive analysis' and the need to identify the company's 'value drivers'.

- The five value drivers are: buyer power, supplier power, entry opportunities, substitute possibilities and competitor rivalry. Their analysis determines the business areas the company might expand into and withdraw from.

- Out of this analysis, Porter suggests that the company selects one strategic approach out of the four possibilities: broad or narrow product differentiation or, broad or narrow cost leadership.

- Once the overall business strategy is formulated, management then needs to formulate the company's investment strategy and its financing strategy.

- The role of financial management can be split into five broad elements:

  — the translation of the business plan into financial terms;
  — the financial evaluation of the plan;
  — the raising of finance for the plan;
  — the implementation and control of the plan;
  — the reporting to interested parties as to the financial outcome of the plan's implementation.

- The mis-match in liquidity requirements between households and firms can be resolved through the use of financial intermediaries and capital markets. However, there is a significant difference in the risk a household/investor is exposed to through each means and this is reflected in the expected returns on investment each provides the household.

Notes

1.   The duration of a company's planning horizon is, in itself, a problematical area. How far ahead in time companies will try and plan depends partially upon the type of business that the company is engaged in and partially on the stability of its operating environment. Some types of business require the acquisition of very long-lived assets, and in such companies the planning process, out of necessity, also has to be very long-term – attempting to look 15–25 years into the future. On the other hand, if the company's assets are essentially short-term and it operates in a very unstable and ever-changing environment, the planning horizon will be likely to be far shorter.

Further reading

1.   For a discussion of the development of the matrix approach to corporate strategy, see K. Davidson, 'Strategic Investment Theories', *Journal of Business Strategy*, Summer 1985.
2.   The two classic books by Porter that introduced the ideas of competitive analysis are M.E. Porter, *Competitive Strategy*, Free Press 1980 and *Competitive Advantage*, Free Press 1985.
3.   For more specific articles on financial planning see J.F. Weston, 'Forecasting Financial Requirements', *Accounting Review*, July 1958 and W.T. Carleton, C.L. Dick and D.H. Downes, 'Financial Policy Models: Theory and Practice', *Journal of Financial and Quantitative Analysis*, December 1973.
4.   Finally, on the role of the financial management function, a useful booklet to read is J.A. Donaldson, *The Corporate Treasury Function*, Institute of Chartered Accountants of Scotland 1988.

Quickie questions

1.   What are the three key strategy questions?
2.   What is SWOT analysis?
3.   Describe the Boston Box.
4.   List the five 'value drivers' of a business.
5.   What does the firm's investment strategy cover?
6.   Why is financing strategy important?
7.   What are the typical responsibilities of the chief accountant?
8.   Sketch out a basic flow of funds diagram for an economy.
9.   What role does the stock market play?
10.   What do we assume about investors' risk attitude?

Problems

1. Outline the strategic business planning process.
2. Investors want to be able to get their money back at short notice; companies want to borrow money for long-term investments. How is this mis-match in liquidity requirements overcome in practice?

3 Traditional methods of investment appraisal

Introduction

In its simplest form, an investment decision can be defined as one which involves the firm making a cash outlay with the aim of receiving, in return, future cash inflows. Numerous variations on this definition are possible, such as a cash outlay with the aim of reducing or saving further cash outlays, but these can all generally adapt to the initial definition with little trouble.[1]

Decisions about buying a new machine, building a factory, extending a warehouse, improving a delivery service, instituting a staff training scheme or launching a new product line are all examples of the investment decisions that may be made in industry. In order to help in making such decisions, and to ensure that they are consistent with each other, a common method of appraisal is required which can be applied equally to the whole spectrum of investment decisions and which should, in terms of the decision structure so far outlined, help to decide whether any particular investment will assist the company in maximizing shareholder wealth (via share price maximization).

A warning

In looking for such an investment appraisal method we shall begin by examining two of the most widely used[2] methods: payback, and return on capital employed, to see how well they fit in with our financial decision objective and value base. However, before doing so we should be clear that neither of these two methods, nor any other method of investment appraisal can give a definitive decision. They cannot tell a company's financial decision maker to 'invest' or 'not invest', but can only act as a decision *guide*. This extremely important point will become obvious as we develop our theory, but it is all too easy to slip back into the erroneous (and sometimes comforting) belief that the techniques that we shall develop here will make decisions for us. They will not do this. All they will do is help to communicate information to the decision maker; but when the actual decision is finally made, it is based on a whole range of very diverse considerations which are beyond our present capabilities to encompass in 'overall' decision-making formulae.[3]

There has sometimes been a considerable amount of resistance and resentment on the part of financial managers to the introduction of any new investment appraisal technique, based partially on the belief that with such methods their decision-making function would be replaced by a formula, 'handle-turning' function. Such a belief is ill-founded, not only for the reason already given, but also because investment is about the future. Almost all investment decisions will involve making forecasts/ estimates/guesses about the investment's future performance, and appraisal techniques are applied to the numbers that emerge from that process. The future is, almost without exception, uncertain and so any investment appraisal technique can only produce *advice* based on these forecasts and not a decision that is guaranteed to turn out to be optimal given hindsight. So, investment appraisal techniques can never replace managerial judgement, but they can help to make that judgement more sound.

The payback method

Let us start by looking at the first of these two traditional methods of investment appraisal: the payback method.[4] This is one of the most tried and trusted of all methods and its name neatly describes its operation, referring to how quickly the incremental benefits that accrue to a company from an investment project 'pay back' the initial capital invested – the benefits being normally defined in terms of after-tax cash flows.

The payback method can be used as a guide to investment decision making in two ways. When faced with a straight accept-or-reject decision, it can provide a rule where projects are only accepted if they pay back the initial investment outlay within a certain predetermined time. In addition, the payback method can provide a rule when a comparison is required of the relative desirability of several mutually exclusive investments.[5] In such cases projects can be ranked in terms of 'speed of payback', with the fastest paying-back project being the most favoured and the slowest paying-back project the least favoured. Thus the project which paid back quickest would be chosen for investment.

Given below are examples of the payback method operating in both decision-making situations. With Project A, assuming that the criterion for project acceptance is a four-year (maximum) payback, then we can see that it should be accepted because it pays back the initial outlay of £4000 within this time period:

Project A Year[6]	Cash flow (£)
0	−4000
1	+1000
2	+1000
3	+2000 payback period
4	3000
5	1000

If Projects B and C are mutually exclusive, Project C has the faster 'speed of payback' and so is the preferred investment. B pays back within three years (i.e. $2\frac{3}{5}$ years: years 1 and 2 cash flow plus three-fifths of year 3 cash flow), whereas C pays back in two years exactly:

Project B		Project C	
Year	Cash flow (£)	Year	Cash flow (£)
0	− 10 000	0	− 12 500
1	+ 3000	1	+ 5000
2	+ 4000	2	+ 7500
3	+ 5000	3	+ 1000
4	+ 6000	4	+ 1000
		5	+ 1000

Working capital

Most projects involve an expenditure not only on capital equipment, but also on working capital. For example, suppose a company was considering investing in a sausage-making machine. Not only would the company have to incur the capital expenditure on the machine itself, but they would also have to invest in working capital: raw material stocks, finished goods stocks and debtors. However, the point to be recognized is that, at the end of the project's life, although the capital equipment will only have (at best) a scrap value, the working capital should be recovered in full. This is because, at the end of the project's life, the firm can run down its stocks of raw materials and finished goods and, hopefully, all outstanding debtors will pay up.

The following question then arises: should working capital be included as part of the project's outlay and so be included in the payback calculation? Example 1 illustrates such a situation. It is probably the case that for payback calculations (only), working capital should be excluded from the analysis, and so the advice given by payback is to accept the sausage machine project.[7] However it should be noted that there are no real rules in making decisions such as this. We will use the cash flows that we judge to be most appropriate.

Example 1

Ajax plc is considering the purchase of a sausage machine. The machine would cost £12 000, have an expected life of five years and a zero scrap value (net of disposal costs) at the end of that time. In addition, an expenditure of £8000 on working capital will be required throughout its life. The firm's management accountants have estimated the net, after-tax, operating cash flows of the project as follows:

Year	Operating cash flow (£)
1	+6000
2	+6000
3	+6000
4	+4000
5	+3000

Ajax evaluates investment opportunities using a three-year maximum payback criterion. The problem here is what set of cash flows should be evaluated using payback: Alternative 1 or 2?

Year	Alternative 1 Capital expenditure (£)	Working capital (£)	Operating cash flow (£)	Year	Alternative 2 Capital expenditure (£)	Operating cash flow (£)
0	−12 000	−8000		0	−12 000	
1			+6000	1		+6000
2			+6000	2		+6000
3			+6000	3		+6000
4			+4000	4		+4000
5		+8000	+3000	5		+3000

If working capital is taken into account, the project should be rejected, as it takes more than three years to recover the total initial outlay of £20 000. But if working capital is excluded from the analysis, the project is acceptable as it has a two-year payback.

The logic behind the approach of excluding working capital is as follows. Payback is concerned about how long it will take the project to reach its break-even point where at least the outlay has been recovered. Management are interested in this point, because they recognize the uncertainties that surround any estimate of a project's future cash flow. Thus the more quickly a project achieves payback, the less risky is that project in the eyes of many managements. As a project's working capital is likely to be recovered whenever the project comes to the end of its life (i.e. working capital is automatically paid back), it is excluded from the analysis of the break-even point.

Advantages of payback

As can be seen from the two initial illustrations, payback is quick and simple to calculate (once the project's cash flow forecasts have been made) and is likely to be readily understood by management. This is one of its greatest advantages as an appraisal technique, but it has other advantages in addition.

A second advantage is that it is thought by many managements to lead to automatic selection of the less risky project in mutually exclusive decision situations. The point has already been mentioned that one of the most difficult tasks in investment appraisal is the forecasting of future project cash flows. In this respect, generally speaking, the further ahead in time is the cash flow estimate, the less reliable is that estimate. Therefore by emphasizing 'speed of return' and selecting the project, from a series of alternatives, that pays back quickest, the appraisal method is – almost by definition – choosing the least risky project, in that it chooses the one which reaches break-even most quickly. However, this is a complex point and we shall return to it later when the problem of risk is more fully discussed.

A further advantage of payback, and one that is connected to what has been said previously, is that it saves management the trouble of having to forecast cash flows over the whole of a project's life. Given that the forecasting process is difficult, and the further ahead in time the forecast has to be made the greater the difficulty, the fact that project cash flows need not be forecasted beyond the maximum payback criterion (by which time the project either is or is not acceptable) is an obvious advantage. For instance, in Example 1, although the sausage machine was thought to have had a five-year life, there really was no need to forecast its cash flows beyond three years (the decision criterion) in order to evaluate it.

A final advantage of payback, that is seen by many managers, is that it is a convenient method to use in capital rationing situations. Capital rationing is a subject which we shall return to later to look at in more detail. However, it basically refers to a situation where a company does not have unlimited capital expenditure funds. (Perhaps the limit has been imposed by the company itself in the form of an annual capital expenditure budget.) Example 2 illustrates the situation.

Example 2

Alpha plc has identified five independent[8] investment opportunities and wishes to evaluate their desirability. The company normally uses payback with a three-year criterion and has specified a maximum capital expenditure budget for the year of £200 000. The project's net after-tax cash flows are estimated as follows:

Project:	1	2	3	4	5
			(all cash flows in £000s)		
Year					
0	−100	−300	−100	−200	−250
1	+ 50	+100	+ 20	+ 50	+ 50
2	+ 50	+100	+ 80	+ 50	+100
3	+ 50	+100	+ 50	+100	+ 80
4		+ 80	+ 30	+ 50	+ 80
5		+ 50			

Using payback, Projects 1 to 4 are all acceptable as they each pay back within the three-year criterion. Project 5 is unacceptable. However, Alpha has a problem. To undertake all four acceptable projects will require total expenditure of £700 000 and only £200 000 has been budgeted. How is the firm to 'ration out' the available cash among the competing projects?

The solution is to reduce the payback criterion from three down to two years. Projects 2 and 4 are now undesirable, leaving just 1 and 3 which, between them, will utilize the available capital.

Example 2 shows how the capital rationing problem can be met by reducing the payback criterion and so reducing the number of acceptable projects. In addition, the approach can also claim to have yet another advantage in that, in such a situation, it appears to accept the most 'sensible' projects. If capital is in short supply, it could be argued that the best projects to accept would be those which returned the expenditure rapidly – which is exactly what the payback method does.

The decision criterion

Nothing has so far been said about how the decision criterion is set. There are a number of possible methods that management might utilize. One would simply be to base the criterion on past experience; for example if the firm's experience is that most successful projects have paid back within four years, then that time period might be set as a criterion. Alternatively, general 'industry practice' might be taken as the guideline.

One obvious, and very sensible, basis for setting the decision criterion would be forecasting ability. For example, if a firm believed that, realistically, it could not forecast project cash flows with sufficient accuracy beyond five years ahead, then five years might be set as the criterion. Here management would be recognizing their forecasting limitations and would be sensibly deciding not to evaluate a project on cash flow forecasts which might be seen more as guesses than estimates.

Disadvantages of payback

Having looked at the advantages – true or otherwise – claimed for the method, let us now turn to the disadvantages. The first is the problem of what is meant by the term 'investment outlay'. If we look at Projects D and E, just how should the investment outlay be defined in each case?

Project D		Project E	
Year	Cash flow (£)	Year	Cash flow (£)
0	−10 000	0	−5000
1	+ 5000	1	+1000
2	+ 5000	2	−5000
3	+ 5000	3	+3000
4	− 2000	4	+3000
		5	+4000

Is Project D's outlay £10 000 or £12 000? Is Project E's outlay £10 000 or £9000? The point is that in each case we *can* come to a decision, say, Project D's outlay is £10 000 and E's is £9000, but the decision rule as it stands is too ambiguous in its definition of terminology to give a definitive ruling.

The problem of ambiguity can also be seen in the definition of the *start* of the payback time period. In other words, from what point do we begin counting? Suppose that Project E will be accepted only if it pays back within three years. If this means that E must pay back its outlay by Year 3 – that is, three years after its commencement – clearly, it should not be accepted. On the other hand, if the payback criterion means that it should pay back within three years of the completion of its outlays – that is, by Year 5 – then it is acceptable. Once again, as it stands, the decision rule is too ambiguous to give a definitive ruling.

This ambiguity is an important problem. When any technique, designed as a decision-making aid, is open to ambiguity in interpretation, then it is likely to be manipulated so as to lend backing to the *desired* decision, rather than the *right* decision. Any decision rule open to such misuse is dangerous and must be viewed with suspicion.

A further problem, and probably the most important one, arises from the fact that the decision is concentrated purely on the cash flows that arise *within* the payback period, and flows that arise outside this period are ignored. Projects F and G illustrate the problem that this can cause:

Project F		Project G		Project H (do nothing)	
Year	Cash flow (£)	Year	Cash flow (£)	Year	Cash flow (£)
0	−100 000	0	−100 000	0	0
1	+ 10 000	1	+ 50 000		
2	+ 20 000	2	+ 50 000		
3	+ 40 000	3	+ 10 000		
4	+ 80 000				
5	+160 000				
6	+320 000				

According to the payback rule, if the two projects are mutually exclusive, Project G is preferred because it pays back the outlay more quickly. If the two projects are independent (i.e. either one or both could be accepted or rejected) and the company has a three-year payback period criterion, again Project G would be accepted and F rejected. In both situations, looking at the cash flows over the whole life of each project, we can see that the wisdom of the decision advice given by the payback method is open to some doubt.

There is a further problem with the logic of payback. The option not to invest is generally one of the options open to the decision maker. If we call this project H and compare it with F and G above we find that it pays back immediately (because no cash was paid out!). An investment of zero will always produce an immediate payback.

The time value of money

A final problem with the payback method is that, in the format used above, it suffers from the fundamental drawback of failing to allow for the 'time value of money'.[9] However, this difficulty can easily be overcome by applying the method – not to ordinary cash flows – but to 'present value' cash flows. In such circumstances, the technique is usually referred to as 'discounted' payback. The concept of the time value of money has a central place within financial decision theory and will be developed formally in the next two chapters. Nevertheless, it will be useful to introduce the idea briefly, at this point.

Essentially what is meant by the term 'the time value of money' is that a given sum of money has a different value depending upon when it occurs in time. The idea is not directly concerned with inflation or deflation (let us assume that neither exists, so that price levels are stable through time) but really concerns the fact that money can be invested so as to earn interest.

Suppose you were owed £100 and were given the choice of having your £100 returned to you either now or in one year's time (assume that if you choose £100 in a year's time the event is 'certain' – i.e. you are certain to be alive then and you are certain to be paid the money). Most people would instinctively take the £100 now – even if they did not need the money – and this would be the correct decision in terms of the time value of money.

The reason why £100 in a year's time has a smaller value than £100 now is because if you took the £100 *now*, the money could be placed on deposit at (say) a 6% interest rate and so turn into £106 in one year's time. Therefore if the person who was in debt to you offered the choice of £100 now or £106 in one year's time (again both events are certain to occur), you would have no preference for either alternative. Thus we could say that the present value of £106 received in a year's time is £100, or that the future value of £100 now is £106 in a year's time, assuming a 6% interest rate.

This concept of the time value of money will be much more fully discussed when we talk about the discounted cash flow methods of investment appraisal in Chapter 5, but the point to be made here is that the payback method does not make any allowance for the time value of money, its emphasis on the speed of return being purely a consideration of project risk. For example, the payback method would be indifferent between Projects I and J whereas, as the reader may well discern, if allowance is made for the time value of money, Project J is preferable to Project I, as money received nearer in time is more valuable than money received later in time.

Project I			Project J	
Year	Cash flow (£)		Year	Cash flow (£)
0	−4000		0	−4000
1	+ 500		1	+3000
2	+ 500		2	+ 500
3	+3000		3	+ 500
4	+ 500		4	+ 500

A worked example of discounted payback will be shown when the time value of money concept is more fully explored in Chapter 5.

In conclusion

Despite these criticisms, it is still possible to say that, to a great extent, payback has been unfairly maligned in the literature on financial decisions. However, it obviously has a robust ability to survive, because surveys reveal it to be the most widely used of all appraisal methods. This popularity stems mainly from two of the reasons that we have already given, that of ease of comprehension and its apparent bias towards less risky projects. Indeed it can be strongly argued that the payback method does provide a very useful 'rule of thumb' check mechanism for the very many minor investment decisions that companies have to make, which are financially too small (either in relative or absolute terms) to justify the time and expense that would necessarily be incurred in using a complex, but more theoretically correct appraisal method.[10] Furthermore, as shall be seen at the end of Chapter 5, a particularly supportive case can be made for the discounted payback technique.

The real problem does not stem from the payback concept itself, but more from the way the method is *used* in the decision-making process. Except in the case of very minor investment decisions, it should not really be used to give decision *advice* at all, but only to give *information* on the speed of return of the initial outlay, which may or may not be of relevance (depending upon the firm's liquidity) in the decision process. It cannot really be considered as an investment appraisal technique because of its major defect: its inability to report the expected return over the *whole* life of an investment, through its disregard of the investment's post-payback period flows. Using the payback method to choose between alternative investments or to set a minimum criterion for investment acceptance is really applying it to a task which is well beyond its ability to handle. At best, for large investments, it can act successfully only as an initial screening device before more powerful methods of appraisal are applied.[11]

The return on capital employed

The second traditional approach to investment appraisal is the return on capital employed (ROCE) which, like payback, has many different names (perhaps the most common is the accounting rate of return) and a wide variety of different methods of computation. In its basic form, it is calculated as the ratio of the accounting profit generated by an investment project to the required capital outlay, expressed as a percentage. There are many variations in the way these two figures are actually calculated, but normal practice in its use for investment appraisal is to calculate profit after depreciation but before any allowance for taxation, and to include in capital employed any increases in working capital that would be required if the project were accepted.

There are two common ways of expressing the ROCE in practice. One is the ratio of the average annual profit generated over the life of the project, to its average capital value (i.e. the average capital employed). The other approach is to take the average annual profit as a ratio of the initial outlay. Example 3 illustrates these calculations.

The ROCE can be employed in the investment appraisal of both independent projects and mutually exclusive projects. First, a decision criterion is set in terms of a minimum acceptable level of ROCE. (The figure used here often reflects the firm's overall return on capital.) Then, for an independent project to be acceptable, its ROCE must at least equal the 'hurdle' or criterion return specified. In a situation of mutually exclusive projects, the best of the alternatives is the project with the highest ROCE. However, this 'best' project will only be accepted by the firm if it, too, meets the set criterion.

Advantages of ROCE

The ROCE investment appraisal technique is widely used in practice, although it is probably declining in popularity. It has three main advantages. The first is that by evaluating the project on the basis of a percentage rate of return it is using a concept with which all management are familiar. For example, being told that a project had a four-year payback would not immediately convey whether that was good or bad; but being told that a project is expected to produce a 35% return on capital would appear obviously desirable (given that we know the going rate of return on, say, the overall company).

The second advantage is connected to the first. It is the fact that the method evaluates the project on the basis of its profitability, which many managers believe (despite comments in Chapter 1) should be the focus of the appraisal. Finally, a third advantage that exists is that of logic. Managers' own performance is often evaluated by shareholders in terms of the company's *overall* return on capital employed. Therefore there does seem to be a certain logic in evaluating individual capital investment opportunities on a similar basis. (This line of thinking then often leads to the specification of the ROCE criterion being set equal to the company's actual or desired overall return on capital.)

Example 3

The Beta Company wished to evaluate an investment proposal using the ROCE technique. The project requires an initial capital expenditure of £10 000, together with £3000 of working capital. The project will have a four-year life, at the end of which time the working capital will be fully recovered and the project will have a scrap value of £2000.

The project's net pre-tax cash flows are as follows, and the company uses straight-line depreciation:

Year	Net cash flow (£)
1	+4000
2	+6000
3	+3500
4	+1500

In these circumstances (and lacking further information) 'profit' can be calculated as equal to cash flow minus depreciation. The annual depreciation charge would be:

$$\frac{£10\,000 - £2000}{4} = £2000/\text{year depreciation.}$$

Year	(£)			
Annual profit or (loss): 1	4000 − 2000	=	2000
2	6000 − 2000	=	4000
3	3500 − 2000	=	1500
4	1500 − 2000	=	(500)
	Total profit	=	£7000

$$\text{Average annual profit} = \frac{£7000}{4} = £1750$$

The initial capital employed would equal £13 000 (capital expenditure plus working capital). The average capital employed would be calculated as:

$$\frac{\text{Capital expenditure} - \text{scrap value}}{2} + \text{scrap value} + \text{working capital}$$

that is:

$$\frac{£10\,000 - £2000}{2} + £2000 + £3000 = £9000.^{12}$$

Hence return on initial capital employed equals

$$\frac{£1750}{£13\,000} = 0.135 \text{ (approx.) or } 13.5\%$$

and return on average capital employed equals

$$\frac{£1750}{£9000} = 0.194 \text{ (approx.) or } 19.4\%.$$

Disadvantages of ROCE

To set against these advantages, there are a number of major disadvantages, the first of which is the ambiguous nature of the ROCE concept. There are so many variants that no general agreement exists on how capital employed should be calculated, on whether initial or average capital employed should be used or on how profit should be defined. As a result, the method lays itself open to abuse as a technique of investment appraisal by allowing the decision maker to select a definition of ROCE which best suits his preconception of a project's desirability.

Second, because the method measures a potential investment's worth in percentage terms it is unable – in an unadjusted form – to take into account the financial size of a project when alternatives are compared.

For example, suppose a company was considering whether to build a large factory, at a cost of £10 million, or a small factory at a cost of £3 million. If the large factory turned out to have an ROCE of 20% while the small factory's

ROCE was 24%, then the latter investment would be the one chosen (assuming 24% exceeded the ROCE criterion). However, it is not at all certain that the small factory would be a wise choice. While the small factory would result in an aggregate profit of £720 000 (24% of £3 million), the large factory would produce a profit of £2 million for the firm.

However, these two criticisms are relatively insignificant when compared to two further difficulties. The first concerns the fact that accounting profit rather than cash flow is used as the basis of evaluation. As our earlier discussion in Chapter 1 showed, this is an entirely incorrect concept to use in a decision-making context. Accounting profit is a *reporting* concept; it is a creation of accountants. A capital investment decision is an economic or resource allocation decision and the economic unit of account is cash, because it is cash which gives power over resources.

The other major criticism of the ROCE is that it also ignores the time value of money. Furthermore, unlike payback, where discounted payback can be used, there is no way that the ROCE can be modified to take the time value of money into account.

However, despite these criticisms, the method is still widely applied to investment decisions in industry and it may be fair to say that, like payback, although there are many problems associated with its application, it may give acceptable decision advice when applied to relatively minor, short-run investment projects.

Nevertheless, there is survey evidence which does indicate a decline in the technique's popularity. There are perhaps two reasons for this, both of which arise from the high rates of inflation suffered by the economy in the late 1970s and the 1980s. The first is that high rates of inflation led to high interest rates and this high time value of money sharply brought home to management the importance of taking it into account in decision making. With interest rates of around 20% it becomes obvious that the timing of cash flows is important. A second reason for the ROCE's decline in popularity could be that the high rates of inflation – and the failure of the inflation accounting debate – taught management about the doubtful validity of the accounting profit number. Thus a method that uses accounting profit and ignores the time value of money has little to recommend it as a decision-making tool.

The use of ROCE tends to result in the adoption of short-term approaches to decision making; so-called *short-termism*. This is related to its use for measuring the performance of managers and the fact that it emphasizes the effects of the investment on reported earnings rather than long-term cash flows.

In conclusion

Comparing these two 'traditional' investment appraisal techniques, each has its own advantages and disadvantages and it is not clear whether either is superior. Each has its own group of advocates and it is common to find both used in conjunction so as to produce a 'two-tier' decision rule, e.g. projects may be accepted only if (say) they pay back within five years *and* have a minimum ROCE of 12%.

In the final analysis, our conclusion must be that, apart from the possible exception of the evaluation of relatively small, short-lived investments, neither method has sufficient advantages to offset its disadvantages, and particularly the failure of both normally to allow for the time value of money.[13] In the next chapter we shall start to examine investment appraisal methods that do attempt to make such an allowance.

Summary

This chapter has covered the following major points:

- The two 'traditional' methods of capital investment appraisal – payback and the return on capital employed – were examined to see how they are calculated and how they are applied, both to individual project evaluation and to situations involving mutually exclusive projects.

- As far as payback was concerned, the technique was usually applied to a project's after-tax cash flows, but working capital was excluded entirely from the evaluation.

- Basically there were four advantages to payback:
  — quick and simple;
  — seen as automatically selecting the less 'risky' project from amongst alternatives;
  — seen as helpful in capital rationing situations;
  — saves management from having to forecast project cash flows beyond the criterion time period.

- Payback's main disadvantage was its failure to consider project cash flows outside the payback period. However, it was argued that, to some extent, this omission might be understandable where management felt that their forecasting ability was suspect beyond the criterion time period.

- The other disadvantage is payback's failure to account for the time value of money, but this can be taken into account through the use of discounted payback.

- The ROCE also had advantages:
  — it is evaluated using the familiar percentage concept;
  — it evaluated projects on the basis of profitability;
  — management's success or failure in taking financial decisions in aggregate is judged on the basis of the company's return on capital employed (amongst other things). Therefore it appears sensible that individual investment decisions should be taken on the same basis.

- However, to be set against these advantages were two major disadvantages: a failure to consider cash flow and a failure to take the time value of money into account.

- In sum, these two techniques may be suitable as initial screening devices, or to evaluate small, short-lived projects. However, they should not be used otherwise, with the possible exception of discounted payback.

Notes

1. Although this point will be expanded upon later, it is worth specifying now that an investment's 'cost' can be defined as all cash outflows and/or reduced cash inflows through time that result (either directly or indirectly) from the investment decision. Similarly, an investment's 'benefit' can be described as all cash inflows and/or reduced outflows through time that result (directly or indirectly) from the investment decision. Thus all costs and benefits of an investment are defined in terms of being incremental to the firm through time and are expressed in cash terms.

2. Various empirical surveys both in the UK and the USA and elsewhere have shown that these two investment appraisal methods have widespread popular appeal. Their familiarity and directness will make the task of replacing them by superior appraisal techniques a difficult one.

3. Not least amongst these diverse considerations is the decision maker's own psychology; one survey (Scapens, Sale and Tikkas, CIMA 1982) concludes that concern with an investment's financial viability is of almost secondary importance to whether or not it 'fits in' with the company's strategic plans.

4. There are a variety of names given to this method. Others include pay-back period, pay-off period, capital recovery period, cash recovery factor.

5. The term 'mutually exclusive' when applied to investment projects is best explained by means of an example. Suppose a company requires a new warehouse and there are two possible sites under consideration, then the decision could be analysed in terms of two mutually exclusive investments: building the warehouse at Site A and building the warehouse at Site B. The projects are said to be mutually exclusive because only *one* new warehouse is required, so if it is built at Site A, the acceptance of this project excludes the other project from being chosen, and vice versa. More generally a pair of projects are mutually exclusive if the acceptance of one means that the other would not or could not be accepted. This definition can be extended to any number of alternative investment projects of which only one can be chosen.

6. It is important to note that throughout this book we shall use the following convention when dealing with all types of financial flows (e.g. profit, dividend, cash or tax flows): all flows will normally be assumed to occur instantaneously on *the last day of the year in which they arise*. Thus a cash flow in the second year of a project's life will be assumed to occur on the last day of the second year. The main exception to this rule is that a project's outlay (or cost) which arises in the first year of its life is assumed to occur on the first day of the year.

   These rather unrealistic assumptions are made for arithmetical convenience, but, in most circumstances, they do not affect the realism of our results in any substantial way. (See the Appendix to Chapter 5 on Compounding and Discounting.) Diagrammatically:

Thus 'Year 0' (or t_0) refers to the start of the first year (i.e. 'now'). 'Year 1' refers to the *end* of the first year and – simultaneously – the start of the second year. 'Year 3' refers to the end of the third year, and so on. References in the text to, for example, 'the second year' will refer to events that happen during the second year, whilst references to 'year 2' (or t_2) will refer to a financial flow that is assumed to arise at the end of the second year (or, the start of the third year).

7.   However, it is important to notice that payback is the *only* appraisal technique which excludes working capital from the analysis.

8.   Project independence can be defined as a situation where the expected financial flows that arise from a project will occur irrespective of any other project being or not being undertaken.

9.   There do exist special cases where the ordinary payback decision rule effectively allows for the time value of money, but such situations are simply fortuitous and of little more than arithmetical interest.

10. This may be especially true of very small companies which may be lacking the resources and knowledge to undertake a more complex appraisal.

11. Even this is really open to doubt. Original writers on the topic such as Joel Dean and Ezra Solomon believed that payback could be used as a coarse screening device to pick out projects whose desirability (in terms of profitability) is so obvious as to remove the need for more refined appraisal. For similar reasons it is held that the method could also be used to reject 'obviously' highly unprofitable projects. There is little evidence to support this belief, neither has there been an operational definition of 'obvious' in this context.

12. The rationale for this calculation can be most easily seen with the help of a diagram:

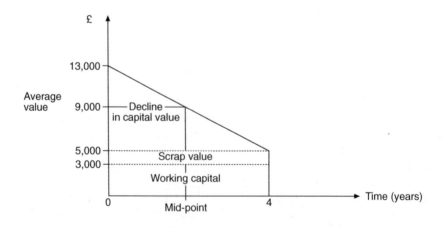

13. Even allowing for the discounted payback variant referred to earlier, payback still suffers the major criticism of not considering a project's financial flows outside the payback period.

Further reading

1. Most of the literature concerning payback and ROCE is fairly old, and the more up-to-date contributions have tended to contrast them with the DCF techniques which are to be discussed in Chapter 5. Nevertheless, an interesting starting point is the discussion in: D. Bodenhorn, 'On the problem of capital budgeting', *Journal of Finance*, December 1959.
2. Even older, but also of interest is: J. Dean, 'Measuring the Productivity of Capital', *Harvard Business Review*, Jan–Feb 1954; as is: E.A. Ravenscroft, 'Return on Investment: Fit the Method to your Needs', *Harvard Business Review*, Mar–Apr 1960.
3. Specifically on payback, see: M.J. Gordon, 'The Payoff Period and the Rate of Profit', *Journal of Business*, October 1955; A. Rappaport, 'The Discounted Payback Period', *Management Science*, Jul–Aug 1965; H. Levy, 'A Note on the Payback Method', *Journal of Financial and Quantitative Analysis*, December 1968; and M.H. Weingartner, 'Some New Views on the Payback Period and Capital Budgeting Decision', *Management Science*, August 1969.
4. Two interesting articles which discuss reasons for the continuing popularity of payback are: M. Statman, 'The Persistence of the Payback Method: A Principal–Agent Perspective', *Engineering Economist*, Winter 1982; and R.H. Pike, 'Owner Manager Conflict and the Role of the Payback Method', *Accounting and Business Research*, Winter 1985.
5. The ROCE method is generally recognized as being inadequate, but see: M.J. Mepham, 'A Reinstatement of the Accounting Rate of Return', *Accounting and Business Research*, Summer 1968, and C.G. Hoskins and G.A. Mumey, 'Payback: A maligned method of Asset Ranking?', *Engineering Economist*, Autumn 1979.

Quickie questions

1. What is the payback decision rule for mutually exclusive projects?
2. What is the payback of Project W:

		Net cash flow:		
Capital expenditure: £11 000			Yr 1	+4000
Working capital: £4000			Yr 2	+4000
Scrap value: £1000			Yr 3	+4000
Life: 5 years			Yr 4	+3000
			Yr 5	+2000

3. What are the advantages of payback?
4. How is payback used in capital rationing situations?
5. How might the payback criterion be set?
6. What is 'discounted payback'?
7. What is the single most important criticism of payback?
8. Why does money have a 'time value'?
9. What is Project W's (see question 2) ARR/ROCE, assuming straight-line depreciation?
10. What are the main advantages of ARR/ROCE?
11. What are the two most serious disadvantages of ARR/ROCE?

Problems

1. Gamma plc is a diversified industrial conglomerate. Its head-office accounting staff are currently evaluating investment proposals put up by different divisions for approval.

    The Electronics division have put forward a proposal to produce a new type of calculator which, because of rapid technological change, can only be expected to have a four-year life, once the production facilities have been set up during the first twelve months.

    The Property division propose taking a four-year lease on a building which already has a tenant paying an annual rent.

    The Mining division propose to spend £1.5 million developing a small copper mine. The mine would only have a three-year life. At the end of that time, the environmental damage the company had caused would need to be rectified at a cost of £0.75 million.

    The net cash flows of the projects (excluding working capital) are as follows (£000s):

Year	Electronics	Property	Mining
0	−1000	−1000	−1500
1	−1000	+ 200	+ 500
2	+ 800	+ 400	+1000
3	+ 800	+ 400	+ 800
4	+ 800	+ 400	− 750
5	+ 800		

    Gamma normally uses payback to evaluate projects with a decision criterion of three years.

    Required:
    (a) Calculate the payback of all three projects and determine the decision advice.
    (b) If the Electronics and Property division projects were mutually exclusive, which project would you advise the company to accept? Think carefully before reaching a decision and then justify your decision.
    (c) If the Property and Mining division projects were mutually exclusive, which project would you advise the company to accept? Again, think carefully and justify your decision.
    (d) Comment on the company's use of the same decision criterion for projects from all three divisions. Would you think this wise?

2. Zeta plc is a manufacturer and distributor of ice-cream. The management are presently considering a project which will require capital expenditure of £200 000, together with £50 000 of working capital. The capital equipment is expected to have a scrap value of £80 000 at the end of its four-year life and 80% of the working capital will also be recovered. (The remaining 20% of unrecovered working capital will consist of bad debts and spoilt stocks.)

    The project's annual revenues and operating cash costs are estimated as follows (£000s):

Year	Revenues	Operating costs
1	200	150
2	260	200
3	400	290
4	100	80

    The company calculates depreciation on a straight-line basis. Normally projects are evaluated using both payback and the return on initial capital employed. The criterion used is three years for payback and 13% for the ROCE.

Required:
(a) Evaluate the project using the company's normal decision criteria. What advice would you give?
(b) The chairman, after receiving your advice, is puzzled over your treatment of working capital in the payback calculation. Explain to her your reasonings.
(c) The chairman also wondered whether the returns on *average* capital employed should be used instead of initial capital. What would your advice be and would the decision advice change? Think carefully before giving your answer; your promotion depends upon it!
(d) If Zeta decides to use only one appraisal technique, which would you advise – payback or ROCE/ARR – and why?

4 The single-period investment consumption decision model

Introduction to the model

In the previous chapter, two widely-used investment appraisal decision rules, payback and ROCE/ARR, were examined. One criticism of payback was that it ignored the time value of money – unless discounted payback was used. A similar criticism was made of the ROCE/ARR approach but, in addition, that was also criticized for evaluating projects on the basis of profit, not cash flow.

The other two main methods of capital investment appraisal are net present value (NPV) and the internal rate of return (IRR). These will be examined in detail in Chapter 5. However, in this chapter we take the opportunity to expand upon our initial discussion about the time value of money, and then look at how, in theory, capital investment decisions should be taken. This will then enable a judgement to be made as to how closely the four alternative investment appraisal techniques accord with the theoretically correct approach.

In order to look at the theory of investment decision making, we are going to develop a simple graphical analysis.[1] *In no way does this analysis purport to represent the real world*, but it will be useful in that it allows conclusions to be reached that do have real-world validity.

The basic assumptions

So as to simplify the analysis and to lay bare the problem of investment decision making, we shall specify six assumptions about the real-world environment within which investment decisions are made.

Assumption 1

The decision maker is only concerned with making investment decisions over a single period time horizon, which we will treat as one year for the sake of simplicity. Given this horizon, there are only two points of time that concern us – the start of the year or now (i.e. t_0 or Year 0) and the end of the year (i.e. t_1 or Year 1). Therefore all the available investment opportunities possess the general characteristic of requiring a cash outlay now, in return for a cash inflow at the end of the year. No investment cash flows extend beyond t_1.[2] (We will show later that this analysis can be easily expanded to cash flows that extend over many years and, indeed, different times during those years.)

Assumption 2

The size and timing of any investment's cash outflow and subsequent cash inflow is known with certainty by the decision maker and so no risk is involved in the investment decision.[3]

Assumption 3

Only 'physical' investment opportunities are available, i.e. investments involving the use of factors of production (land, labour and machinery) to produce a future return. This means that there is no 'capital market' where money can be lent or borrowed at a rate of interest.[4]

Assumption 4

All investment projects are infinitely divisible; therefore fractions of projects may be undertaken, and they exhibit decreasing returns to scale.

Assumption 5

All investment project cash flows are entirely independent of each other. Therefore the return produced at the end of the year from any investment now is fixed and known for certain and is unaffected by any other investment decision.

Assumption 6

The person in receipt of the benefits from investment decisions is rational, in that 'more cash' is always preferred to 'less cash' in any period.

These are the six major assumptions that we are going to make initially (although there are several other assumptions which we shall specify later as we develop the analysis), and obviously most of them are very unrealistic and in no way reflect the real world: investors are almost invariably faced with making decisions where the effects stretch over many periods; the future is largely unknown and so future cash flows cannot be certain; non-physical investments, such as placing money on deposit at a bank, are usually available to investors; investment projects are often indivisible and so must either be undertaken completely or not at all; many investment project cash flows depend upon what other investment decisions have or have not been made. However, such simplifying assumptions do provide a starting point for our analysis; we shall examine later the effect of replacing them with more realistic descriptions of the real world, but for the moment let us accept them.

The time value of money

We have already defined an investment decision by a company as one which involves the company in cash outlay (now) with the aim of receiving a (future) cash inflow in return. If we also make the simplistic but basically correct assumption that a company can do either of two things with any 'spare' cash[5] it has – pay it out to shareholders as a dividend[6] or retain it within the company and invest it – then if a company makes a decision to invest, it is in fact deciding not to pay that cash to shareholders now but instead to put it into a project with the aim of obtaining an increased amount of cash in the future, which can then be paid out as a dividend.

Therefore, a decision to invest by a company means that shareholders forgo the opportunity of consumption now (i.e. a dividend now) with the aim of increasing future consumption (i.e. an enlarged dividend later). At this stage we will ignore the complications caused by the possibility of selling shares and the linkage of their value to investment decisions. So investment decisions are about the delaying of current consumption in order to increase future consumption. (Or in non-economic terms, not spending money on consuming goods and services now, but investing the money instead so as to produce more money later which can then be spent on an increased quantity of goods and services.)

To look more closely at the investment decision, let us first consider the case of the single-owner firm (i.e. one in which the company has only one shareholder, who owns all the shares, and whose entire wealth is represented by the company) in which the owner is also the decision maker. In deciding to invest, the owner is forgoing some present consumption in order to increase future consumption and, in taking such action, he must also have decided that the future consumption so gained is somehow of greater value than the present consumption sacrificed in making the investment.

To make such investment decisions in a consistent manner,[7] the owner requires a specific criterion that will enable him to judge whether or not any particular investment opportunity will produce sufficient compensation, in terms of increased future consumption, for having to reduce current consumption in order to make the investment.

Suppose our owner-manager requires a minimum of £1.20 back at the end of the year in order to persuade him to invest £1 now. Thus he requires compensation of 20p for every £1 of current consumption he forgoes. This requirement – which is a type of exchange rate of money between points in time and is, in fact, the owner's time value of money (TVM)[8] – can be expressed as a percentage:

$$\frac{£1.20}{£1.00} - 1 = 0.20 \text{ or } 20\%.$$

So an investment appraisal decision rule could be formulated in which a project is only undertaken if it produces at least a 20% return on capital.

The owner-manager would not be willing to invest in a project which produced less than a 20% return, because 20% represents his time value of money.

It is important to realize that this time value of money is unlikely to remain a constant but will probably increase as more and more present consumption is sacrificed for investment so as to produce a greater amount of future consumption. That is to say, with each successive reduction in current consumption the owner is likely to demand a higher and higher minimum future return in order to persuade him to invest, because each additional £1 of current consumption forgone is likely to be of increasing value (in terms of the benefits received from consumption), and each additional £1 of future consumption gained is likely to be of decreasing value. This is an example of the economic concept of diminishing marginal utility.

The basic graphical analysis

The single-owner firm case

The one-period graphical analysis, made under our six assumptions, is shown in Fig. 4.1. The curve AB is called the physical investment line[9] (PIL) and is composed of all the physical investment opportunities available to the company at t_0, arranged in order of decreasing return.[10] Thus the most 'profitable' investments – in terms of greatest return – would be undertaken first by the firm.

The physical investment line represents the complete range of maximum consumption combinations that the owner can obtain between the two points in time[11] by applying varying amounts of the company's existing resources to physical investment opportunities. Therefore as the owner gives up increasing amounts of current consumption in order to make physical investments, the company locates further and further up and around the physical investment line. (For instance if it locates at point A, no investment

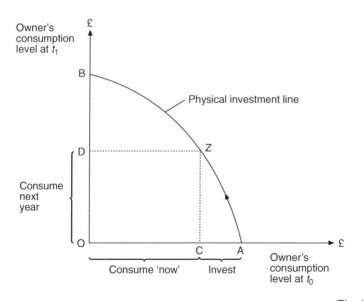

Fig. 4.1 *The physical investment line*

is undertaken and if it locates at point B, all possible physical investments are undertaken.)

Using Fig. 4.1, OA represents the owner's total wealth now (i.e. at t_0) and can be regarded as the (unforced) liquidation value of the company. If all this wealth is consumed now and none is invested, then there will be zero wealth available for consumption next year (i.e. t_1). If only part of this year's wealth is consumed, say OC, and the rest, CA, is invested, then the company locates itself at point Z on the physical investment line and this level of investment will produce OD available for consumption next year.

The return received by the company from the last (i.e. marginal) £1 of investment made at t_0 – the final piece of investment that brings the company to locate at point Z – can be found from the slope of the physical investment line at that point.[12] But besides being the return on the marginal investment, this slope represents something else. The company has located at point Z because the owner must feel that further investment is not worthwhile. In other words, the gain in next year's consumption generated by a marginal increase in investment now, does not provide sufficient compensation for the further reduction in present consumption that would be necessary to finance the increased investment. Therefore the marginal return on investment being obtained at Z must be equal to the owner's time value of money (TVM).

If the marginal return at Z was greater than the owner's TVM, the company would continue to invest, and if it were less than the TVM, the company would have stopped investing *before* reaching point Z, because the return gained from a move along the PIL from below Z to point Z would have been insufficient compensation for the present consumption that would have to be forgone to make the investment.

Introduction of indifference curves

We can derive this result better by asking the question: given that the physical investment line represents a whole series of infinitely divisible and independent opportunities for investment projects, arranged in decreasing order of rate of return, so that the investment with the greatest return is ranked (and undertaken) first and the one with the smallest return last, how does the company know when to stop investing? In order to answer this fully, we have to use another economic concept: the indifference curve.

It is assumed that the reader is familiar with the derivation and meaning of this term – it is explained in most basic economic textbooks. In rough terms, indifference curves are curves of constant utility or welfare, and when mapped on to our graph of consumption 'now' and consumption 'next year', an individual indifference curve indicates all possible combinations of consumption at the two points in time which give the same level of utility. The curves are convex to the origin, indicating that there is diminishing marginal utility attached to consumption at any single point of time, and each indifference curve, moving from left to right, gives the individual a higher overall level of utility.

Their place here concerns the fact that the set of indifference curves belonging to the company's owner can be mapped on the Fig. 4.1 graph, as shown in Fig. 4.2, and can be used to indicate at what point the company should stop investing; it is that point on the physical investment line which enables the owner to achieve his highest indifference curve, that is, his highest level of utility. This is found at the point of tangency between an indifference curve and the physical investment line. In terms of Fig. 4.2, the company invests CA 'now' because the two time-point pattern of consumption that results for the owner – OC 'now' and OD 'next year' – places him on his highest possible indifference curve and so maximizes his welfare.

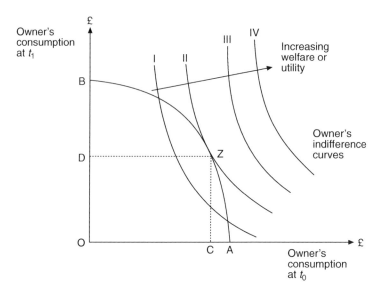

Fig. 4.2 *Indifference curves*

The point of tangency between the two curves represents a point where the slopes of each equate. As the slope of the indifference curve reflects an individual's marginal time value of money and the slope of the physical investment line represents the rate of return on the marginal project, then the point where the slopes of these two curves equate must be the point at which the owner's TVM equals the return on the marginal investment made by the company. Thus the investment decision rule is that the company continues to make physical investments until the return from the marginal investment (i.e. the last one made) equals the owner's marginal time value of money. Any further investment will not produce the necessary return required and so will have the effect, in terms of our indifference curve analysis, of placing the owner on a lower indifference curve.[13]

Introduction of capital markets

From this simple analysis, under a series of restrictive assumptions about the real world, we have seen how investment decisions would be made and why money is said to possess a 'time value'. If we now make our analysis slightly more realistic by relaxing our third assumption so as to make available to the single-owner firm the opportunity of being able to lend and borrow money on a capital market at a rate of interest, we can then develop a second reason for money having a time value.

With the introduction of capital markets, the firm is faced with three possible courses of action at t_0: consumption, physical investment or capital market investment. Making the very important assumption that there is a perfect capital market[14] and therefore only one market rate of interest[15] (which is both the borrowing and lending rate), we can use the one-period graphical analysis to illustrate how the company makes investment decisions so as to allow the owner to distribute his consumption between the two points in time in such a way that he maximizes his welfare.

The financial market line

In terms of Fig. 4.3, suppose the single-owner firm has amount OG available for consumption at t_0 and OH available at t_1. The capital market can be represented by a straight line, AE, which passes through point F, the coordinate of the existing consumption distribution. The slope of this line[16] is given by $-(1 + r)$, where r is the perfect capital market rate of interest, and the line is termed the financial investment line (FIL).

This line shows the range of capital market transactions available to the single-owner firm, given the existing distribution of cash resources of OG now (i.e. t_0) and OH next year (i.e. t_1). A move *down* the financial investment line from F to (say) point L means that the firm borrows GM on the capital market now – so increasing consumption at t_0 from OG to OM – and repays (capital plus interest) HN next year – so reducing consumption at t_1 from OH to ON. Notice that the maximum that can be borrowed now is amount GA; if the firm attempts to borrow more than this, there will not be sufficient resources available next year to repay the capital and accrued interest.

A move *up* the financial investment line to (say) point I means that the firm is lending JG on the capital market so as to reduce consumption now (to OJ) and to increase consumption next year (to OK). Again notice that a maximum of OG can be lent now – reducing current consumption to zero – and this results in having OE available for consumption next year.

Fig. 4.3 *The financial investment line*

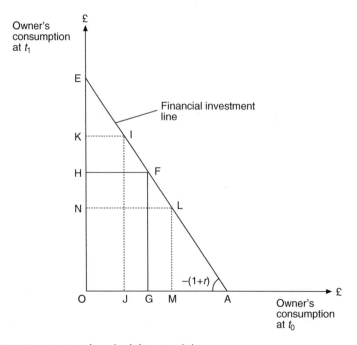

The separation theorem

Having seen how the financial investment line works, we can now combine the physical and financial investment lines on a single graph. This allows us to examine how both physical investment decisions and capital market borrowing or lending decisions are made in conjunction with each other, in order to allow the owner to achieve his highest possible indifference curve and so optimize his consumption spread over the period and maximize his utility.

However, up to this point we have taken as our decision-making entity the single-owner firm, where the investment decision maker and the owner are one and the same person. Introducing the possibility of using the capital market allows us to analyse the investment decision process not only in the single-owner case, but also in the much more important situation where there are many owners (i.e. shareholders) and they are separate from the investment decision makers (i.e. management). This is the Separation Theorem.[17]

The capital investment decision rule now becomes: the company (i.e. managers) undertakes physical investments until the return from the marginal physical investment equates with the perfect capital market interest rate/rate of return. This level of physical investment results in some particular dividend flow, at t_0 and t_1, to the shareholders. The shareholders then make financial investment decisions (by either borrowing or lending on the capital market) until their individual marginal time values of money equate with the capital market rate of interest. Such action will result in them achieving their highest possible indifference curves by producing a distribution of consumption over the period, which maximizes their individual levels of utility.

Graphical derivation of the decision rule

We can see how these separation theorem decision rules are derived and why they help to maximize the shareholder's utility by examining Fig. 4.4. Here the financial investment line is superimposed on the Fig. 4.1 situation. Let us assume for the moment that although ownership is separate from management, the company has only one shareholder.

The current liquidation value of the company is OA. In the absence of a capital market we know that the company management will invest amount AC, and so make physical investments up to point Z on the physical investment line. This represents the point of tangency between the physical investment line and the owner's indifference curve (UT_1), and therefore at this point the return from the marginal investment (derived from the slope of the physical investment line) equates with the shareholder's time value of money (given by the slope of the indifference curve tangential to point Z). Thus in our one-period world, the shareholder would receive a 'dividend' of OC now and OD next year. This distribution of consumption over the period places him on his highest attainable indifference curve: UT_1, and so maximizes his utility.

With the introduction of a capital market, the company's management now invest amount QA, so as to undertake physical investments up to the point where the return on the marginal physical investment equates with the capital market interest rate/rate of return (derived from the slope of the

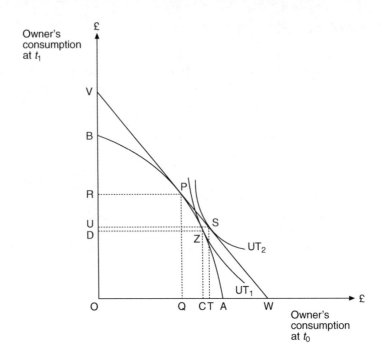

Fig. 4.4 *The separation theorem*

financial investment line). This occurs at point P where the financial investment line is tangent to the physical investment line. Thus the shareholder now receives a different dividend distribution: OQ now and OR next year. The company has undertaken physical investments up to point P because this has the effect of placing the shareholder on the highest possible financial investment line (VW).

Unlike the situation where capital market opportunities did not exist, the shareholder now does not have to accept the pattern of dividend distribution given by the company for consumption. Instead, he can borrow or lend on the capital market (i.e. move down or up VW from point P) so as to adjust his received dividend flow to suit whatever consumption pattern is preferred.

This preferred pattern is given by the point on the financial investment line which is tangent to one of his indifference curves, because this indifference curve will be the highest attainable. Thus the shareholder either lends or borrows on the capital market until his marginal time value of money (derived from the slope of the indifference curve) equates with the perfect capital market rate of interest. In Fig. 4.4 the shareholder achieves this point, S, by moving down the financial investment line and borrowing an amount QT to make a total of OT available for consumption 'now' and OU available for consumption 'next year'. (A dividend of OR is received from the company next year, but part of this, RU, is used to repay the borrowed capital and accrued interest.)

Whether the shareholder lends or borrows or even omits to use the capital market at all depends solely upon the location of the point of tangency between the financial investment line and the shareholder's indifference curve, as Fig. 4.5 shows. What Fig. 4.4 illustrates is how, by taking advantage of both physical *and* financial investment opportunities, the shareholder can attain a higher indifference curve, UT_2 (and so increase his utility),

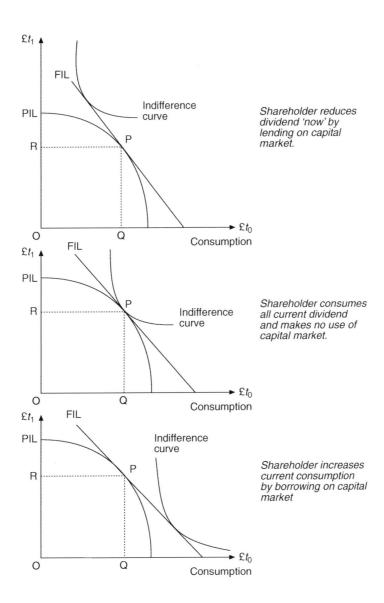

Fig. 4.5 *Lending and borrowing decisions*

Shareholder reduces dividend 'now' by lending on capital market.

Shareholder consumes all current dividend and makes no use of capital market.

Shareholder increases current consumption by borrowing on capital market

than would have been possible from making physical investments alone. In fact this can unambiguously be seen occurring in Fig. 4.4, because the shareholder has managed to increase his consumption in both periods through using the capital market: by amount CT 'now' and UD 'next year'.[18]

The multi-owner firm

The development of this separation theorem is extremely important. It results in a company's management making only *physical* investment decisions and leaving individual shareholders to adjust their received dividend pattern to fit their particular consumption requirements by using the capital market. In the owner-manager firm and in the situation where ownership and management are separate but there is only one owner, it makes no difference to the analysis whether the individual owner/shareholder uses the capital market or the company uses the capital market on the owner's/shareholder's behalf (as long as, in the case where owner and management are separate, the managers are aware of the owner's marginal time value of money).

However, the crucial importance of the separation theorem comes when ownership is separated from management *and* there is more than one owner. Quite simply, different individuals have different time values of money, and so a company would be able to undertake the physical investment decisions but not the financial investment decisions, because there would be more than one marginal time value of money.[19] The use of the separation theorem avoids this problem by leaving the financial investment decisions to the individual shareholders.

Fig. 4.6 shows a situation where a company is owned by two shareholders: one with 75% of the equity (Shareholder 1) and the other with 25% of the equity (Shareholder 2). The firm continues to make physical investments until the marginal return on investment equates with the market rate of interest, and then pays out the resulting dividends to each shareholder in proportion to his equity holding. In so doing, the company would still be ensuring that each individual shareholder is placed on the highest possible financial investment line. It is then up to the individual shareholder to make whatever decision is best, in the knowledge of his own set of indifference curves and time value of money, with regard to using the capital market in order to adjust his received dividend flow.

In the example shown in Fig. 4.6, Shareholder 1 (75% holding) will use the capital market to borrow and so increases consumption 'now' at the expense of a reduced future consumption level. Shareholder 2 will use the capital market to lend, thereby reducing consumption 'now' but, in return, having an increased level of consumption 'next year'.

Fig. 4.6 *The multi-owner case*

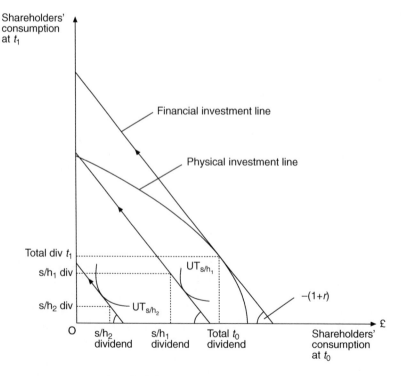

The conclusions of the basic model

This development of the single-period investment–consumption model, as it is called, is important not only for illustrating how and why money has a time value, but also as acting as an introduction to financial decision making in general. In this respect, we stated that management's objective must be to try to maximize shareholders' wealth and this would be achieved through the maximization of the dividend flow through time. The separation theorem places this latter statement in a clearer light.

Management must make investment decisions so as to maximize the dividend flow to shareholders. But this is only the first stage of a two-stage process, because the individual shareholder then uses the capital market to adjust the timing of this dividend flow so that it accords with his desired pattern of consumption.

The conclusions of our one-period investment–consumption model, *and the assumptions upon which it is based*, are important and wide-ranging (as we shall see later). The model implies that we require a technique of investment appraisal which will ensure that companies undertake physical investment until the return from the marginal investment equates with the perfect capital market rate of return. In other words, companies should undertake capital investment projects as long as the return generated (from each one) is *not less* than the market rate of interest.

Introducing uncertainty

At this point, it should also be noted that, just as individuals have their own personal time value of money, so the capital market interest rate represents the economy's average time value of money. Therefore the capital investment decision rule for companies could be restated as: undertake capital investment projects as long as the rate of return generated from each one is not less than the market's time value of money. However, it should also be noted that this decision rule, as it stands, is set in a world of certainty. In an uncertain world, as we shall see, there is a whole range of different market interest rates. Therefore this decision rule will require some slight modification.

The problem of uncertainty will be developed fully in later chapters, but it will be helpful to introduce the basic idea at this stage. In a certain world, an investment's outcome is known with certainty by the decision maker. In an uncertain world, an investment's outcome is uncertain and hence is referred to as a 'risky' investment. With such investments, decision makers are not entirely uninformed about the possible outcome, in that they *expect* a particular outcome (or cash inflow) from an investment, but realize that the *actual* outcome may differ from what was expected. (Notice too, therefore, that risk is a two-way street. An investment's actual outcome may be either better or worse than was expected.)

Generally speaking, investors dislike uncertainty of outcome. This does not mean that they are unwilling to take on a risky project. Instead it means that they require a reward for doing so and this reward is a higher level of expected return. Therefore, in an uncertain world, there is not just a single capital market interest rate/rate of return, but a whole series of different rates of return – one for each level of risk: the higher the risk, the higher the capital market rate of return.

As a result, in an uncertain world, our capital investment decision rule for companies now has to be modified. Projects should only be undertaken as long as they generate a rate of return which is not less than the capital market's rate of return *for a risk level equivalent to that of the project*.

Payback and ROCE

Clearly, the payback investment appraisal method does not meet the requirements of our decision rule that has been derived through this graphical analysis. The reason being that – even allowing for the fact that it can be adapted to allow for the time value of money – it uses speed of return, rather than rate of return, as its criterion of project desirability.

Equally unsuitable is the return on capital employed because, although it is a rate-of-return concept, it ignores the time value of money.[20] In the next chapter we shall turn to the discounted cash flow methods of investment appraisal and examine the extent to which they meet the requirements of our model.[21]

Summary

This chapter dealt with the Hirshliefer single-period investment-consumption model to examine what was required of a capital investment appraisal decision rule. The following were the main points covered:

- The model was developed initially under six basic assumptions:
  - single time period horizon;
  - certainty of investment outcome;
  - only physical investment opportunities;
  - investments exhibit infinite divisibility and diminishing returns to scale;
  - investments are all independent;
  - investors are rational.

- The concept of the investor's marginal time value of money was introduced, which would be likely to be an increasing function of the amount invested.

- The firm's physical investment line was introduced and it was seen that the slope of the function represented the marginal rate of return on investment projects at any point.

- As a result, firms would locate on the physical investment line at the point where the slope of the line (the marginal project rate of return) equated with the investor's own marginal time value of money.

- In terms of indifference curves, this optimal investment point occurs at the point of tangency between the PIL and the investor's indifference curve set: the slope of the indifference curve reflecting the investor's marginal time value of money.

- With the introduction of capital markets and the financial market line, the graphical analysis can now handle cases other than the single-owner firm. The decision rule is that the firm should invest in projects as long as their return is not less than the market rate of return – given by the slope of the FIL, which reflects society's average time value of money.

- This capital investment decision rule then allows each individual shareholder to adjust the received pattern of dividends/cash flow by using the capital market to locate on the highest possible indifference curve.

- This analysis is known as the Hirshliefer Separation Theorem in that the capital investment decision (made by managers) can be separated from the capital market decision (made by owners/investors/shareholders).

- Finally, the concept of risk was briefly examined. It was argued that, in an uncertain world, the investment decision rule that arose out of the Hirshliefer analysis had to be modified: the firm should accept projects as long as they were expected to produce a return that was not less than the capital market rate of return for that level of risk.

Notes

1. This approach was first used by the American economist Irving Fisher (and hence has become known as Fisherian Analysis) in *The Theory of Interest* (New York, Macmillan 1930). Its use was revived specifically in terms of financial decision theory by Jack Hirshliefer, 'On the Theory of Optimal Investment Decisions', *Journal of Political Economy*, August 1958.

2. Alternatively we could say that all investment opportunities have a life-span of just one period of time, t_0 to t_1.

3. In this assumption of no risk, we are also implicitly assuming that our investor will be alive to enjoy the fruits of his or her decisions.

4. We are also assuming here that the relative price levels of these factors of production are unchanging and so no 'holding gains' (in inflation accounting parlance) are possible.

5. Here we are using the term 'spare cash' in the sense of the residual cash resources of a company after allowing for the claims of all creditors.

6. In this simple case we are obviously ignoring the possible constraining influence of legislation in respect of company dividends.

7. We can define a consistent criterion for investment decisions as one which would produce the following decision: if Project A is preferred to Project B and Project B is preferred to Project C, then the decision criterion should result in Project A being preferred to Project C. If not, the criterion is not producing consistent decisions. Technically, the decision making must exhibit 'transitivity'.

8. This time value of money could be either positive or negative. For instance, an individual could be willing to take 5p less 'next year' for every

£1 invested 'now', so his exchange rate would be $95/100 - 1 = -0.05$ or -5%. However, there is considerable evidence to suggest that TVMs are usually positive, with the ultimate, although somewhat morbid, argument being the inevitability of death. So in a one-period case, in order to be persuaded to forgo £1 of consumption 'now', the owner will have to be offered £1 + 'next year', just to cover the risk that he may not be around next year to collect the return from the investment – he may be dead!

As an individual's time value of money is likely not to remain constant but to change with events, it is more correct to call any TVM a *marginal* time value of money.

9. The literature gives this curve a variety of names, e.g. investment opportunity line, productive opportunity line or time-exchange function.

10. As a result of this arrangement and of our assumption that all physical investment opportunities are infinitely divisible and display decreasing returns to scale, the physical investment line is likely to be generally smooth and concave to the origin. In the real world of investments that are not infinitely divisible it is anything but smooth.

11. The term 'maximum consumption combinations' is meant in the sense that with any given amount of current consumption, no higher consumption next year is possible with the company's existing resources and similarly, with any given amount of consumption next year, no higher level of current consumption is possible.

12. The return on the marginal investment – the marginal return – can properly be found from the first derivative of the function of the physical investment line. For illustration purposes it can be very roughly approximated by:

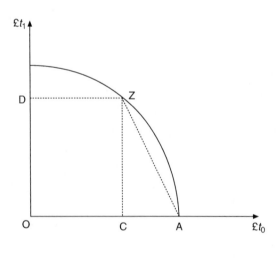

$$\frac{OD - CA}{CA} = \frac{OD}{CA} - \frac{CA}{CA} = \frac{OD}{CA} - 1.$$

Therefore if the company has a total value now of £1000 (OA) of which the owner consumes £600 (OC) and invests the remainder (CA) in order to produce £450 (OD) next year, we can obtain a rough approximation of the return on the marginal project (point Z) as:

$$\frac{450}{400} - 1 = 0.125 = 12\tfrac{1}{2}\%.$$

Graphically, we are finding the slope of the dotted line ZA. In fact this calculation of $12\tfrac{1}{2}\%$ does not provide the return on the marginal investment, but the *average* return on the *total* investment.

13. It is worth noting that under our present assumptions it makes no difference to our analysis whether or not the company represents the owner's sole source of consumption. However, we shall see later that when some of the assumptions are varied, this factor becomes important.

14. The concept of a perfect capital market will prove extremely important to us, in later developments of the theory. For the time being we shall define it – under the assumption of a world of certainty – as a market where everyone can borrow or lend as much money as they wish (within their ability to repay) at a single rate of interest which is applicable to all, whether borrowing or lending. Additionally there are no transaction costs involved in using the market, no single investor or group of investors dominate the market and all information is freely available.

15. Up to this point, no mention has been made of taxation. It is easiest to assume that taxation does not exist, but it makes little difference to the analysis if tax is levied on gain as long as all investors face the same level of taxation and there is no differentiation between gain from physical and capital market investment. In such circumstances the return on investment referred to in the analysis is, of course, the after-tax return.

16. This term is negative because the line AE has a negative slope – it slopes downwards from left to right.

17. This is often referred to as the Hirshliefer Separation Theorem.

18. The reader must be careful not to be misled here. The test of being 'better off' or increasing utility is whether or not a higher indifference curve is reached. So we could just as easily get a situation where the shareholder achieves a higher indifference curve through using the capital markets but this results (say) in a decrease in consumption 'now' and an increase 'next year'. As a higher indifference curve has been reached the reduction in consumption 'now' must be more than offset (in the shareholder's mind) by the gain in consumption 'next year'.

19. It would be possible, although somewhat unlikely, for all of a company's shareholders to have an identical set of indifference curves/time value of money. In such cases the separation theorem would lose its importance.

20. In fact there do exist chance circumstances when ROCE will provide correct investment appraisal advice, but such situations are likely to be highly artificial and of little practical significance.

21. It may be wise to correct here a mistaken impression that the reader could possibly gain from this presentation and development of the theory. Historically, payback and ROCE were derived (largely) in ignorance of the single-period investment–consumption model. It is therefore not surprising that neither method meets the model's requirement for an investment appraisal technique. However, the two major discounted cash flow methods, which are to be discussed in the next chapter, were *not* developed

in isolation from the model but arise out of the logic which lies behind the model's construction.

The reader should not hold the belief that it is just fortuitous that these later two methods of investment appraisal accord (as we shall see) with the model.

Further reading

1. The basic reading for the ideas discussed in this chapter is: J. Hirshliefer, 'On the Theory of Optimal Investment Decisions', *Journal of Political Economy*, August 1958. The article is not easy reading, especially the second half, but is very much worthwhile.
2. Although the idea of risk has only been introduced very briefly at this stage, an accessible article to read would be: J. Hirshliefer, 'Risk, the Discount Rate and Investment Decision', *American Economic Review*, May 1961.

Quickie questions

1. Why is an individual's personal time value of money likely to increase as more investment is undertaken?
2. What does the physical investment line represent?
3. What determines the slope of the physical investment line?
4. What is an indifference curve?
5. Given a single owner-manager firm, how does the firm decide on its level of capital investment?
6. If an owner wants to lend money at t_0, does he move up or down the financial investment line?
7. What is the two-part decision rule that arises out of the Hirshliefer separation theorem?
8. Define a risky capital investment.
9. Taking risk into consideration, what is the capital investment decision rule that managers should follow if they wish to maximize shareholder wealth?
10. What are the four main assumptions (remember, two were dropped at later stages in the analysis) of the single period investment–consumption model?
11. What is the generally assumed attitude of investors to risk?
12. If your personal marginal time value of money was less than the market interest rate, would you want to lend or borrow?

Problem

1. Phonetic plc has £500 of cash resources available at t_0. It has identified three investment projects, as follows:

Project	I	II	III
Outlay at t_0	100	200	200
Inflow at t_1	120	300	210

Assume that all projects exhibit *constant* returns to scale.

Required:
(a) Draw, to scale, the physical investment line facing the firm.

(b) Given that the market interest rate is 8% show, graphically, the firm's investment decisions and the resulting t_0 and t_1 cash flow to the owner.

(c) How might the investment decisions of the firm change if the market interest rate moved:
- (i)   to 25%?
- (ii) to 10%?
- (iii) to 20%?

(d) Given the market interest rate of 8%, before the firm can implement the investment plan given in your answer to part (b) an extra project is identified:

Project	IV
Outlay at t_0	250
Inflow at t_1	330

Show the new situation graphically. What is your revised investment decision advice to management?

5 The discounted cash flow approach

Net present value

Having examined the two 'traditional' methods of capital investment appraisal, it is now time to turn to the other two main appraisal techniques. These are net present value (NPV) and internal rate of return (IRR) both of which are described as discounted cash flow (DCF) methods. We shall start by first examining the net present value technique.

The NPV investment appraisal method works on the simple, but fundamental, principle that an investment is worthwhile undertaking if the money got out of the investment is greater than the money put in (assuming of course that our objectives can be described in financial terms). On this very commonsense principle, project A is worth investing in. For an outlay of £500, it produces a total cash inflow of £600. Thus it has a net value of plus £100.

Project A

Year	Cash flow (£)
0	−500
1	+200
2	+200
3	+200
	+100 net value

It is clear that, with such a straightforward approach, the decision rule would be: accept all investments with a positive or zero net value (as they produce a return either equal to or greater than their cost), and reject all those with a negative net value.

However, let us take a totally different situation. Suppose you were made an offer: if you pay £500 now, you will immediately receive 200 French francs, 200 Japanese yen and 200 German marks. How would you go about deciding whether the offer was worthwhile? What you certainly would *not* do is to say: I have to give up 500 pieces of paper and, in return, I'll get 200 + 200 + 200 = 600 pieces of paper. As I end up with 100 more pieces of paper, the deal is worthwhile! Instead, you would recognize that in order to evaluate the offer, you have to convert all the different currencies to a *common* currency, and *then* undertake the comparison.

Although it does not *look* as silly as that which was initially suggested with the currency offer, our suggested approach to evaluating Project A *is* just as silly. In the same way that money in different currencies cannot be compared directly, but first have to be converted to a common currency, cash flows in the same currency (as in Project A), but occurring *at different points in time* cannot be compared directly, but must first be converted to a common point of time. This is because of the *time value of money*.

Therefore the net present value investment appraisal decision rule basically takes the same approach as that used with Project A, but with one vital difference. That difference is that the time value of money is taken into account in assessing whether the investment has a positive or negative net value.

The discounting process

The time value of money is taken into account through the discounting process. The arithmetic of discounting is dealt with in an appendix to this chapter and the reader is advised to become familiar with its contents. However, it will help to explain the NPV technique if the basic concepts of discounting are developed here.

We have already seen from our initial discussion on the time value of money in Chapter 3 that, given the choice between £100 now, or £100 in twelve months' time, most people would intuitively take the £100 now. This is because the £100 could be placed on deposit at (say) 6% interest and so turn itself into £106 in twelve months' time. (And, being rational investors, £106 in twelve months' time will be preferred to only £100 in twelve months' time.) Therefore, in this case, 6% – the interest rate – represents the time value of money.

The mathematics of this process works through the compound interest formula:

$$A(1 + r)^n$$

where A is the initial amount invested or deposited, r is the (annual) rate of return (which could be interest) and n is the number of years for which A is left deposited. In the example used above, these three variables have the respective values of: £100, 0.06 and 1. So, £100 left on deposit for twelve months is turned into:

$$£100(1 + 0.06)^1 = £100 + £6 = £106.$$

Using this compound interest formula, but switching it around, we can also calculate that to receive £106 in twelve months' time, the amount to be invested now is:

$$\frac{£106}{(1+0.06)} = £106\frac{1}{(1+0.06)} = £100.$$

Therefore £100 is the 'present value' (PV) of £106 received in twelve months' time and £106, the 'future' or 'terminal' value (FV) of £100 deposited twelve months' previously, assuming a 6% interest rate in each case.

Similarly, £100 invested for two years at a 6% compound interest rate would turn into:

$$£100(1 + 0.06)(1 + 0.06) = £100(1 + 0.06)^2 = £112.36$$

and £112.36 received in two years' time is equal to:

$$\frac{£112.36}{(1+0.06)^2} = £112.36\frac{1}{(1+0.06)^2} = £100 \text{ now.}$$

Thus the terminal value in two years' time of £100 invested now is £112.36, whilst the present value of £112.36 received in two years' time is £100. In each case we are assuming an annual compound interest rate of 6%.

In general terms, $A(1 + r)^n$ is the terminal value of an amount A that has been placed on deposit for n years at an annual compound interest rate of r. Similarly: $A[1/(1 + r)^n]$ is the *present value* of an amount A received in n years' time, where r is the annual compound interest rate.

In the calculation of the terminal value, an amount of money is being 'compounded' *forward* through time, whereas in the calculation of the present value, an amount of money is being 'discounted' *backwards* through time. To distinguish between these two processes, it is usual to refer to the compound interest rate, when used in the discounting process, as the *discount rate*. Also, usually a slightly easier notation is used for the present value expression: $A(1 + r)^{-n}$. Thus in the previous example, the present value of £112.36 received in two years' time, when the annual rate of discount was 6%, is given by:

$$\frac{£112.36}{(1+0.06)^2} = £112.36(1+0.06)^{-2} = £112.36 \times 0.8900 = £100.$$

A discounting example

The NPV method makes use of the idea of present values by expressing the project's cash flows in terms of its net *present* value, although the cash flows could just as easily be expressed in terms of net *terminal* values. It is really for no reason other than convention that present values are used.

To see how the NPV method works, let us return to Project A, but this time, instead of just netting out the cash inflows and outflows to produce a net value of plus £100, we first of all convert (or 'discount') the cash flows to *present value* cash flows, in order to allow for the time value of money, and then net out the inflows and outflows. Thus with a discount rate of (say) 8%, the net present value of Project A is £15.40:

Project A

Year	Cash flow (£)	×	Discounting factor			=	Present value cash flow (£)
0	−500	×	$(1+0.08)^0$	=	−500 × 1	=	−500.00
1	+200	×	$(1+0.08)^{-1}$	=	+200 × 0.9259	=	+185.18
2	+200	×	$(1+0.08)^{-2}$	=	+200 × 0.8573	=	+171.46
3	+200	×	$(1+0.08)^{-3}$	=	+200 × 0.7938	=	+158.76
					NPV		+ 15.40

From this analysis we can see that Project A is worth undertaking, because the cash outflows associated with it are exceeded by the cash inflows produced by it. The time value of money has been taken into account by the fact that all the cash flows of the project, for the purposes of comparison, are converted to values at one point in time: the present.

To emphasize this important point further, it is vital to understand that once the fact is accepted that money has a time value, then it follows that money at different points in time is not directly comparable: £1 now cannot be directly compared with £1 next year, and so the cash flows of a project that arise at different points through time all have to be converted to a value at one particular point in time. By convention, and because it has many practical advantages, the point in time normally chosen is the present.

Thus our original netting procedure with Project A which produced a net value of +£100 was nonsensical, because we were not comparing like with like, but were trying to compare directly the net money flows arising at different points in time without first converting them to a common point in time. The NPV approach tells us that in terms of present values (i.e. converting all the cash flows to money values *now*) Project A produces a return which is £15.40 in excess of the investment outlay (i.e. in present value terms the cash outflow is £500 and the total cash inflow is £515.40) and is therefore a worthwhile investment.

Project B

Year	Cash flow (£)	×	Discounting factor		=	Present value cash flow (£)
0	−1000	×	$(1+0.08)^0$	=	−1000.00
1	+ 100	×	$(1+0.08)^{-1}$	=	+ 92.59
2	+ 200	×	$(1+0.08)^{-2}$	=	+ 171.46
3	+ 200	×	$(1+0.08)^{-3}$	=	+ 158.76
4	+ 550	×	$(1+0.08)^{-4}$	=	+ 404.25
Net value	+ 50			NPV		− 172.94

As another example, evaluating Project B without taking into account the time value of money, the cash inflows exceed the cash outflows by £50 and so the project appears to be a worthwhile investment. However if we do take into account the time value of money by discounting the cash flows into present values at an 8% discount rate, then we can see that Project B is *not* a worthwhile investment, because the cash outflow required exceeds the cash inflows produced, resulting in a *negative* net present value.

Calculating present values

The discounting factors, such as $(1 + 0.08)^{-3}$, can be calculated quite easily on any basic calculator that has a 'powers' function, i.e. x^y. In addition, a table of discounting factors for a variety of values of n and i is given on page 606. These tables can be used to find that $(1 + 0.08)^{-3}$ equals 0.7938. In other words, the present value of £1 in three years' time at an 8% rate of discount is 79.38 pence. Therefore, £200 in three years' time has a present value of: £200 × 0.7938 = £158.76.

It is also very easy to use computer spreadsheets to find the present value of a series of cash flows. If you have access to a PC with a spreadsheet, use it to caculate the NPV of example B above. If you use the NPV function built into the spreadsheet you will probably have come up with the answer −£160.1. This is because the function was incorrectly defined in the first spreadsheets to have an NPV function and, presumably for the sake of consistency, it has been incorrectly defined ever since. It is actually present value and not net present value. Using the notation below, the function in the spreadsheet is

$$\sum_{t=1}^{n} \frac{A_t}{(1+r)^t}$$

but for NPV t should equal 0 to n and not 1 to n. Thus the spreadsheet function is incorrect by one power of $1 + r$ for each period calculated.

The timing of cash flows

For the sake of simplicity we will continue to assume, in the examples that follow, that cash flows are discrete and occur at the end of the time period in question. Obviously, in the real world this will often not be the case. Many cash flows in business happen throught the year (e.g. sales, purchases and expenses). To be strictly accurate we should work on the basis that both cash flows and compounding are continuous. The formula for calculating the present value of cash flows like this is an exponential function:

$$1/r \, (1 - e^{-r}).$$

Applying this to a discount rate of 11% gives a discount factor of 0.947 for cash flows taking place during the first year. Thus if we received £100 every day this would total £36 500 (spread over the year) and its present value would be £36 500 × .947 = £34 566.

However, it is not always convenient to work figures out using exponential functions and there is an extremely good approximation that is much easier to use. All we need to do is to assume that the cash flows take place discretely but half way through the year, so in year one (still using 11%) this would produce the discount factor

$$1/(1.11)^{0.5} = 0.95.$$

Applying this to our cash flow of £36 500 produces a present value of £34 675 which is less than 0.5% out. Had we assumed a year end cash flow, 1/1.11 gives us a discount factor of 0.90 and if we apply this to £36 500 we find a present value of £32 850 which is nearly 5% out.

Discount tables using mid-point cash flows are included in the tables that start at page 251.

The NPV decision rule

In general terms, we can express the net present value of an investment project as the sum of its net discounted future cash flows:

$$\sum_{t=0}^{n} \frac{A_t}{(1+r)^t}$$

where A_t is the project's cash flow (either positive or negative) in time t (t takes on values from year 0 to year n, where n represents the point in time when the project comes to the end of its life) and r is the annual rate of discount or the time value of money (which is here assumed to remain a constant over the life of the project). If the expression has a zero or positive value, the company should invest in the project; if it has negative value, it should not invest.[1] (This general mathematical expression for the net present value of an investment project is more fully explained in the appendix on compounding and discounting at the end of this chapter.)

Let us take a closer look at Project B to see why the NPV method tells us not to invest. Project B requires an outlay of £1000 and would produce cash inflows for the four following years. However, if we did not invest £1000 in B we could, presumably, put the money on deposit (i.e. lend the money on the capital market) at the going rate of interest of 8%. At the end of four years' time this would produce £1000 × (1 + 0.08)⁴ = £1360.50.

Suppose we *did* invest in Project B and as the generated cash inflows arose we placed them on deposit (at 8% compound interest). How much cash would we be able to accumulate by the end of four years (i.e. by the time the life of the project was completed)? This is shown below, where the £100 Project B produces in twelve months' time can be invested for three years, the £200 it produces in 24 months' time can be invested for two years, and so on:

Year	Project's cash inflow (£)	×	Compounding factor	=	Terminal value (end of year 4) (£)
1	+ 100	×	$(1+0.08)^3$	=	+ 125.97
2	+ 200	×	$(1+0.08)^2$	=	+ 233.28
3	+ 200	×	$(1+0.08)^1$	=	+ 216.00
4	+ 550	×	$(1+0.08)^0$	=	+ 550.00
			Total terminal value	=	+ 1125.25

So putting the £1000 on deposit for four years produces £1360.50, whereas if we invest our £1000 in Project B and place on deposit any cash flows that arise, at the end of four years this will produce only £1125.25.

Therefore, looking at the two alternatives, the project is not the most desirable investment: we should be better off placing the £1000 on deposit in the capital market. This is the basis of the advice given by the NPV appraisal method because the present value of £1360.50 received in four years' time with an 8% discount rate is:

$$£1360.50(1 + 0.08)^{-4} = £1000$$

whilst the present value of £1125.25 received in four years' time with an 8% discount rate is:

$$£1125.25(1 + 0.08)^{-4} = £827.06.$$

The difference between these two sums (£1000 − £827.06) is £172.94, which is the amount of Project B's negative net present value.

So we can see that the NPV method of investment appraisal evaluates projects by looking at the *alternative* to an investment in that project, such as lending the money out on the capital market at the market rate of interest. It automatically carries out this comparison of alternatives through the decision rule: only invest in projects which produce zero or positive NPVs. As we have seen, the value of a project's NPV represents the increase or decrease (depending upon whether the NPV is positive or negative) in return that would arise from investing in the project rather than lending the money on the capital market at the market rate of interest, and it is this rate that is used as the discount rate.

Alternative interpretations of NPV

There are some equally valid, alternative interpretations of the meaning behind a project's net present value which might be helpful to examine in order to gain a deeper understanding. We will take another project as an example. Project C is expected to produce the following net cash flows:

Year	Cash flow (£)
0	−100
1	+ 30
2	+ 40
3	+ 50
4	+ 20

Referring back to our brief discussion at the end of the previous chapter about risk, suppose that the capital market rate of return available from an investment of similar risk to Project C is 10%. Thus 10% is the relevant time value of money and so is the appropriate discount rate to use in an NPV analysis.

Project C's NPV is calculated as:

Year	Cash flow (£)		Discount factor		PV cash flow (£)
0	− 100	×	$(1 + 0.10)^{0}$	=	− 100.00
1	+ 30	×	$(1 + 0.10)^{-1}$	=	+ 27.27
2	+ 40	×	$(1 + 0.10)^{-2}$	=	+ 33.06
3	+ 50	×	$(1 + 0.10)^{-3}$	=	+ 37.57
4	+ 20	×	$(1 + 0.10)^{-4}$	=	+ 13.66
					+ £11.56 NPV

Project C has a positive NPV and therefore, according to the decision rule, is worthwhile undertaking. There are three obvious interpretations that can be made of this result:

1. An investment of £100 in Project C produces £11.56 more, in t_0 terms, than investing on the capital market. In this sense, the £11.56

is an *excess* return or a measure of *economic profit*. (This is our original interpretation.)

2. As Project C produces a positive NPV, it is generating a return which is greater than 10%, the discount rate used.
3. If £100 were borrowed at 10% interest, in order to undertake Project C, then the project would generate a sufficient cash flow to pay the interest, repay the loan *and* leave a surplus of £11.56 in present value terms.

Given these three interpretations, the logic of the NPV decision rule becomes even more obvious:

1. A negative NPV project is unacceptable because it indicates that the project makes a loss *relative* to a capital market investment (i.e. an opportunity loss).
2. A negative NPV project is unacceptable because it is producing a return less than that available for a similar level of risk on the capital market.
3. A negative NPV project is unacceptable as it would not generate sufficient cash flow to repay the financial cost of undertaking it.

Also notice, given these interpretations, that a zero NPV project *would* be acceptable – but we would not be overjoyed if we identified one.

Finally, there is a fourth interpretation of a project's NPV that can be made. In many ways, this is the most important interpretation and how it arises will be seen in the next section when we return to the Hirshliefer analysis. Quite simply, a project's net present value indicates the increase in shareholders' wealth that it will generate if it is undertaken. Hence, the technique links directly into our fundamental objective of financial management decision making.

NPV and the investment–consumption model

When looking at our single-period investment–consumption model, we saw that in order to act in the best interests of its owners, a company should move along the physical investment line until the return from the marginal investment becomes equal to the return given by the capital market (i.e. the market rate of interest). How does the NPV method of investment appraisal help us achieve this point?

Returning to Project A, we saw that, using an 8% discount rate, the project had an NPV of plus £15.40 whilst Project B had an NPV of minus £172.94. On the basis of what we already understand about the net present value, we can also say – using the two examples above – that as Project A has a positive NPV when discounted at 8%, it must be producing a rate of return *greater* than 8%, and similarly, as Project B has a negative NPV when discounted at 8%, then it must be producing a rate of return of *less than* 8%.

Just what the exact rate of return is in each case we shall consider later, but looking at Project D, since it gives a zero NPV when discounted at 8%, we can conclude that it has a rate of return exactly *equal* to 8%:

Project D

Year	Cash flow (£)	×	Present value factor		Present value cash flow (£)
0	− 400	×	$(1 + 0.08)^0$	=	− 400.00
1	+ 200	×	$(1 + 0.08)^{-1}$	=	+ 185.18
2	+ 100	×	$(1 + 0.08)^{-2}$	=	+ 85.73
3	+ 162.62	×	$(1 + 0.08)^{-3}$	=	+ 129.09
				NPV	£0

Therefore, if a company follows the NPV rule and invests in all physical investment opportunities available to it that possess either zero or positive net present values, using the market rate of interest as the discount rate, it will automatically move along the physical investment line until a point of tangency is reached with the financial investment line.

If a company makes physical investments beyond this optimal point, these projects will have a rate of return which is less than the market rate of interest and therefore *negative* net present values. As long as investment decision makers within companies follow the NPV decision rule and *only* invest in projects with zero or positive NPVs, then the company is ensured of optimally locating on the physical investment line.

The graphical interpretation

In Fig. 5.1, if management assess the company's total resources (i.e. the full, liquidated value of the company at time t_0) as OA and they have sought out all the investment alternatives available to them, expressed by the physical investment line AB, then using the NPV method of investment appraisal, they will invest in all projects with positive or zero NPVs when discounted at the market rate of interest.

Fig. 5.1 *Using the NPV rule*

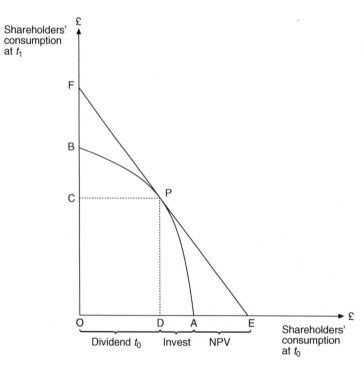

This simple decision rule will lead to DA of the company's resources being put into productive investments at t_0 and the remainder, OD, being paid out to shareholders as dividends. This investment will result in a total dividend of OC being paid out at t_1. Shareholders can then adjust their individual dividends to fit their desired consumption pattern by lending or borrowing on the capital market. This two-stage process, with the company first making physical investment decisions and then the individual shareholder making financial investment decisions, will ensure that individual shareholders will achieve their highest possible indifference curves and hence maximize their level of utility.

We should also note that if the company does invest up to the optimal point P in Fig. 5.1 (i.e. the point of tangency between the physical and financial investment lines), then the present value of the cash *inflows* generated by all the company's investment project undertakings is given by DE, the cash expenditure made on these investments is given by DA and so, by difference, AE represents the total *net* present value of the investment projects undertaken by the firm. (Alternatively, OE can be said to represent the present value of the sum of dividend OD at t_0 and dividend OC at t_1.)

From this we can see the derivation of that important fourth interpretation of the idea of net present value. Notice that with no investment undertaken, the total worth of the company's resources (in t_0 terms) is given by AO. If amount AD is invested to yield OC at t_1, then the worth of the company (again, in t_0 terms) increases to amount OE. Thus undertaking the investments required to locate at point P on the physical investment line has resulted in an increase in the current worth of the company – in other words, in shareholders' wealth – of AE, which of course represents the total NPV of the investments undertaken. Therefore the net present value of a project represents the amount by which shareholders' wealth (measured in t_0 terms) will change as a result of accepting the project. (It thus becomes obvious why management should not accept *negative* NPV projects – they will cause shareholders' wealth to be reduced.)

In general, the single-period investment–consumption diagram can measure the NPV of a company's total physical investments as the distance between the point at which the physical investment line cuts the horizontal axis and where the financial investment line, passing through the point at which the firm has located on the physical investment line, also cuts the horizontal axis.[2] As can be seen from Fig. 5.2, if a company either under-invests and locates at (say) point X, or over-invests and locates at (say) point Y, or optimally invests and locates at point Z on the physical investment line, in each case the total NPV earned by the company's investment decisions is given by the distance on the horizontal axis between the physical investment line and the financial investment line passing through the location point: respectively AB, AC and AD.[3] Locating at the optimal point on the physical investment line (at the point of tangency with the market line) also maximizes NPV and so here is yet another surrogate for the financial decision-making objective of maximizing shareholder wealth, that of maximizing total net present value.

One final point of interest from this graphical analysis is to use it to look at the effect of a change in the market rate of interest. A *fall* in the market rate of interest will cause the financial investment line to pivot anticlockwise and become flatter. This would then have the effect of moving the point of tangency (and hence the optimal physical investment point) higher

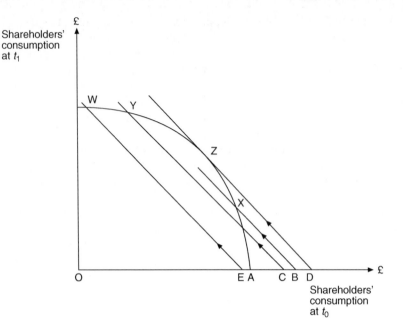

Fig. 5.2 *Under and over investments*

up the physical investment line, thus increasing the amount of investment that a company must undertake to reach its point of optimality. This is just as we would expect, as is the case where the market rate of interest rises and the reverse effect is observed.

(The reader no doubt has noticed how the analysis has slipped in and out of the assumption of a single-period time horizon. The assumption was made in the Hirshliefer analysis in order to allow a graphical/two-dimensional presentation. However, the conclusions drawn can be quite simply applied to a multi-time period example, such as that of Project D.)

Internal rate of return

Before looking more carefully at this analysis and specifically at the implicit and explicit assumptions that lie behind the NPV method, let us turn to the second major discounted cash flow investment appraisal technique, the internal rate of return (IRR) or yield.[4] As we shall see later on in the discussion, the IRR has some very great theoretical and practical difficulties as a method of investment appraisal, and indeed it may be questioned whether it is truly a method of appraisal at all, or just an arithmetic result.

The IRR model

To discover what the IRR is, let us return briefly to our discussion of NPV. We stated that if a project had a positive NPV at a certain discount rate (say) 10%, this meant, amongst other things, that the project's return was actually greater than 10%, whilst if the project had a negative NPV then its return was less than the discount rate, and if it had a zero NPV, then its return was equal to the discount rate.

The IRR of a project can be defined as the rate of discount which, when applied to the project's cash flows, produces a zero NPV (hence the method could be seen as just an arithmetic result of the NPV method). In general terms, the IRR is the value for r which satisfies the expression:

$$\sum_{t=0}^{n} \frac{A}{\left(1+r\right)^t} = 0.$$

For a very simple project, such as E, where cash flows only extend over two periods, the internal rate of return is easy to calculate using simple algebra:

Project E

Year	Cash flow (£)
0	+ 200
1	+ 218

The IRR of Project E is equal to r, where:

$$-200 + \frac{218}{1+r} = 0.$$

Multiplying both sides by $(1 + r)$ gives:

$$-200(1 + r) + 218 = 0$$

and rearranging: $218 - 200 = 200r$

$$18 = 200r$$

$$\frac{18}{200} = r = 0.09 \text{ or } 9\%.$$

Thus if Project E's cash flows were discounted by 9% they would have a zero NPV:

Project E

Year	Cash flow (£)	×	Present value factor		Present value cash flow (£)
0	− 200	×	$(1 + 0.09)^0$	=	− 200
1	+ 218	×	$(1 + 0.09)^{-1}$	=	+ 200
				NPV	£0

And with a slightly more complex project, with cash flows occurring at three points of time, t_0, t_1, and t_2, the IRR can still easily be found through the solution to a quadratic equation, as with Project F:

Project F

Year	Cash flow (£)
0	− 100
1	+ 60
2	+ 55

IRR $= r$, where:

$$-100 + \frac{60}{1+r} + \frac{55}{\left(1+r\right)^2} = 0.$$

Multiplying both sides by $(1+r)^2$, we produce a quadratic equation in $1+r$ that can be solved via the quadratic formula:

$$-100(1+r)^2 + 60(1+r) + 55 = 0$$

$$(1+r) = \frac{-60 \pm \sqrt{60^2 - (4 \times -100 \times 55)}}{(2 \times 100)}$$

$$(1+r) = +1.10 \text{ or } (1+r) = -0.50.$$

This second (negative) result can be discarded as meaningless for our purposes, so that $1 + r = 1.10$ and $r = 0.10$ or 10%. This is the internal rate of return of Project F, and therefore if the project's cash flows were discounted at this rate they would have a zero NPV.

Estimating the IRR via linear interpolation

To find the IRR of projects whose cash flows extend over more than three points in time, we become involved with finding solutions to complex polynomial equations. There are many computer programs that will carry out this task, including spreadsheets. Try the example in the last section using the spreadsheet package on your PC to calculate IRR if you have access to one. If you don't have access to a computer (and this must be very rare for corporate decision makers) a fairly good *approximation* of an investment project's IRR can be found through the mathematical technique called linear interpolation.

Returning to Project F, although we have found its IRR to be 10%, let us now estimate it by using the *linear interpolation* method.

If a whole series of different discount rates were applied to Project F's cash flow, the resulting NPVs could be plotted out on a graph against the discount rate. Fig. 5.3 illustrates the sort of result that might occur, termed the *NPV profile*. Notice that the project's IRR is given by the point where the NPV profile cuts the horizontal axis.

We will first deal with the *mechanics* of linear interpolation, and then examine its rationale. The approach used is to select a pair of discount rates so that one of them, when applied to the project's cash flow, produces a positive NPV and the other produces a negative NPV. From observing Fig. 5.3, it can be seen that as the discount rate (the time value of money) gets larger, the positive NPV gets progressively smaller, passes through zero, and then becomes an increasingly large negative value. (This result is, of course, not surprising, knowing as much as we do about the time value of money concept.) Therefore a low and a high discount rate should be chosen to provide the required positive and negative NPVs.

Using 4% and 20% discount rates (the extreme discount rate values given in the table on page 606), the NPV of Project F can be calculated as:

$0 - 100 (1.04)^0 = -100.00$	$0 - 100 (1.20)^0 = -100.00$
$1 + 60 (1.04)^{-1} = +57.69$	$1 + 60 (1.20)^{-1} = +50.00$
$2 + 55 (1.04)^{-2} = +50.85$	$2 + 55 (1.20)^{-2} = +38.19$
$\text{NPV} = +8.54$	$\text{NPV} = -11.81$

Given the IRR is that discount rate that produces a *zero* NPV, Project F's

IRR must lie somewhere between 4% and 20%. As the IRR is more than 4%, *how much* more than 4% is estimated by taking the NPV at 4% as a proportion (0.42) of the difference between the two NPVs calculated. That proportion is then taken of the difference between the two discount rates used (16%):

$$\text{IRR} = 4\% \left[\frac{+8.54}{+8.54 - (-11.81)} \times (20\% - 4\%) \right]$$

$$\text{IRR} = 4\% + [0.42 \times 16\%] = 10.72\%.$$

Figure 5.3 shows the linear interpolation method diagrammatically. The IRR is only estimated, because the NPV profile is being approximated by a straight line.

This 'bracketing' of discount rates around the true IRR so as to produce a positive and negative NPV is not strictly necessary, but it does make the

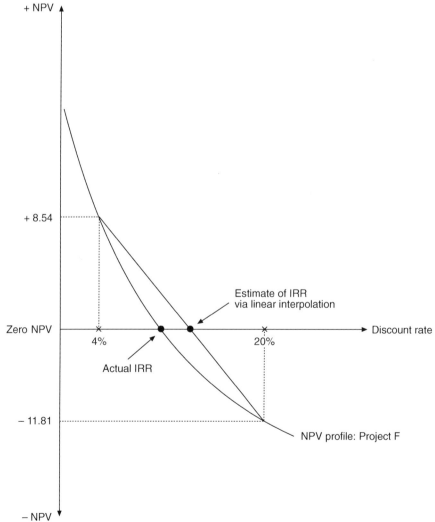

Fig. 5.3 *Estimating the IRR (not to scale)*

approximation calculation easier. Furthermore, the narrower the bracketing around the actual IRR, the more accurate the estimate of the IRR. For example, using 8% and 12% discount rates, linear interpolation estimates Project F's IRR as:

At 8% discount rate: +2.70 NPV

At 12% discount rate: −2.58 NPV

$$IRR = 8\%\left[\frac{+2.70}{+2.70-(-2.58)}\times(12\%-8\%)\right]=10.04\%.$$

This gives a much closer result to the actual IRR. However, for most investment appraisal purposes, a highly accurate estimate of the IRR is not justified and an estimate with the accuracy of our initial calculation is usually more than sufficient.

Finally, notice that the arithmetic of linear interpolation can still be used, even if the two discount rates used do *not* produce one positive and one negative NPV, as they have done in the examples used so far.

The general rule for using linear interpolation is as follows. Select any two discount rates, a lower rate and a higher rate. Calculate the project's NPV at each discount rate. Given that:

LRNPV = NPV of the project when calculated at the lower discount rate
HRNPV = NPV of the project when calculated at the higher discount rate
LDR   = Lower discount rate, and
HDR   = Higher discount rate, then:

$$IRR = LDR + \left[\frac{LRNPV}{LRNPV - HRNPV}\times(HDR-LDR)\right].$$

This is illustrated in Example 1.

Example 1

Arnold Ltd wish to estimate the IRR of a project that is under evaluation. Its cash flows are as follows:

Year	Cash flow (£)
0	−10 000
1	+ 5000
2	+ 8000
3	+ 3000

Again using 4% and 20% as the two discount rates, the NPV of the project is as follows (but remember, any two discounts could be used although, of course, they will give a different answer because the linear interpolation method is only estimating the IRR. Thus, using a different pair of discount rates will produce a different estimate):

At a 4% discount rate, the NPV is + £4871
At a 20% discount rate, the NPV is + £1458

Therefore the project's IRR can be estimated as:

$$IRR = 4\% + \left[\frac{£4871}{£4871 - £1458}\times(20\%-4\%)\right]=26.8\%.$$

The IRR decision rule

Having seen how to calculate a project's internal rate of return, how are we to use it for investment appraisal purposes? The decision rule is that only projects with an IRR greater than or equal to some predetermined 'cut-off' rate should be accepted. This cut-off rate is usually the market rate of interest (i.e. the discount rate that would have been used if an NPV analysis were undertaken instead). All other investment project opportunities should be rejected. Therefore Project F would be acceptable if the decision criterion has been set at 10%, or less.

The reasoning behind the IRR decision rule is similar to that behind NPV. The market interest rate reflects the *opportunity cost* of the capital involved. Thus to be acceptable, a project must generate a return at least equal to the return available elsewhere on the capital market.

IRR and the investment–consumption model

Again, just as the NPV method fitted into our single-period investment–consumption model, so too does the IRR method. We originally described the physical investment line as representing the whole series of infinitely divisible physical investment projects which were available to the company, arranged in order of decreasing rate of return. This rate of return can be viewed as the individual project's internal rate of return and can be derived (as we have already seen) from the slope of the physical investment lines.[5]

In Fig. 5.4 therefore, moving progressively along the line from point A to B, the slope gets less and less steep, indicating that the company initially

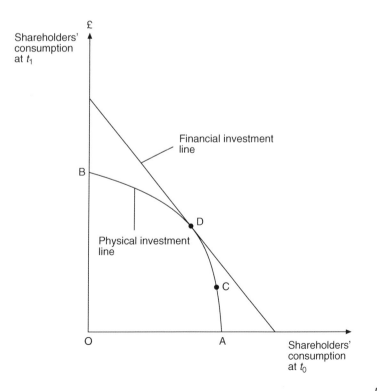

Fig. 5.4 *Using the IRR rule*

invests in projects with high internal rates of return and then works its way through to projects with much smaller IRRs. Thus from the slope of the physical investment line at point C can be derived the IRR of the marginal physical investment represented by that point.

The IRR decision rule tells a company to invest in all projects with IRRs greater than or equal to the market rate of interest. Thus a company will move up and around its physical investment line until it reaches the point of tangency with the financial investment line. Up to this point, all investment projects that the company has undertaken will have IRRs *greater than* the market rate of interest. At point D on Fig. 5.4, the marginal project will have an IRR *equal* to the market interest rate, and it is at this point that the company will cease further investment, because the remaining investment opportunities will all have IRRs which are *less than* the market interest rate. Therefore, the internal rate of return investment appraisal rule, like the NPV rule, will ensure that a company locates at the optimal point on its physical investment line.

Discounted payback

Having examined the basic application of the two discounted cash flow techniques of capital investment appraisal, it is appropriate to return briefly to look at the discounted payback technique, which was referred to in Chapter 3. There it was stated that a major limitation of payback was that it did not take the time value of money into account. However, this criticism could be overcome through the use of discounted payback.

All that discounted payback does is to see how quickly a project takes to pay back its outlay in *present value* (rather than undiscounted), cash flow terms. Example 2 illustrates the approach.

Example 2

Phonate plc wishes to evaluate an investment opportunity using discounted payback, for which it uses a four-year decision criterion. For discounting purposes, the company uses a 10% discount rate which, it is judged, reflects the return available elsewhere in the capital market for a similar risk investment. The project, code-named G, has a five-year life and the following estimated cash flows are as follows:

Year	Cash flow (£)
0	−250 000
1	+100 000
2	+100 000
3	+102 000
4	+ 50 000
5	+ 35 000

The discounted payback of Project G is calculated as follows:

Year	Cash flow (£)	×	Discount factor	=	PV cash flow (£)
0	– 250 000	×	1	=	– 250 000
1	+ 100 000	×	0.9091	=	+ 90 910
2	+ 100 000	×	0.8264	=	+ 82 640
3	+ 102 000	×	0.7513	=	+ 76 633 3-year payback
4	+ 50 000	×	0.6830	=	+ 34 150
5	+ 35 000	×	0.6209	=	+ 21 731

Project G has a discounted payback of approximately three years and so is acceptable, according to the company's decision criterion.

Truncated NPV

Discounted payback can be looked upon as a variation of the basic payback technique. However it is perhaps instructive to see it more as a variation on the NPV method.

In Example 2 the decision rule used by the company implied: accept the project as long as its NPV is at least zero (if not positive) at the end of four years. If a project complies with this requirement then it does pay back within the criterion period. Thus discounted payback is no more than a truncated version of NPV. Instead of calculating the project's NPV over the whole of its life, the NPV is effectively calculated up to some specified cut-off point which, in this example, happened to be four years.

Discounted payback still suffers from the criticism made of standard pay-back – that of ignoring project cash flows that lie outside the payback time period. However, as before, the point should be made that setting this artificial time horizon on a project's life may be no more than making a realistic allowance for management's limited forecasting abilities.

Finally, despite the foregoing, it should be pointed out that the use of discounted payback will not necessarily lead to the firm's optimal physical investment line location. This is because some positive NPV projects may well be rejected because they do not generate that positive NPV sufficiently quickly. A further criticism will be made of discounted payback in the following chapter.

Summary

This chapter has looked at the basic application of the two discounted cash flow (DCF) methods of investment appraisal. The main points covered were as follows:

- The fact that money has a time value (i.e. an opportunity cost in terms of a rate of interest) means that cash flows that arise at different points in time cannot be compared directly but must first be converted to common point of time (usually t_0, the present time).

- The NPV decision rule states:
  — accept a project if its NPV ≥ 0 (i.e. positive or zero);
  — reject a project if its NPV < 0 (i.e. negative).

- Although a number of different (but correct) interpretations can be made about the meaning of NPV, the most important is that the magnitude of a project's NPV represents the increase in shareholder wealth that can be expected to come about through its acceptance.

- It was seen that the NPV decision rule (see above) would lead the company to locate at the optimal point on the physical investment line of the Hirshliefer analysis. It was from this analysis that the connection between NPV and shareholder wealth can be seen.

- The internal rate of return (IRR) of a project is that discount rate which, when applied to a project's cash flow, produces a zero NPV. It is therefore a simple arithmetic result.

- The IRR decision rule is:
  - accept a project if its IRR $\geq$ decision criterion or 'hurdle rate';
  - reject if its IRR < decision criterion.

- Like NPV, use of the IRR decision rule will also lead to the company optimally locating on its physical investment line.

- Discounted payback, in which the speed of payback is computed in present value cash flow terms, was seen to be simply a version of NPV with an artificially truncated project life.

Appendix: compounding and discounting

Tables A to H can be found on pp. 251–4.

1 Compound interest factors

The amount to which a sum of £1 accumulates when placed on deposit for N years at a constant annual rate of interest of i is given by:

$$(1 + i)^N.$$

Thus, £500 placed on deposit for six years at an annual rate of interest of 12%, accumulates to:

$$£500 \, (1.12)^6 = £500 \times 1.9738 = £986.90.$$

Similarly, if £200 is placed on deposit for three years at 10% and two years at 8%, then the accumulated sum at the end of five years is:

$$£200 \, (1.10)^3 \, (1.08)^2 = £200 \times 1.3310 \times 1.1664 = £310.50.$$

Table A provides compound interest factors for various values of N and i.

2 Present value factors

The value now (i.e. the present value) of £1 arising in N years' time when the rate of discount (interest) is i, is given by:

$$1/(1 + i)^N \text{ or } (1 + i)^{-N}.$$

Thus, £500 arising in six years' time, when the annual rate of discount is 12%, has a present value of:

$$£500\,(1.12)^{-6} = £500 \times 0.5066 = £253.30.$$

Similarly, £200 arising in five years, where the annual rate of discount is 10% for three years and 8% for two years, has a present value of:

$$£200\,(1.10)^{-3}\,(1.08)^{-2} = £200 \times 0.7513 \times 0.8573 = £128.82.$$

Table B provides present value factors for various values of N and i.

3 Perpetuities

A perpetuity is a special pattern of cash flows. It is a fixed cash flow that continues for ever. The best known examples of this are undated government securities. The first of these were created during the Napoleonic wars at a time when the British Government did not have the money to repay some debt that was falling due. Thus they 'consolidated' the loan stock and promised to pay 2.5% (which was then above the market rate) for ever rather than repaying the principal. This was called Consolidated Loan Stock (Consols for short). If you had held £100 of this loan stock in 1805 you would have received £2.50 per annum in interest.

So PV (£100) $\times r$ (the interest rate of 2.5%) = C (the 'coupon' or cash flow of £2.50).

Rearranged this becomes PV = C/r.

The Consols still pay 2.5% but the market rate of interest varies and so does their present value. So if the rate of interest is now 6%, the PV of the block of Consols will be £2.50/6% = £41.67.

Have a look at today's price for 2.5% consolidated loan stock in a good newspaper (*Guardian, The Times, Telegraph, Financial Times*). It comes under undated government securities and the price quoted is for a block of Consols with a nominal (face) value of £100.

A perpetuity cannot have a terminal value simply because it does not have a foreseeable end.

4 Annuities

An annuity can be defined as a constant amount of cash which arises for a given number of consecutive years. Three main types of annuity can be specified:

1. an annuity due, where the first sum arises immediately;
2. an immediate annuity, where the first sum arises in one year's time;
3. a deferred annuity, where the first sum arises in two or more years' time.

Examples of the cash flows of four-year £100 annuities of each type are given below:

Year	0	1	2	3	4	5
1. Annuity due	£100	£100	£100	£100		
2. Immediate annuity		£100	£100	£100	£100	
3. One-year deferred annuity			£100	£100	£100	£100

5 Present value of an annuity

The present value of an *immediate* annuity of £1 per year for N years, where the rate of discount is i, is given by:

$$\frac{1-(1+i)^{-N}}{i}, \text{ denoted as } A_{N\neg i}.$$

Thus the present value of a four-year £100 immediate annuity, where the rate of discount is 16%, is:

$$£100\frac{1-(1.16)^{-4}}{0.16} = £100\,A_{4\neg 0.16} = £100\times 2.7982 = £279.82.$$

The present value of a four-year £100 annuity *due*, where the rate of discount is 16%, is:

$$£100+£100\,A_{3\neg 0.16} = £100+(£100\times 2.2459) = £324.59.$$

Whereas the present value of a four-year £100 annuity, deferred for (say) one year (so that the first sum arises at year 2), at a rate of discount of 18%, is:

$$£100\,A_{4\neg 0.18}(1.18)^{-1} = £100\times 2.6901\times 0.8474 = £227.96.$$

Notice the precise function of the $A_{N:i}$ factor. It gathers the annuity together and brings it to a point in time that is *one year earlier than the point of time when the first annuity amount arises*. For an *immediate* annuity, one year earlier than when the annuity commences is t_0. Thus $A_{N:i}$ will provide the present value of an immediate annuity; but for a deferred annuity the $A_{N:i}$ factor will have to be applied with an additional discount factor – as in the example above – to get it back to present value. Table C provides factors for the present values of £1 immediate annuities for various values of N and i.

Another way of defining an immediate annuity is that it is effectively the difference between a perpetuity that starts immediately (i.e. first cash flow in one year's time) and a perpetuity that starts in n periods' time. A perpetuity starting in n periods' time would be worth $C/r \times 1/(1+r)^n$ and, as we know, a perpetuity starting immediately is worth C/r. So the value of an annuuity is $C\,[(1/r) - (1/(r(1 + r)^n))]$.

6 Terminal value of an annuity

The amount to which an annuity of £1 per year for N years accumulates when the annual rate of interest is i takes the form of a geometric progression, which simplifies to:

$$\frac{(1+i)^N - 1}{i}, \text{ denoted as } S_{N\neg i}.$$

Thus the 'terminal value' of a four-year £100 immediate annuity (the amount to which it accumulates at the end of its life), where the rate of interest is 14%, is:

$$£100\frac{(1.14)^4 - 1}{0.14} = £100\,S_{4\neg 0.14} = £100 \times 4.9211 = £492.11.$$

Table D provides the terminal values of annuity factors for various values of N and i.

7 Annual equivalent factors

The annual value of an immediate annuity which lasts for N years, where the prevailing rate of discount is i, and which has a present value of £1, is given by:

$$\frac{i}{1-(1+i)^{-N}}, \text{ denoted as } A_{N\neg i}^{-1}$$

In other words, the reciprocal of the $A_{N\neg i}$ factor.

Thus the annual value of an immediate annuity which lasts for five years, where the rate of discount is 8%, and which has a present value of £2000, is:

$$£2000\frac{0.08}{1-(1.08)^{-5}} = £2000 \times 0.2505 = £501 \text{ per year.}$$

If this was a five-year annuity, deferred for (say) three years, then its annual value would be:

$$£2000\,A_{5\neg 0.08}^{-1}(1.08)^3 = £2000 \times 0.2505 \times 1.2597 = £631.11.$$

In other words, a £631.11 five-year annuity, deferred for three years, would have a present value of £2000 if the annual rate of discount was 8%. Table E provides these factors for immediate annuities with a present value of £1, for various values of i and N.

8 Sinking fund factors

Sinking funds were once fairly commonly used as a way of saving to replace assets or paying for some other obligation in the future. The idea is that the terminal value (i.e. the amount that is going to be paid out) is converted into a series of annual cash payments.

The annual value of an annuity which lasts for N years, where the prevailing rate of interest is i, and which has a terminal value of £1, is given by:

$$\frac{i}{(1+i)^N - 1}, \text{ denoted as } S_{N\neg i}^{-1}.$$

Thus the annual value of a four-year annuity which has a terminal value of £100, where the interest rate is 16%, is:

$$\text{£}100\,\frac{0.16}{(1.16)^4 - 1} = \text{£}100 \times 0.1974 = \text{£}19.74 \text{ per year.}$$

In other words, a four-year £19.74 annuity would have a terminal value of £100 when the annual interest rate is 16%. Hence, the annual amount of £19.74 would be known as the sinking fund. Table F provides sinking fund factors for annuities with terminal values of £1, for various values of i and N.

Notes

1.   There is a widely advocated DCF method of investment appraisal (but not widely used), variously called the 'excess present value index', the 'profitability index', the 'discounted profitability index', or even the 'benefit–cost ratio'. This method arises directly out of the NPV method (and so gives equivalent decision advice) and can be defined as:

$$\frac{\text{Present value of project cash inflows}}{\text{Present value of project cash outflows}}.$$

If the index is less than 1, the project should be rejected (equivalent to a negative NPV). If the index is greater than or equal to one, the project should be accepted. Thus in terms of Project B:

$$\text{Index} = \frac{827.06}{100\,000} = 0.8271$$

and as the index is less than 1, Project B should be rejected.

2.   To a limited extent a similar analysis can be performed on the vertical axis in terms of net *terminal* values (i.e. at t_1) rather than net present values. For instance, in the situation illustrated in Fig. 5.1, OF represents the terminal value of the sum of dividend OD in t_0 and OC in t_1; OC represents the terminal value of the cash inflows generated from the company's investments; and CF represents the net terminal value of the investments undertaken.

3.   Notice that if the company were to over-invest up to point W, the *total* net present value of its investment decision would be negative. In other words, the shareholders would have been better off if management had undertaken no investment at all, rather than over-investing to such an extent. This analysis does serve to support management's general inclination to invest conservatively (i.e. a tendency to under-invest, or to invest less than the optimal amount). Under-optimal investment must always lead to an increase in shareholders' wealth, relative to their wealth if management undertook zero investment, as long as negative NPV projects are not undertaken. However, with over-investment, a situation like point W is possible where shareholders are actually worse off as a result of the company's investment decisions. In the real world, a management with poor appraisal ability may well do right to err on the side of conservatism, rather than taking a very sanguine or cavalier attitude to investment decisions.

4. This method of investment appraisal has unfortunately suffered a confusing array of alternative names in the past, such as the 'marginal efficiency of capital', 'true yield' and even (to really add to the confusion) 'discounted cash flow'. Some of these alternatives still persist in the literature, but it is now most widely known as the 'internal rate of return'.

5. Strictly speaking, this is not correct. The IRR of a project is its *average* rate of return, whilst under our assumptions of infinite project divisibility and diminishing returns, the IRR of each incremental piece of a project will be slightly lower than that of the previous increment. Hence the physical investment line is composed of the IRRs of each incremental investment in the projects that are available, rather than of the IRRs of each complete project that is available.

Further reading

1. At this stage we are only midway through our evaluation of the two discounted cash flow investment appraisal techniques. Therefore many relevant articles will not yet be appropriate. However, a very interesting starting point is two articles which question the whole basis of the investment decision making developed here: P.F. King, 'Is the Emphasis of Capital Budgeting Theory Misplaced?', *Journal of Business Finance and Accounting*, Spring 1975; and D. Cooper, 'Rationality and Investment Appraisal', *Accounting and Business Research*, Summer 1975.
2. In addition, a further article which is of interest at this stage is: E.M. Lerner and A. Rappaport, 'Limit DCF in Capital Budgeting', *Harvard Business Review*, September–October 1968.
3. Finally, it is perhaps a good idea to introduce a dose of realism at this early stage and an interesting article to pursue is T. Crick and S.H. Kim, 'Do Executives Practice what Academics Teach?', *Management Accounting*, November 1986.

Quickie questions (including questions on the appendix)

1. Using a 14% discount rate, what is the NPV of the following project?

Year	Cash flow
0	−1000
1	+ 500
2	+ 600
3	+ 400

2. If a project costing £1000 has an NPV of +£120 at a 10% discount rate, how would you interpret the NPV figure and what should be the investment advice?
3. Estimate the IRR of the following project:

Year	Cash flow
0	−500
1	+200
2	+300
3	+200

4. Using the project in question 3, what is its discounted payback, given a 10% discount rate?
5. In the real world where the outcomes of investment projects are uncertain, what should the NPV discount rate represent?
6. What is the connection between the NPV discount rate and the IRR hurdle rate?
7. Given a 10% discount rate, what is the present value of the following annuity?

Year	Cash flow
0	−1000
1	+ 350
2	+ 350
3	+ 350
4	+ 350

8. What are the three main types of annuity?
9. A project costs £1000 and produces a cash inflow of £100 per year for ever. What is its IRR?
10. Using annuity factors, what is the NPV of this project at a 16% discount rate?

Year	Cash flow
0	−1000
1	+ 200
2	+ 200
3	+ 500
4	+ 500
5	+ 500

Problems

1. Trionym plc is a manufacturer of confectionery, based in the West Midlands. It has recently merged with a sugar refiner, West Indian Sugar Supplies plc (WISS). For some weeks, the accountants in the two companies have been discussing investment appraisal techniques. Trionym traditionally uses payback and the return on average capital employed, while WISS has used NPV for a number of years.

   The discussion on appraisal techniques has now reached a crisis as a decision is required on a proposal to invest £1.8 million on a new chocolate-coating machine in order to move into the chocolate biscuit market. The financial details are as follows:

Outlay:	£1.8 million at t_0
Life:	10 years
Net cash flow:	Years 1–6 +£500 000/year
	Years 7–10 +£300 000/year
Scrap value:	£0.5 million

   The company uses straight-line depreciation and has a target rate of return, for both ROCE and NPV of 18%, and a payback criterion of five years.

   Required:
   (a) Calculate the project's NPV.
   (b) Calculate the ROCE in line with company practice.
   (c) Calculate the project's payback.

(d) On the basis of your calculations, formulate your investment decision advice. Write a report to the chairman which justifies your decision and mention any reservations which you might have.

(e) In order to try and resolve the conflict between the two managements you suggest that the company uses discounted payback as a compromise. Estimate the project's discounted payback and write a memo to the chairman outlining its advantages and disadvantages.

(f) Comment critically on the company's existing decision criteria.

2. Congo Ltd is considering the selection of one of a pair of mutually exclusive investment projects. Both would involve purchasing machinery with a life of five years.

Project 1 would generate annual cash flows (receipts less payments) of £200 000; the machinery would cost £556 000 and have a scrap value of £56 000.

Project 2 would generate annual cash flows of £500 000; the machinery would cost £1 616 000 and have a scrap value of £301 000.

Congo uses the straight-line method for providing depreciation. Its cost of capital is 14% per annum. Assume that annual cash flows arise on the anniversaries of the initial outlay, that there will be no price changes over the project lives and that acceptance of one of the projects will not alter the required amount of working capital.

Required:

(a) Calculate for each project:
   (i)   the accounting rate of return (ratio, over project life, of average accounting profit to average book value of investment) to nearest 1%;
   (ii) the net present value;
   (iii) the internal rate of return (DCF yield) to nearest 1%;
   (iv) the payback period to one decimal place.

(b) State which project you would select for acceptance, if either, giving reasons for your choice of criterion to guide the decision.

Ignore taxation.

3. Stadler is an ambitious young executive who has recently been appointed to the position of financial director of Paradis plc, a small listed company. Stadler regards this appointment as a temporary one, enabling him to gain experience before moving to a larger organization. His intention is to leave Paradis plc in three years, with its share price standing high. As a consequence, he is particularly concerned that the reported profits of Paradis plc should be as high as possible in his third and final year with the company.

Paradis plc has recently raised £350 000 from shareholders, and the directors are considering three ways of using these funds. Three projects (A, B and C) are being considered, each involving the immediate purchase of equipment costing £350 000. One project only can be undertaken and the equipment for each project will have a useful life equal to that of the project, with no scrap value. Stadler favours Project C because it is expected to show the highest accounting profit in the third year. However, he does not wish to reveal his real reasons for favouring Project C and so, in his report to the chairman, he recommends Project C because it shows the highest internal rate of return. The following summary is taken from his report:

Project	Net cash flows (£000)									Internal rate of return
	Years									
	0	1	2	3	4	5	6	7	8	%
A	−350	100	110	104	112	138	160	180	–	27.5
B	−350	40	100	210	260	160	–	–	–	26.4
C	−350	200	150	240	40	–	–	–	–	33.0

The chairman of the company is accustomed to projects being appraised in terms of payback and accounting rate of return, and he is consequently suspicious of the use of internal rate of return as a method of project selection. Accordingly, the chairman has asked for an independent report on the choice of project. The company's cost of capital is 20% and a policy of straight-line depreciation is used to write off the cost of equipment in the financial statements.

Required:
(a) Calculate the payback period for each project.
(b) Calculate the accounting rate of return for each project.
(c) Prepare a report for the chairman with supporting calculations indicating which project should be preferred by the ordinary shareholders of Paradis plc.
(d) Discuss the assumptions about the reactions of the stock market that are implicit in Stadler's choice of project C.
Ignore taxation.

6 Net present value and internal rate of return developed

NPV and project interdependence

In Chapter 3, when examining the payback and ROCE/ARR techniques, two investment decisions were dealt with:

1. decisions involving single, independent projects where a straightforward 'accept' or 'reject' decision was required;
2. decisions involving mutually exclusive projects, where a decision on the single best project from a series of alternative projects was required.

In Chapter 5 when examining the two discounted cash flow techniques of NPV and IRR, our discussion only covered the decision rule for single independent project decisions. In this chapter, we start by looking at the NPV and IRR decision rules when faced with mutually exclusive projects and other forms of project decision interdependence.

NPV and mutually exclusive projects

We have already seen from the single-period investment–consumption model that, in terms of net present value, the higher the aggregate NPV of a firm's investments, the higher will be the level of wealth achieved by its shareholders. Therefore, as far as deciding between mutually exclusive investment alternatives is concerned, the decision rule would appear to be quite straightforward in terms of using the NPV: accept whichever alternative projects that result in the greatest positive NPV, because this will produce the greatest addition to the shareholders' wealth.[1]

As an example, suppose a company has to make an investment decision concerning two mutually exclusive projects, A and B, whose cash flows and NPV calculations are set out below:

Project A

Year	Cash flow (£)	×	10% discount factor	=	Present value cash flow (£)
0	− 1500	×	1	=	− 1500
1	+ 500	×	0.9091	=	+ 454.55
2	+ 800	×	0.8264	=	+ 661.12
3	+ 1000	×	0.7513	=	+ 751.30
				NPV	+ 366.97

Project B

Year	Cash flow (£)	×	10% discount factor	=	Present value cash flow (£)
0	− 1900	×	1	=	− 1900
1	+ 500	×	0.9091	=	+ 454.55
2	+ 800	×	0.8264	=	+ 661.12
3	+ 1000	×	0.7513	=	+ 751.30
4	+ 700	×	0.6830	=	+ 478.10
				NPV	+ 445.07

Assuming that the appropriate discount rate is 10%, when the project cash flows are converted to present values, Project B is preferred to A because it has the larger positive NPV. It is important to realize that the appraisal method in such circumstances is entirely unaffected by the fact that these two projects have differing capital outlays and life-spans. The whole decision is based purely on the absolute size of the positive NPV.

The mutually exclusive investment decision can be made in this way because of two important assumptions underlying the analysis. When developing the single-period investment–consumption model, a number of simplifying assumptions about the real world were specified. However, when we then moved on to examine the DCF investment appraisal techniques, many of these assumptions (such as a single time period and a world of certainty) were either implicitly or explicitly dropped. Nevertheless, there are two important assumptions that underlie the use of DCF techniques. They are:

1. The existence of a perfect capital market. Reference has already been made to this concept, when the existence of a capital market was introduced in the Hirshleifer analysis in Chapter 4. A perfect capital market describes a market where investors can lend and borrow money and which has a number of particular characteristics. We will examine the concept in greater detail at a later stage but, for the present, all that is required is to specify that characteristic which is of particular importance as far as the DCF techniques are concerned. It is that investors/companies will always be able to raise finance to undertake any project that they identify as having a non-negative NPV (or whose IRR meets the decision criterion hurdle rate). Therefore, decision makers will never find themselves in a position where they are unable to take on a positive NPV project because of

lack of finance. In addition, we should add to this condition the assumption that the cost of the finance raised will always be at the going rate of return for investments of that particular risk level.

2. The discount rate used in an NPV analysis, or the hurdle rate used in an IRR analysis, correctly reflects the degree of risk involved in the project. This refers to the fact that the discount rate should represent the return available elsewhere in the (perfect) capital market on a similar risk investment. Therefore notice how this assumption is, itself, dependent upon the first assumption.

As a result of these two assumptions the choice between Projects A and B can be made on the basis used. The fact that B is a more costly project than A is irrelevant, given the first assumption. Project B is preferred to A simply because it is capable of generating a cash flow that will pay back its outlay and its financing costs and leave an economic profit, in present value terms (a rise in shareholder wealth), of £445.07. Project A will also repay its outlay and its financing costs, but will only cause shareholder wealth to rise by £366.97.

Also, the fact that B is more expensive than A, and has a longer life than A, might suggest that it is more risky. (Neither fact will *necessarily* make B more risky than A.) However, these differences can also be ignored in the decision analysis because of our second assumption. In other words, the whole problem of riskiness is taken account of in the discount rate. The fact that both projects are being discounted at 10% implies that a judgement has been made that they are equally risky.

In this respect, if it were felt that two mutually exclusive projects were of different risk levels, then different discount rates should be used to evaluate each one. However, the decision – with its focus on maximizing the increase in shareholder wealth – would remain unchanged. Example 1 illustrates such a situation.

The point to notice about Example 1 is that the decision has been taken on the basis of what would be the resulting increase in shareholder wealth. The fact that the amusement park development produces a return in excess of 18% (in fact its IRR is approximately 18.6%), whilst the private housing development only produces a return in excess of 10% (its IRR is approximately 12.5%), is irrelevant. Rates of return cannot be compared in isolation, but must be looked at relative to the risk involved. In this example, given the risk involved, the private housing development is the better project from the viewpoint of shareholder wealth.

Finally, the operation of this modified NPV rule for mutually exclusive projects requires an additional assumption in the face of unequal project lives (but not unequal investment outlays). This is that the mutually exclusive projects are 'isolated' investments in the sense that they do not form part of a replacement chain. In other words, it is assumed that the nature of the mutually exclusive projects is such that, whichever project is chosen, it will not be replaced when it reaches the end of its life. If this assumption does not hold, then we are involved with a different type of project interdependence which requires a more complex decision rule. This issue is treated separately when the Replacement Decision is examined.

Epitasis plc is a small company engaged in house-building. The company is presently considering whether to purchase a piece of land that has come up for sale at a cost of £10 million. Two suggestions have been made for the use of the land. One is to construct a number of private houses for sale and the other is to construct and operate an amusement park.

The company's management accountants have made the following estimates of both projects' net cash flows (including the cost of the land):

Year	Private house development (£m)	Amusement park (£m)
0	−10	−10
1	− 5	− 8
2	+ 7	+ 4
3	+ 9	+ 6
4	+ 4	+ 8
5		+ 7
6		+ 9

The company uses NPV to evaluate projects and normally takes 10% as a discount rate, as this reflects the return available elsewhere on house-building investments. In the present situation this appears to be a suitable rate for the private housing development, but not for the amusement park. After much research, the company has decided that the minimum required rate of return that they should expect on this more risky project is 18%.

On this basis, the project's NPVs were calculated:

Private housing development: + £0.733 million.
Amusement park development: + £0.264 million.

Therefore the company's decision was to purchase the land and undertake a private housing development.

Interlinked projects

Another type of project interdependence can arise when a project's cash flows are affected by investment decisions taken elsewhere. It would be highly unusual to find *any* project which had truly independent cash flows, as almost certainly the magnitude and timing of a project's cash flows will be affected to some extent by other investment decisions. This problem really arises out of uncertainty about the future, and will be examined later in that context.

The case of interdependence to be examined here is the simpler case in which the cash flows of an investment opportunity are directly affected by the company's decision regarding another investment project. For example, when two non-mutually exclusive projects, C and D, are appraised it is found that Project C has the following cash flows, which are independent of any other investment decisions made by the company:

Project C

Year	Cash flow (£)	×	10% discount factor	=	Present value cash flow (£)
0	− 1000	×	1	=	− 1000
1	+ 400	×	0.9091	=	+ 363.64
2	+ 500	×	0.8264	=	+ 413.20
3	+ 200	×	0.7513	=	+ 150.26
			NPV		− £72.90

When discounted by 10% (assumed to be the appropriate rate), Project C has a negative NPV of £72.90. Viewed in isolation, and following the NPV rule for independent projects, it would be rejected as an unsuitable investment.

However, suppose Project D, which is also under consideration, has two alternative sets of cash flows and NPVs, depending upon whether Project C is accepted by the company (cash flow 1) or rejected (cash flow 2):

Project D

Year	Cash flow 1 (£)	×	10% discount factor	=	Present value cash flow (£)
0	− 2000	×	1	=	− 2000
1	+ 500	×	0.9091	=	+ 454.55
2	+ 800	×	0.8264	=	+ 661.12
3	+ 1000	×	0.7513	=	+ 751.30
4	+ 1000	×	0.6830	=	+ 683.00
			NPV		+ 549.97

Year	Cash flow 1 (£)	×	10% discount factor	=	Present value cash flow (£)
0	− 2000	×	1	=	− 2000
1	+ 500	×	0.9091	=	+ 454.55
2	+ 800	×	0.8264	=	+ 661.12
3	+ 1200	×	0.7513	=	+ 901.56
4	+ 600	×	0.6830	=	+ 409.80
			NPV		+ 427.03

The correct way to analyse this situation, within the assumptions made, is to treat the problem as three mutually exclusive investments: Project C, Project D, and Project C + D. Whichever alternative produces the largest positive NPV should be accepted. In this example:

Project C $= -£72.90$
Project D $= +£427.03$
Project C + D $= -£72.90 + £549.97 = +£477.07$

Thus the correct investment decision, in terms of maximizing shareholder wealth, is to accept Projects C and D jointly, because it is this alternative which produces the largest net present value.

IRR rule and interdependent projects

Introduction

We have seen that in the face of these two types of non-independent cash flow, the NPV investment decision rule can be fairly easily modified so as to produce the correct decision advice. In terms of the single-period investment–consumption model, these modified decision rules would ensure a company's attainment of the optimal point on the physical investment line and the consequent maximization of shareholder wealth. But what modifications would have to be made to the IRR decision rule?

In a situation of mutually exclusive investment projects, a modification, apparently similar to that made to the NPV rule, is traditionally advocated: accept whichever project has the greatest IRR, as long as it exceeds the decision criterion/hurdle rate. Such an approach is incorrect, but it has been widely advocated because of a misunderstanding concerning the process involved in using both NPV and IRR as criteria for investment decisions.

We have already seen that when an individual project is evaluated by NPV, an 'automatic' comparison is made between the cash flows produced by the project and the cash flows that would have been produced (but were forgone, and so represent an opportunity cost under the assumption of a perfect capital market) if the project's outlay had been invested on the capital market for the period of the project's life-span. Therefore, the decision whether to accept or reject the project is not an absolute decision, but a *relative* one – relative to what the forgone alternative would have yielded. As a result, when faced with mutually exclusive investments, the choice between projects is carried out on the basis of this automatic comparison with the capital market. Whichever project performs best, *relative to the capital market*, is chosen – given that the chosen alternative out-performs the capital market alternative, i.e. has a positive NPV.

Incremental cash flows

We can approach this idea another way. Suppose we have a pair of mutually exclusive projects, E and F, which have the following cash flows, lives and present values when discounted at the appropriate market rate of return of 10%:

Project E

Year	Cash flow (£)	×	10% discount factor	=	Present value cash flow (£)
0	−1500	×	1	=	− 1500
1	+ 550	×	0.9091	=	+ 500.00
2	+1400	×	0.8264	=	+ 1156.96
				NPV	+ 156.96

Project F

Year	Cash flow (£)	×	10% discount factor	=	Present value cash flow (£)
0	−1900	×	1	=	−1900
1	+ 400	×	0.9091	=	+ 363.64
2	+ 800	×	0.8264	=	+ 661.12
3	+ 800	×	0.7513	=	+ 601.04
4	+ 700	×	0.6830	=	+ 478.10
				NPV	+ 203.90

Project F would be preferred to E, as it has the larger, positive NPV.

Now, let us look at the present value of the extra, or incremental, cash flows that the firm would obtain from investing in Project E, rather than F and vice versa:

Year	Project E c/f		Project F c/f	= E–F c/f	×	10% PV factor	=	Present value cash flow
0	(–1500)	–	(–1900)	= + 400	×	1	=	+ 400
1	(+ 550)	–	(+ 400)	= + 150	×	0.9091	=	+ 136.36
2	(+1400)	–	(+ 800)	= + 600	×	0.8264	=	+ 495.84
3		–	(+ 800)	= – 800	×	0.7513	=	– 601.04
4		–	(+ 700)	= – 700	×	0.6830	=	– 478.10
							NPV –	46.94

Year	Incremental F–E c/f	×	10% PV factor	=	Present value cash flow
0	– 400	×	1	=	– 400
1	– 150	×	0.9091	=	– 136.36
2	– 600	×	0.8264	=	– 495.84
3	+ 800	×	0.7513	=	+ 601.04
4	+ 700	×	0.6830	=	+ 478.10
				NPV +	46.94

In our initial analysis of this decision problem, Project F was preferred to E. The incremental analysis shown above helps to explain further the reason for the decision: if F is chosen in preference to E, this will produce an NPV which will be £46.94 greater than if E was preferred to F.

(Notice the NPV of Project F, less that of Project E, is: £203.90 – £156.96 = £46.94.)

Therefore, F is chosen.

Use of the IRR

In the case of mutually exclusive investments, use of the IRR decision rule causes problems. Unlike the NPV calculation which automatically compares the project with the alternative capital market investment forgone, the IRR method makes the comparison on a somewhat different basis by using the decision rule: does the project yield a greater or lesser return than the capital market? In doing so, however, it does not give a consistently reliable indication of how much better or worse the project is, relative to the capital market investment alternative.

Thus the IRR decision rule is safe to apply to single, independent decision situations (when all that is required is an answer to the question: does the project produce a return better or worse than that of the capital market?), but it cannot reliably be used to judge between alternative projects. This is a rather subtle, but important point, and it requires some further explanation.

Using linear interpolation, the IRRs of the two projects, E and F can be estimated. For E the IRR is estimated at 17%, and for F at 15%. As E has the larger of the two IRRs and this is greater than the decision criterion hurdle rate (10%), the IRR decision rule would suggest that Project E is accepted and F rejected. However, to formulate decision advice on this basis is to forget that the IRR method only compares a project with the capital market alternative in the operation of the accept/reject decision rule. (Indeed the fact that this standard IRR decision rule gives unreliable decision advice is made obvious in this example, because the decision reached is the *opposite* of that reached by NPV.)

The IRR method can correctly advise in this case that both projects are worthwhile: Project E is worthwhile as it produces a return that is greater than that of the capital market, likewise with Project F. But it does not necessarily follow that E is *better* than F because it has an IRR of 17% as opposed to 15%. Indeed we know from operating the NPV decision rule that the advice is incorrect: F is a better investment than E; and selecting E will result in a £46.94 loss of NPV.

IRR and incremental cash flows

The correct approach to evaluating mutually exclusive investments using the IRR is to examine the incremental cash flows that arise between the alternatives. In order to clarify the problem and derive the correct IRR decision rule in such circumstances, we shall make use of a device which was used earlier to examine the IRR concept: the net present value profile.

Fig. 6.1 graphs the NPV profiles of Projects E and F and both the differential cash flows (E–F, F–E). This demonstrates one of the real problems of using the IRR as a decision criterion when choice between alternatives is involved.

Project E always has a higher IRR than F, whatever the rate of discount, and therefore, basing the choice between mutually exclusive investments on size of IRR, the decision is independent of the capital market rate of

Fig. 6.1 *NPV versus IRR*

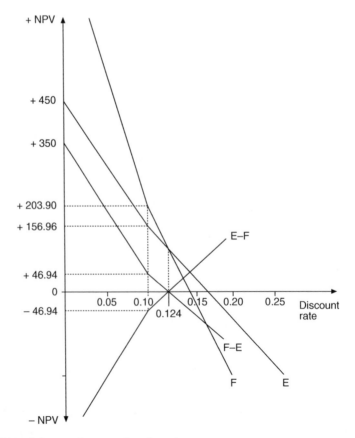

interest. In contrast, when the decision is based on the NPV rule, the choice of project changes as the discount rate/market rate of interest changes. It can be seen from Fig. 6.1 that at rates of discount below 12.4%, Project F is preferred because it has the higher NPV: but at discount rates above 12.4%, Project E is preferred.

The intersection point of the two cash flow profiles is at a discount rate of 12.4% and so, at this rate, the decision would be indifferent between the two projects because they both produce the same NPV. Also notice that, as we would expect at that discount rate, the NPV of both differential cash flows is zero: both projects are equally acceptable, and the differential cash flows reflect this indifference.

On the basis of Fig. 6.1, a number of firm conclusions can be made about the use of both methods in appraising mutually exclusive projects. The NPV can be used to give the correct decision advice with just a small (and commonsense) modification to the basic rule: accept whichever alternative has the highest positive NPV when discounted at the perfect capital market rate of interest. The use of the IRR involves a more complex decision rule. This complexity arises both from the fact that the IRRs of the differential cash flows have to be computed and (as can be seen from Fig. 6.1) from the fact that the IRRs of both incremental cash flows are identical. The complete modified decision rule is as follows.

Calculate the IRRs of the two projects and the IRR of *either* of the differential cash flows, then:

1. If the differential cash flow IRR is *greater* than the cut-off rate, and
    (a) less than both project IRRs, then accept the project with the *smallest* IRR;
    (b) greater than both project IRRs, then accept the project with *highest* IRR.
2. If the differential cash flow IRR is *less* than the cut-off rate, and
    (a) the IRRs of one or both projects are higher than the cut-off rate, then accept the project with the *highest* IRR;
    (b) if neither project's IRR is greater than the cut-off rate, *reject* both.

In the example used, therefore, using the NPV decision rule, Project F should be accepted because it has the highest positive NPV when discounted at 10% – the perfect capital market interest rate. The modified IRR decision rule also leads to the acceptance of F because the IRR of the differential cash flow (12.4%) is greater than the cut-off rate (10%) and less than the IRR of both projects (15% and 17%). Therefore, the project with the smallest IRR, Project F, is chosen.

A less complex, but somewhat incomplete decision rule can also be used in most cases:

1. If the IRR of the differential cash flow is less than the cut-off rate, accept the project with the largest IRR.
2. If the IRR of the differential cash flow is greater than the cut-off rate, accept the project with the smallest IRR.

In the example used above, as the IRR of the differential cash flow, at 12.4%, is greater than the 10% cut-off rate, then project F should be accepted as it has the smallest IRR – 15% as against 17% for Project E.

The conclusion that can be drawn from this example is that the IRR decision rule is excessively complex and unwieldy when compared against the

NPV decision rule. What is more, the example used only two mutually exclusive projects. If faced with a choice between (say) a dozen alternatives, the NPV rule simply requires the calculation of each project's NPV and the project with the largest positive NPV is selected. With the IRR rule, the IRRs of *pairs* of projects and their differential cash flow have to be calculated, making a choice between each pair of projects in turn, until an outright 'winner' is found – an extremely tedious operation.

A further example

Example 2 may help to clarify this approach to resolving the conflict that can occur between the advice given by the NPV decision rule and the advice given by the standard IRR decision rule for mutually exclusive decision situations.

Given Example 2, it should be made clear that it is very unlikely that any company actually uses this modified IRR decision rule in practice. To use it in this way implies a belief in the correctness of the NPV decision rule – because the modified IRR rule is designed always to give the same advice as NPV. But in that case it is both simpler and easier to use the NPV rule itself. Example 2 illustrates how it would be possible to use the IRR decision rule in mutually exclusive project situations so as to provide correct (i.e. shareholder wealth-maximizing) decision advice.

Example 2

Parabiotic plc is involved in making a decision between a pair of mutually exclusive projects: X and Y. The cash flows of the two projects are as follows:

Year	Project X (£000s)	Project Y (£000s)
0	− 1000	− 450
1	+ 400	+ 300
2	+ 600	+ 150
3	+ 187	+ 106

Given the risk involved, it is judged that 6% would be an appropriate NPV discount rate and IRR hurdle rate.

NPV calculation

Year	Cash flow (£) X		Discount factor		
0	− 1000	×	1	=	− 1000
1	+ 400	×	0.9434	=	+ 377.36
2	+ 600	×	0.8900	=	+ 534.00
3	+ 187	×	0.8396	=	+ 157.00
					+ 68.36 NPV

Year	Cash flow (£) Y		Discount factor		
0	− 450	×	1	=	− 450
1	+ 300	×	0.9434	=	+ 283.02
2	+ 150	×	0.8900	=	+ 133.50
3	+ 106	×	0.8396	=	+ 89.00
					+ 55.52 NPV

Using the NPV decision rule for mutually exclusive projects, Project X is preferred to Project Y as it has the largest positive NPV and so will give the greatest increase in shareholder wealth.

IRR calculation

Project X:	At 6% it has an NPV of +68.36 NPV				
At 20%:	−1000	×	1	=	−1000
	+ 400	×	0.8333	=	+ 333.32
	+ 600	×	0.6944	=	+ 416.64
	+ 187	×	0.5787	=	+ 108.22
				=	− 141.82 NPV
Project Y:	At 6% it has an NPV of +55.52 NPV				
At 20%:	− 450	×	1	=	− 450
	+ 300	×	0.8333	=	+ 249.99
	+ 150	×	0.6944	=	+ 104.16
	+ 106	×	0.5787	=	+ 61.34
					− 34.51 NPV

Linear interpolation can now be used to estimate the IRR of both projects:

$$\text{Project X} : 6\% + \left[\frac{68.36}{68.36-(-141.82)} \times (20\% - 6\%)\right] = 10.5\%\ \text{IRR}$$

$$\text{Project Y} : 6\% + \left[\frac{55.52}{55.52-(-34.51)} \times (20\% - 6\%)\right] = 14.6\%\ \text{IRR}$$

Using the *standard* IRR decision rule for mutually exclusive projects, Project Y is the better project as it has the higher IRR and should be accepted because its IRR exceeds the hurdle rate of return of 6%.

Therefore, in this case, we are getting a *conflict* between the advice given by NPV and the advice given by the IRR decision rule. However, if the *modified* IRR decision rule is used, we require to calculate the IRR of the differential cash flow: X minus Y.

Year	*Cash flow X (£)*	-	*Cash flow Y (£)*	=	*Differential cash flow*
0	−1000	-	(− 450)	=	− 550
1	+ 400	-	(+ 300)	=	+ 100
2	+ 600	-	(+ 150)	=	+ 450
3	+ 187	-	(+ 106)	=	+ 81

At a 4% discount rate:

− 550	×	1	=	− 550
+ 100	×	0.9615	=	+ 96.15
+ 450	×	0.9246	=	+ 416.07
+ 81	×	0.8890	=	+ 72.01
				+ 34.23 NPV

At a 20% discount rate:

− 550	×	1	=	− 550
+ 100	×	0.8333	=	+ 83.33
+ 450	×	0.6944	=	+ 312.48
+ 81	×	0.5787	=	+ 46.87
				− 107.32 NPV

Again, using linear interpolation:
Differential cash flow IRR:

$$4\% + \left[\frac{34.23}{34.23-(-107.32)} \times (20\% - 4\%)\right] = 7.9\%.$$

Note that linear interpolation has been used here for illustrative purposes. It is to be expected that the calcualtions would normally be carried out using a computer spreadsheet

Now, using the simplified, modified IRR decision rule for mutually exclusive projects: as the IRR of the differential cash flow is *greater than* the hurdle rate of 6%, Project X – the project with the *smaller* IRR – should be accepted. Notice that there is now no conflict with the advice given by NPV.

The 'opportunity cost of cash' assumption

The fact that, in a decision choice involving mutually exclusive projects, selecting the project with the highest positive NPV will give a correct decision but selecting the project with the highest IRR will, *only by chance*, also give the correct decision, has been explained on the basis that the IRR ranks projects in an order of preference which is independent of the capital market rate of return. But we have not really answered the question of why, in the example used, the NPV rule accepts Project F and rejects E. After all, Project E produces a higher return (17%) than F (15%). The reason lies in what is (somewhat misleadingly) called the *reinvestment assumption* of each decision rule. Perhaps a more apt description would be the *opportunity cost of capital* assumption.

The NPV decision rule assumes that project-generated cash flows are reinvested to earn a rate of return equal to the discount rate used in the NPV analysis. (More strictly, remember, it is not so much a reinvestment rate of return, but an opportunity cost or benefit.) In contrast, the IRR method assumes project-generated cash flows are reinvested to earn a rate of return equal to the IRR of the project which generated those cash flows. Therefore using Project E as an example:

Project E:	Year	Cash flow (£)	
	0	− 1500	NPV at a 10% discount
	1	+ 550	rate = +£156.96
	2	+ 1400	

IRR is approximately 17%

The NPV decision rule assumes that the £550 and £1400 cash flows generated at Years 1 and 2 respectively can be reinvested to earn a 10% rate of return. The IRR method assumes they can be reinvested to earn a 17% rate of return.

This difference can be seen in the general forms of the two models. With the NPV model, the discount rate used is the market rate of interest:

$$\sum_{t=0}^{N} \frac{A_t}{(1+i)^t} = \text{NPV}$$

where
A_t = project cash flow at time t;
i = market discount rate;
N = number of years of the project's life.

However, with the IRR model, the discount rate used is the project's own internal rate of return:

$$\sum_{t=0}^{N}\frac{A_t}{(1+i)^t}=0 \quad \text{where } r = \text{project's IRR.}$$

A simple example will help to illustrate the point. Suppose that the following project, G, is available, where the market rate of discount is 5%. The project has an NPV of +£12.39 and an IRR of 10%. What these results mean is shown in Example 3, where the reinvestment assumptions can actually be seen to be in operation.

Example 3

Project G:	Year	Cash flow (£)	At a 5% discount rate
	0	− 173.55	NPV = + 12.39
	1	+ 100	
	2	+ 100	At a 5% hurdle rate
			IRR = 10%

The project's NPV is arrived at by calculating the sum of money that can be accumulated from the project by the end of its life (where intermediate cash flows are reinvested at 5%), and comparing this with the amount of money that could be accumulated by placing the project's outlay in a similar-risk capital market investment. £205 can be accumulated from the project and only £191.34 from the capital market investment. This difference of £13.66 in Year 2 terms has a present value of £12.39: the project's NPV.

Year	0	1	2
	− 173.55	+100	+100
		100(1.05) ⟶	105
			205
		173.55(1.05)² ⟶	191.34
NPV = 12.39 ⟵		13.66(1.05)⁻² ⟶	13.66

The project has an IRR of 10%. If it truly does produce a 10% return it must be capable of generating the same amount of cash by the end of its life that would be generated from investing the project's outlay to yield a 10% return. Investing £173.55 for two years at 10% generates £210. The only way that Project G can accumulate £210 by the end of its life is to assume that the intermediate cash flow (£100 at Year 1) can be reinvested to earn 10%.

Year	0	1	2
	− 173.55	+ 100	+100
		100(1.10) ⟶	110
			210
		173.55(1.10)² ⟶	210
NPV = 0 ⟵		0(1.10)⁻² ⟶	0

The IRR approach assumes that the project cash flows can yield a return equal to the IRR of the project that generated those cash flows. Now the important point is that investments yielding such returns may well be available to the company but, the flaw in the IRR's assumption is that these investments will be available *independently* of whether or not the company accepts the particular project under consideration. The NPV model accepts this argument, taking the market rate of interest, as the opportunity cost of the project cash flows.

The market rate of interest is viewed as the opportunity cost because, even if a project's cash flow *is* used by a company to undertake an investment with a very high yield, if that cash flow were *not* available, the high-yielding investment could still be undertaken by using money borrowed from the capital market, *at the market rate of interest.* What the IRR model does is to credit some of the assumed profitability of those other investments to the project being appraised, by assuming that the opportunity cost of the project-generated cash flows is equal to the project's own IRR or yield.

Therefore, we can conclude that, given the presence of a perfect capital market, it is the NPV model and not the IRR model which makes the correct assumption about the opportunity cost of a project's cash flow. Hence it is the NPV decision rule that gives the correct decision advice. As a result, if we are to use the IRR, then we have to make use of the type of complex decision rule that was derived earlier. However there is no real logic to that type of rule – it simply ensures that the same decision is produced as that given by the (much simpler) NPV decision rule.

Finally, there is also a logical inconsistency in the IRR's reinvestment assumption. As an example of this, take Projects H and I.

Project H:	Year	Cash flow (£)	Project I:	Year	Cash flow (£)
	0	− 100		0	− 150
	1	+ 30		1	+ 70
	2	+ 70		2	+ 70
	3	+ 19.80		3	+ 74.41

Project H has an IRR of 10%, while Project I has an IRR of 20%. Therefore the implicit assumption is that Project I's cash flows can be reinvested to earn 20%, but Project H's cash flows can only be reinvested to earn 10%. Therefore why, for example, can the £70 generated at Year 2 by Project I be reinvested at twice the rate as the same amount of cash, generated at precisely the same point in time, by Project H? There is a fault in the logic of the assumption. There is no logical reason why cash flows which arise at the same time from two different sources should be reinvested at different rates (i.e. have different opportunity benefits).

Extending the time horizon

Introduction

Having examined the case of mutually exclusive projects, let us now turn to another issue. This concerns the fact that the Hirshleifer's single-period graphical analysis was undertaken under the assumption of a single-period investment time horizon. Certainly since starting to examine the DCF methods of investment appraisal, examples have been used of projects which involve cash flows extending over more than one period. But what we must now ask is whether the assumption of a single-period time horizon is simply an assumption of convenience which allows the model to be developed graphically.

In short, the answer to the question is that it is not. In a single-period world we have seen that both the NPV and IRR decision rules will give the same, correct decision advice (even if some fairly complex adjustments sometimes have to be made to the IRR rule). Both methods should enable a company to locate optimally on its physical investment line. However, problems can occur for the IRR decision rule once this two-dimensional world is left behind.

Average and marginal rates of return

As soon as the assumption of a single time period (t_0-t_1) is explicitly relaxed, we get new support for the rationale of the NPV approach (to the detriment of IRR) and a new perspective from which to view the 'reinvestment' assumption. So far, in all the examples used, we have implicitly assumed that the capital market interest rate remains fixed over time. However, suppose a company is evaluating Project J, whose cash flows are given below. In this case, the annual market interest/discount rate is expected to be 10% over the coming year and 15% over the following year.

Project J:

Year	Cash flow (£)		Discount factor		
0	− 100	×	1	=	− 100
1	+ 60	×	$(1.10)^{-1}$	=	+ 54.55
2	+ 60	×	$(1.10)^{-1} \times (1.15)^{-1}$ =		+ 47.43
			NPV	=	+ 1.98

The IRR of Project J is approximately 13%.

As far as the NPV decision rule is concerned, known fluctuations in the discount rate do not cause any problems. Project J has a positive NPV after its cash flows have been discounted by the appropriate market discount rate for each time period.

But what of the IRR decision rule? Project J should be accepted if its IRR is greater than the decision criterion/hurdle rate, but in this example, the IRR of J is *greater* than the market interest rate in one period, and *less* than the rate in the other period. In such circumstances, a single-figure IRR is just not valid for decision-making purposes.

This is a very real problem with the IRR decision rule. Unless future market interest rates can be assumed to be, at least, approximately constant, the rule breaks down. What we are seeing in this example is that, although both DCF methods recognize that money has a time value and so cash flows that occur at different points of time cannot be directly compared, but first have to be converted to values at just one point of time via a weighting mechanism,[2] the IRR uses the *average*, or long-run, rate of return for weighting, whilst the NPV uses the *marginal*, or period-by-period, rate of return.

Multiple IRRs

Another problem for the IRR decision rule, which arises out of the mathematics of its computation, comes to light when the investment time horizon is extended. The IRR of a project's cash flow is the root of a polynomial equation,[3] the problem is that, as the fifteenth-century French mathematician Descartes proved with his 'rule of signs', there are possible solutions to polynomial equations for each change of sign. Thus any particular investment project may have more than one internal rate of return (i.e. there may be more than one rate of discount which will reduce the project's cash flow to a zero NPV), or it may not have any IRR at all. This important (and not uncommon) phenomenon can be examined in terms of the NPV profiles of projects on the basis that the IRR is given by the point at which the profile line cuts the graph's horizontal axis (along which the discount rate is measured).

To start with, we must define what have become known as 'conventional' and 'non-conventional' cash flows.[4] A conventional project cash flow is one where a cash outflow, or a series of cash outflows, is followed by a cash inflow or series of cash inflows. The essence of the definition is that in a conventional cash flow, there is only one change in sign $(+, -)$ between the time periods. All three cash flows given below are therefore conventional:

		Year			
Project	0	1	2	3	4
K	− 1000	+ 400	+ 500	+ 800	+ 50
L	− 1000	− 500	− 600	+ 1500	+ 2000
M	− 500	− 600	+ 2000		

The one change of sign for Project K comes between year 0 and year 1, for Project L it comes between year 2 and year 3, and for Project M it comes between year 1 and year 2. In each project cash flow there is only one sign change. Such projects will only have one IRR each (there is an exception to this, to which we shall return), and so no problems arise for the IRR decision rule.

Non-conventional cash flows can therefore be defined as those which involve more than one change in sign, such as shown below:

		Year				
Project	0	1	2	3	4	
N	− 100	+ 20	− 50	+ 80	+ 170	3 changes of sign
P	− 100	+ 60	+ 80	− 20		2 changes of sign

Such projects are likely to have more than one IRR and, as a general rule of thumb, a project will have as many IRRs as its cash flow has changes in sign.

Example 4

Ossett Roadstone Ltd has been given permission to extract gravel. It will cost £1 050 000 to set up the project. It will then produce cash flows of £800 000 for five years. At the end of the five years, it will cost £3 000 000 to landscape the area which is a requirement for planning permission. Assess the project using IRR.

The cash flows produce two solutions 2% and 43% and the pattern of its NPV is graphed in Fig. 6.2.

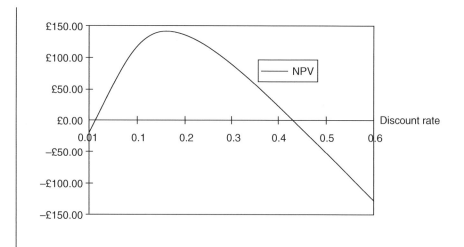

Fig. 6.2 *Multiple IRRs*

As we have already suggested, most people would use a computer spreadsheet to calculate the IRR of a pattern of cash flows. Try Ossett Roadstone using a spreadsheet. You will find that the solution presented by the computer depends upon the level of the guess that you entered into the formula. The lesson here must be that the use of such software without a knowledge of the problems being discussed here could lead to inappropriate decisions.

Non-conventional cash flows can make life very difficult for the IRR decision rule. For example, suppose that Project Q's NPV profile is illustrated in Fig. 6.3. This project has three IRRs: 10%, 15% and 18%. In itself, this is not too disturbing if the cut-off rate is either less than 10% or greater than 18%, because the IRR rule still manages to give unambiguous (and operationally correct) decision advice. But if the cut-off rate is (say) 12%, the IRR decision can only give – at best – highly ambiguous advice (which may be incorrect). In such circumstances, the NPV rule would have no difficulty in giving the correct advice: to reject the project because it has a negative NPV.

However, it can be shown that with most project cash flows that are likely to occur in practice, and where multiple IRRs occur, the variations in the project's NPV between the IRRs are usually very small, and the value of the

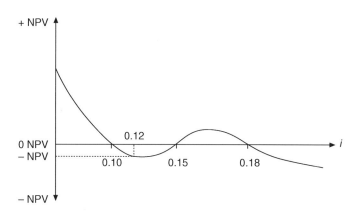

Fig. 6.3 *A misleading IRR*

NPV itself is likely to be close to zero. Therefore it follows that with a simple accept-or-reject decision, the problem of multiple IRRs is not too serious. If a project is accepted on the basis of (say) the majority of its IRRs being greater than the cut-off/discount rate, whereas when evaluated using NPV it turns out to have a negative NPV, then the IRR-based decision would not be disastrous as the magnitude of the negative NPV would be likely to be relatively small. Nevertheless, the problem of multiple IRRs does remain to cause difficulties in the case of mutually exclusive investment decisions. In such circumstances, the differential cash flow may well have multiple IRRs, which causes the decision rule to become non-operational.

Despite the foregoing argument concerning the practical unimportance of multiple IRRs, the conclusion reached must still be that the possible presence of multiple IRRs is yet one more factor to count against the use of that particular DCF technique. The argument that, while the IRR rule may give the wrong decision, it will not be *very* wrong, is not a persuasive one.

Extended yield method

One approach that is often suggested, and sometimes used in practice, to handle the problem of multiple IRRs, is the *extended yield* method. Project R is an example of a project which would cause difficulties for the IRR decision rule. The extended yield method solves the problem by eliminating the offending second change in sign. This is achieved by discounting the unwanted cash flow back to present value at the hurdle rate, and then netting the figure off against the Year 0 outlay. Example 5 illustrates the approach.

However, it should be noted that the extended yield method only *gets around* the problem of multiple IRRs – it does not *solve* the problem.

Although a single IRR has been calculated for Project R, the point remains that in reality Project R has *two* IRRs (and neither is likely to be the 13.4% estimated).

Example 5

A company wishes to evaluate Project R using the IRR decision rule with a 10% hurdle rate:

Year	Cash flow
0	− 100
1	+ 50
2	+ 80
3	− 10

The Year 3 cash flow is discounted back to present value at 10%: $-10(1.10)^{-3} = -7.51$ and this figure is then netted off with the Year 0 cash flow to provide a *revised* cash flow for Project R:

Year	Cash flow
0	− 107.51
1	+ 50
2	+ 80

At 4%, the project has an NPV of: +14.53
At 20%, the project has an NPV of: −10.29

Using linear interpolation, the IRR of Project R can be estimated as:

$$4\% + \left[\frac{14.53}{14.53 - (-10.92)} \times (20\% - 4\%) \right] = 13.4\% \text{ IRR.}$$

Other problems with the IRR rule

Example 6

If we return to the example of Ossett Roadstone we find another problem with IRR. As before it will cost £1 050 000 to set up the project. It will then produce cash flows of £800 000 for five years. However, at the end of the five years, it will cost £3 090 000 to landscape the area which is a requirement of planning permission. Assess the project using IRR.

The answer to Example 6 is shown in Fig. 6.4 and illustrates another problematical situation for the IRR rule where there is only a single IRR for the project, but at no rate of discount does the project yield a positive NPV. If, in this example, the discount rate were 10%, the NPV rule would correctly reject the project. However, the IRR rule would accept it because its IRR (20%) is greater than the hurdle rate.

Fig. 6.5 illustrates an NPV profile which causes the IRR decision rule to break down completely. Here we assume that all the conditions for Ossett Roadstone remain the same except for the fact that the landscaping will cost £3 200 000 and it can be seen that no internal rate of return exists![5]

A further difficulty that arises out of the IRR approach is caused by the fact that it evaluates projects on the basis of a percentage rate of return. In other words, it examines a project's return relative to its outlay, rather than in absolute terms as with NPV.

For example, suppose a company is evaluating a pair of mutually exclusive projects: a large factory or a small factory. The large factory has an outlay of £10 million, the small factory has an outlay of £2 million. Suppose the large factory has an IRR of 18% and the small factory 24%, and the hurdle rate is 15%. Therefore both alternatives are acceptable in their own right, but the standard IRR decision rule would accept the small factory, as it produces the higher IRR. The problem is that the company would end up with a significantly better incremental cash flow from an 18% return on £10 million, than from a 24% return on only £2 million. This is, of course, yet another reason for the possible existence of conflicting advice between NPV and the standard IRR decision rule.

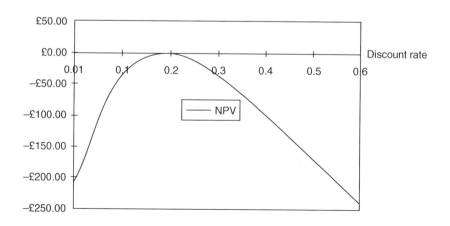

Fig. 6.4 *A non-existent IRR*

Fig. 6.5 A non-existent IRR

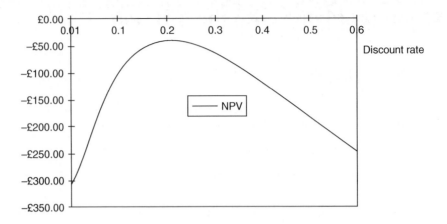

The modified IRR

Whilst there can be little argument about the theoretical superiority of NPV as a decision rule, surveys of managers suggest that many of them feel that they understand the idea of IRR better than NPV simply because it is expressed in percentage terms rather than an absolute figure. Managers are used to dealing with percentages, e.g. return on capital, dividend yields, gross profit margins, etc. It may also be that they (mistakenly) believe that it is not necessary to be able to work out the company's cost of capital in order to use IRR. This has led to the development of modified IRR. It is thus an attempt to overcome the theoretical difficulties of the normal IRR technique, whilst retaining an evaluation of the project based on a percentage rate of return and so avoiding the perceived 'user-unfriendliness' of NPV.

The approach is really founded on an NPV analysis which is then converted into a rate of return. However, instead of *discounting* the project cash flows – at the appropriate opportunity cost of capital – to *present value*, the cash flows (with the exception of the project's outlay) are *compounded* forward to a total *terminal* value. On the basis of these two cash flows – the project's outlay and the terminal value of its net cash inflows – the IRR is then calculated. This is illustrated in Example 7.

This particular modification to the IRR technique has two great technical advantages. First, it eliminates any potential problem of multiple IRRs. Second, it will not provide decision advice involving mutually exclusive projects which conflicts with that given by the NPV technique. If you recall, that particular problem arose out of the fact that the IRR technique made an incorrect assumption about the reinvestment rate of project-generated cash flows. With this modification, the problem is avoided by compounding the project's net cash inflows forward at the correct reinvestment rate – the project's opportunity cost of capital or hurdle rate.

Example 7

Year	(£)	
0	(100)	Hurdle rate is 10%
1	50	
2	40	
3	50	

The terminal value of the project's net cash inflows can be calculated as:

Year	(£)			
1	$50\,(1.10)^2$	=	60.5	
2	$40\,(1.10)^1$	=	44.0	
3	$50\,(1.10)^0$	=	50.0	
Total terminal value		=	£154.50	

The project has a modified cash flow of:

Year	(£)
0	(100)
3	154.5

The IRR can now be estimated, as usual, using linear interpolation:

NPV at 4%	:	37.50
NPV at 20%	:	(10.59)

$$IRR = 4\% + \left[\frac{37.50}{37.50 - (-10.59)} \times (20\% - 4\%) \right] = 16.5\% \; IRR.$$

In Example 7, the project is shown to have an IRR of approximately 16.5%. In fact the modified *actual* IRR is 15.6%. What we have to ask is: does the project genuinely produce a rate of return of 15.6%? The answer is that it does, if the project-generated cash flows can accumulate at the end of the project's life to the same amount that could be accumulated by investing the project's outlay to earn an annual rate of return of 15.6%.

Investing £100 for three years at an annual rate of return of 15.6% yields a terminal value of:

$$£100\,(1 + 0.156)^3 = £154.50$$

This is *precisely* the terminal value of the project's net cash inflows calculated in Example 7. In other words, the project does genuinely earn a rate of return of 15.6%.

In many ways this modified IRR calculation achieves the best of all worlds. Its theoretical underpinning is that of NPV, but its method of evaluation is through the use of a user-friendly rate of return. Therefore it can be seen as a cosmetic restatement of an NPV analysis.

In conclusion

Our analysis puts forward a very strong case for the use of the NPV decision rule for investment appraisal. At best, the IRR method (or the modified IRR) might be used as a support and as a communication device on the basis of management's familiarity with rates of return, rather than net present values, for the decision advice given by the NPV rule.[6]

As a result of this conclusion, from now on, we shall be implicitly assuming that the NPV technique will be the approach that should be used by companies in making investment appraisals. It is the only technique from the four investigated that can be relied upon to give advice that will lead towards the maximizing of shareholder wealth.

The replacement cycle problem

Optimal replacement cycle

It was noted earlier that, when faced with a mutually exclusive investment decision, the NPV decision rule was to accept whichever project had the largest positive NPV. This decision rule was based on the assumption of a perfect capital market *and* on the assumption that the projects involved were 'one-offs'. In other words, they did not form part of a continuous replacement cycle.

However, where a project *does* form part of a continuous replacement cycle, the NPV decision rule needs to be modified. This situation is referred to as the *replacement cycle problem*, and Example 8 illustrates the approach.

Example 8

Photolysis plc uses a 10% discount rate for project appraisal. It is considering purchasing a machine which, when it comes to the end of its economic life, is expected to be replaced by an identical machine and so on, continuously. The machine has a maximum life of three years but, as its productivity declines with age, it could be replaced after either just one or two years. The financial details are as follows (all figures in £000s):

Year	0	1	2	3
Outlay	− 1000			
Revenues		+ 900	+ 800	+ 700
Costs		− 400	− 350	− 350
Scrap value		+ 650	+ 400	+ 150

The choice of when to replace this machine can be seen as a choice between three mutually exclusive alternatives, the cash flows and NPVs of which are as follows:

Cash flows

Dispose of machine at end of:		0	1	2	3
First year	Outlay	− 1000			
	Revenue		+ 900		
	Costs		− 400		
	Scrap		+ 650		
	Net cash flow	− 1000	+ 1150		
Second year	Outlay	− 1000			
	Revenue		+ 900	+ 800	
	Costs		− 400	− 350	
	Scrap			+ 400	
	Net cash flow	− 1000	+ 500	+ 850	

Third year	Outlay	-1000			
	Revenue		$+900$	$+800$	$+700$
	Costs		-400	-350	-350
	Scrap				$+150$
	Net cash flow	-1000	$+500$	$+450$	$+500$

Disposal point

					NPV
Yr 1	-1000	$+1150(1.10)^{-1}$			$=+45.46$
Yr 2	-1000	$+500(1.10)^{-1}$	$+850(1.10)^{-2}$		$=+156.99$
Yr 3	-1000	$+500(1.10)^{-1}$	$+450(1.10)^{-2}$	$+500(1.10)^{-3}$	$=+202.08$

If these were straightforward mutually exclusive projects, then the decision could be based on whichever alternative has the largest positive NPV. However, the machine – whenever the decision is taken to replace it – will be replaced by an identical machine which will itself be replaced by another identical machine and so on. Therefore, purely on the basis of the NPVs alone, like is not being compared with like as each NPV is generated over a different span of time: one, two or three years.

In order to place the three alternatives on a comparable basis, the equivalent *annual* cash flow of each has to be computed:

Disposal point	NPV	$\div$	$A_{n-0.10}$	$=$	Equivalent annual cash flow
Yr 1	$+45.46$	$\div$	$A_{1-0.10}$	$=$	$+50.00$
Yr 2	$+156.99$	$\div$	$A_{2-0.10}$	$=$	$+90.46$
Yr 3	$+202.08$	$\div$	$A_{3-0.10}$	$=$	$+81.26$

In order to understand the meaning of the *equivalent annual cash flow* figures, let us take the two-year replacement option as an example. Quite simply, the cash flow of the machine over its two-year life has an NPV which is equivalent to that of a two-year immediate annuity of £90.46 per year:

Year 0	Year 1	Year 2		
-1000	$+500$	$+850$	$=$	$+156.99$ NPV
	$+90.46$	$+90.46$	$=$	$+156.99$ NPV

As a result, replacing the machine every two years is equivalent to a cash flow of £90.46 at the end of every year:

Year	0	1	2	3	4	5	$6 \rightarrow \infty$
1st machine	-1000	$+500$	$+850$				
2nd machine			-1000	$+500$	$+850$		
3rd machine					-1000	$+500$	$+850$
etc., etc.							-1000
Equivalent c/f		$+90.46$	$+90.46$	$+90.46$	$+90.46$	$+90.46$	$+90.46$

Therefore, the optimal replacement cycle of the machine can be decided on the basis of which replacement cycle gives the most favourable equivalent annual cash flow. In this example, it is two-year replacement. Both one- and three-year replacement will result in a lower equivalent annual cash flow.

Repair versus replace

The repair versus replace decision is very common. How long should the company continue to spend money on keeping an existing machine working, and when should it be replaced with a new machine?

With this situation, it is important to realize two decisions are involved:

1. When should the *existing* machine be replaced?
2. What is the optimal replacement cycle of the *new* machine?

Furthermore, decision 2 *must* be made before decision 1 can be made. Example 9 continues on from Example 8 to illustrate the procedure.

Finally, a major drawback of the repair or replace decision procedure should be pointed out. The drawback is the implicit assumption of unchanging technology. In other words, the assumption in the optimal replacement cycle that the new machine will be replaced by an *identical* machine, *ad infinitum*, is clearly unrealistic. Thus the technique's real-world usefulness should be seen with this limitation in mind.

Example 9

Photolysis plc, referred to in Example 8, already have an existing machine doing the job of the new machine whose optimal replacement cycle has been identified as every two years. Therefore, the only remaining decision is: when should the company's existing machine be scrapped? The financial details are as follows (all figures in £000s):

Existing machine			
Year	0	1	2
Scrap value	+ 250	+ 200	+ 50
Repair cost	– 100	– 250	
Revenue		+ 600	+ 600
Costs		– 300	– 340

On the basis of this information, the existing machine could be kept operational for a maximum of two more years. To be kept operational for the next twelve months would require £100 000 of repairs to be carried out now. To extend the machine's life up to the end of Year 2 would require a further £250 000 to be spent on repairs in twelve months' time. However, the repair costs in any particular year could be avoided by scrapping the machine in that year. The cash flows of the different options are as follows, based on the assumption that when scrapped, the existing machine will be replaced by the new machine (referred to in Example 8) which is itself replaced every two years and so locks the company into an equivalent annual cash flow of + £90.46: in perpetuity.

Scrap the existing machine at:	Year	0	1	2	3 → ∞
Year 0	Scrap value	+ 250			
	New machine		+ 90.46	+ 90.46	+ 90.46
	Net cash flow	+ 250	+ 90.46	+ 90.46	+ 90.46
Year 1	Scrap value		+ 200.00		
	Repair cost	– 100			
	Revenue		+ 600.00		
	Cost		– 300.00		
	New machine			+ 90.46	+ 90.46
	Net cash flow	– 100	+ 500.00	+ 90.46	+ 90.46
Year 2	Scrap value			+ 50.00	
	Repair cost	– 100	– 250.00		
	Revenue		+ 600.00	+ 600.00	
	Cost		– 300.00	– 340.00	
	New machine				+ 90.46
	Net cash flow	– 100	+ 50.00	+ 310.00	+ 90.46

The NPV of each of these perpetuity cash flows is:
Scrap at Year 0: + 250 + (90.46 ÷ 0.10) = + 1154.60 NPV
Scrap at Year 1: – 100 + 500 $(1.10)^{-1}$ + (90.46 ÷ 0.10) $(1.10)^{-1}$ = +1176.92 NPV

Scrap at Year 2: $-100 + 50 (1.10)^{-1} + 310 (1.10)^{-2} + (90.46 \div 0.10) (1.10)^{-2} = +949.20$ NPV

Therefore the best option for the company is to scrap the existing machine in twelve months' time (the largest NPV option) and replace it by the new machine, which itself is replaced every two years thereafter (see Example 8).

Summary

This chapter has looked at the application of the two DCF investment appraisal methods in the context of decisions between mutually exclusive projects. Arising out of this have come a number of difficulties with the IRR decision rule. The main points made are:

- The NPV decision rule for mutually exclusive decisions is: accept whichever project has the largest positive NPV. The logic behind this was obvious, given the objective of shareholder wealth maximization and the meaning of NPV.

- The decision rule holds even when the alternative investments are of unequal magnitude, duration or risk, assuming a perfect capital market and that the discount rate used properly reflects the return available elsewhere on the capital market from a similar-risk investment.

- The standard IRR decision rule for mutually exclusive investments is:
  — the 'best' project has the highest IRR;
  — accept the best project if its IRR > hurdle rate.

- This *standard* IRR decision rule gives unreliable investment decision advice in situations of mutually exclusive projects: the problem arises from the arithmetic of the IRR and the fact that it assumes project-generated cash flows will be reinvested to earn a rate of return equal to the IRR of the project generating those cash flows.

- The reinvestment assumption is, strictly speaking, an assumption about the opportunity cost of project-generated cash flows. Given a perfect capital market, the assumption made by the IRR is incorrect – their opportunity cost equates with the capital market rate of return for the risk level involved. The NPV method makes this, correct, assumption.

- The problem of the IRR can be resolved, in an artificial way, by a modified decision rule which, in its simplest form, states:
  — if IRR of the differential cash flow is > hurdle rate, accept the project with the smallest IRR;
  — if IRR of the differential cash flow is < hurdle rate, accept the project with the largest IRR.

- A further problem for the IRR arises out of the possible existence of multiple IRRs, when the decision rule then breaks down completely.

- The problem of multiple IRRs can be resolved, again in a purely artificial way, through the use of the extended yield technique. However, this was shown not to deal with the problem, merely to avoid it.

- The theoretical objections to the IRR can be overcome by the use of the *modified* IRR technique, but in reality it is more akin to a cosmetic restatement of NPV.

- The strong conclusion to the chapter is that, for several reasons, the IRR investment appraisal technique is – just like payback and ROCE/ARR – unsatisfactory. Therefore only NPV remains as an investment appraisal technique which will give consistently reliable advice leading to shareholder wealth maximization.

- Finally, a related area was examined: the repair-or-replace decision. This was seen to be a special case of mutually exclusive projects involving the use of the annuity discounting factors.

Notes

1.   This, of course, would be the decision rule for revenue-generating projects. For purely cost-generating projects (such as the installation of air conditioning equipment in a factory), the best project would be that which produces the smallest negative NPV.

2.   The processes of discounting and compounding can be viewed simply as a method of assigning weights to cash flows.

3.   The IRR calculation simply involves finding the roots of a polynomial equation of n terms (where n = the number of periods of the project's life). In general, the IRR equation of a project which lasts for n years will have n roots or solutions or IRRs. However, with a conventional type of cash flow, only one of these solutions is a real number and the rest will be imaginary (e.g. $\sqrt{-2}$), with mathematical, but no economic importance. However, a non-conventional project cash flow can produce a polynomial equation of a type which may have several real number roots, each one of which is an equally valid IRR. (Conventional and non-conventional cash flows are defined in the following paragraph in the main text.)

4.   The use of these terms should not lead the reader into the all-too-easy substitution of 'usual' and 'unusual'. Non-conventional cash flows can be extremely common in practice, as we shall discover when we examine the impact of taxation on investment appraisal.

5.   The IRR is said not to exist only as a 'real' number, in such cases. It will exist, and so there will be roots to the polynomial, in terms of imaginary numbers. This mathematical result, however, has little relevance for our purposes.

6.   Even this may be a disadvantage in that management may falsely believe that the IRR is essentially the same as the Accounting Rate of Return (ROCE), when in fact the two measures are totally distinct.

Further reading

1. On the problems with the IRR technique, see R. Dorfman, 'The Meaning of Internal Rates of Return', *Journal of Finance*, December 1981; A Herbst, 'The Unique, Real Internal Rate of Return: Caveat Emptor!', *Journal of Financial and Quantitative Analysis*, June 1978; S.M. Keane, 'The Internal Rate of Return and the Reinvestment Fallacy', *Journal of Accounting and Business Research*, June 1979 and C.R. Beidleman, 'DCF Reinvestment Rates Assumptions', *Engineering Economist*, Winter 1984.
2. For a description of the modified IRR technique, see W.R. McDaniel, D.E. McCarty and K.A. Jessell, 'DCF with Explicit Reinvestment Rates: Tutorial and Extension', *The Financial Review*, August 1988.
3. There are many articles reporting the results of surveys on capital budgeting practice. Amongst these, the following are of particular interest: M. Ross, 'Capital Budgeting Practice in Twelve Large Manufacturers', *Financial Management*, Winter 1986, R.H. Pike and T.S. Ooi, 'The Impact of Corporate Investment Objectives and Constraints on Capital Budgeting Practices', *British Accounting Review*, August 1989, S.H. Kim and L. Guin, 'A Summary of Empirical Studies on Capital Budgeting Practices', *Business and Public Affairs*, Autumn 1986, and S.C. Weaver *et al.*, 'Capital Budgeting: Panel Discussions on Corporate Investments', *Financial Management*, Spring 1989.
4. Finally, two rather thoughtful articles are S.C. Myers, 'Notes on an Expert System for Capital Budgeting', *Financial Management*, Autumn 1988, and M. Bromwich and A. Bhimani, 'Strategic Investment Appraisal', *Management Accounting*, March 1991.

Quickie questions

1. Project A has an outlay of £1 million and when using a discount rate of 10%, to reflect its risk, it has an NPV of + £20 000. Project B has an outlay of £10 million and when discounted at 20%, to reflect its risk, has an NPV of + £15 000. If A and B are mutually exclusive, which project should the firm accept?
2. In question 1, what assumptions are you making in giving your answer?
3. What are the reinvestment assumptions of NPV and IRR, which is correct, and under what circumstances?
4. Under what circumstances can multiple IRRs occur, and what can be done to avoid the problem?
5. Project C has the following cash flows:

0	− 100
1	+ 60
2	+ 80
3	− 20

   Using the 'extended yield technique', what is its IRR, given a 10% hurdle rate?
6. Sketch out a diagram showing how the conflict between NPV and IRR can occur.
7. What is the simple modification to the IRR decision rule?
8. Project D has the following cash flows:

0	− 80
1	+ 40
2	+ 80
3	− 30

   Given the minimum required rate of return is 10%, what is its modified IRR?

Problems

1. Saucy Steamboats Ltd is currently evaluating a proposal to invest in a new inshore rowing boat. Two possible types, A and B, have now been identified, each of which would have a five-year life and zero scrap value. Their costs and associated net revenues are:

Year	Type A (£)	Type B (£)
0	− 1000	− 2000
1	+ 350	+ 640
2	+ 350	+ 640
3	+ 350	+ 640
4	+ 350	+ 640
5	+ 350	+ 640

The appropriate discount rate is 10% per annum. Both alternatives can be considered marginal investments and acceptance of either one would leave the company's risk unchanged. The company operates in a perfect capital market. Ignore taxation and inflation.

Required:
(a) The managing director of Saucy Steamboats Ltd insists that the investment alternatives should be appraised using the internal rate of return. You are therefore required to appraise these projects on that basis alone. State the decision rule you use, making sure that it will produce the correct investment decision advice in terms of maximizing shareholders' wealth.
(b) Present a careful and detailed outline of the argument you might put forward to the managing director for using the net present value appraisal technique, rather than the internal rate of return, given the present conditions surrounding Saucy Steamboats Ltd.
Note that your answer to part (b) should *not* be confined to a discussion of the two investment opportunities under consideration in part (a). Assume that all cash flows arise on the last day of the year to which they relate, with the exception of the project outlays, which occur at the start of the first year.

2. Mr Cowdrey runs a manufacturing business. He is considering whether to accept one of two mutually exclusive investment projects and, if so, which one to accept. Each project involves an immediate cash outlay of £100 000. Mr Cowdrey estimates that the net cash inflows from each project will be as follows:

Net cash inflow at end of:	Project A (£)	Project B (£)
Year 1	60 000	10 000
Year 2	40 000	20 000
Year 3	30 000	110 000

Mr Cowdrey does not expect capital or any other resource to be in short supply during the next three years.

Required:
(a) Prepare a graph to show the functional relationship between net present value and the discount rate for the two projects (label the vertical axis 'net present value' and the horizontal axis 'discount rate').
(b) Use the graph to estimate the internal rate of return of each project.

(c) On the basis of the information given, advise Mr Cowdrey which project to accept if his discount rate is (i) 6%, (ii) 12%.

(d) Describe briefly any additional information you think would be useful to Mr Cowdrey in choosing between the two projects.

(e) Discuss the relative merits of net present value and internal rate of return as methods of investment appraisal.

Ignore taxation.

3. Charles Pooter (Investment) plc are considering which, if any, of four independent projects to undertake. The forecast cash flows for each project are listed below; receipts arise at the end of each year.

	Immediate		Net cash inflows	
Project	outlay	Year 1	Year 2	Year 3
1	– 2500	+ 1000	+ 1000	+ 1000
2	– 1000	+ 100	+ 1400	0
3	– 1000	+ 800	+ 600	0
4	– 4000	0	0	+ 5000

The company faces a perfect capital market, in which the interest rate for the projects' risk level is 10%.

Required:

(a) Using the NPV decision rule, indicate which projects the company should accept. State clearly the reasons for your decisions.

(b) How would your conclusions in (a) differ if the projects were mutually exclusive?

(c) Estimate the IRRs of Projects 2 and 3. Would it be valid to choose between Projects 2 and 3 on the basis of their expected IRRs? If not, present revised calculations so that the internal rate of return method, and the method you have used in (a), lead to the same, unambiguous conclusions.

(d) In practice, the IRR method has been observed to be far more widely used than NPV. Suggest reasons for this relative popularity. Why might the supposed superiority of NPV be an illusion or an irrelevance, in reality?

4. Demeter Ltd owns a machine of type DK which could be used in production for two more years at most. The machine originally cost £45 000 five years ago. Its realizable value is currently £8000 (because a special opportunity for sale has arisen), but it would be zero at all subsequent times. If the machine were to be used for two more years, it would require a major overhaul at a cost of £9000 at the end of one year.

A new model of the machine is now being marketed. It costs £40 000 and has a maximum life of ten years, provided that special maintenance is undertaken at a cost of £10 000 after five years, and at a cost of £20 000 after eight years. The new model would have no realizable value at any time. Assume that no other new models are expected to become available in the foreseeable future, and that no changes are expected in costs or demand for output of the machine. Demeter's cost of capital is 15% per annum.

Required:

Prepare calculations to show whether Demeter's existing machine should be replaced now, or after one or two years.

Investment appraisal and inflation

Up to this stage in the analysis, we have implicitly assumed, within our world of managerial investment decision making, that prices have been stable. That is not to say that we have excluded the possibility of any price changes, but that we have assumed that there are no general price movements within the economy, either upwards (inflation) or downwards (deflation). Indeed it was made clear when dealing with the concept of the time value of money that the concept, fundamentally, has nothing to do with inflation, and so inflation was assumed not to exist.

In this section we will now drop this assumption and examine how the existence of general price movements within an economy affect investment appraisal and decision making, and how appraisal techniques can be adapted, if need be, to cope with such circumstances. These effects will be examined mainly by analysing the inflation case, but the approach used and conclusions drawn will also apply, by analogy, to the case of deflation.

The problem of inflation

Inflation can be simply defined as a situation where prices in an economy are, in general, rising over time. Its expected (or unexpected) presence is likely to cause problems for the appraisal of investment opportunities in two main ways.

The first problem is that it will make the estimation of a project's expected cash flow more difficult. When a project is being appraised, management will have to provide estimates of its inputs and outputs. With inflation, the prices of these inputs and outputs are likely to change, and management will hence have to estimate the magnitude of these changes. In other words, management will have to estimate the expected future rates of inflation. Thus there is a *forecasting* problem caused by the presence of inflation.

The second problem is, in one sense, an extension of the first. Market interest rates, or rates of return, can be viewed as representing the price of money, and so interest rates – like other prices – can be expected to rise when there is general inflation within the economy. Thus management have the additional task of estimating the effects of inflation on the project appraisal discount rate.

'Real' and 'market' rates of interest

The effects of inflation on market interest rates can most easily be seen by way of an example. We know from the discussion about the concept of the time value of money that suppliers of investment capital make a trade-off between consumption now and consumption at some future point in time. Generally speaking, current consumption is preferred to future consumption and so, in order to be persuaded to forgo consumption now (and invest instead), investors have to be rewarded with the promise of increased consumption at a later point in time. Market interest rates reflect this time 'exchange rate' of consumption.

Example 1

For the moment, suppose that within the economy there is no inflation. An investor, we are told, is willing to lend you £100 for a year in return for £110 in twelve months' time. In other words, he is willing to give up £100 worth of consumption now, as long as he is rewarded with an extra 10% consumption in twelve months' time. Thus the 10% interest rate that he is demanding can be seen both in money terms – he wants an extra ten £1 coins – and in terms of consumption or purchasing power. However, it is this latter interpretation that is of fundamental concern to the investor – how much additional consumption he is to receive in the future for giving up current consumption. (Pound coins by themselves are of little use. What makes them desirable is that they give the power to consume; consumption and consumption power – or purchasing power – is the point of importance.)

Now let us take a slightly different situation, with inflation expected to raise the general level of prices in the economy by 5% over the next twelve months. Our investor would still be willing to give up £100 worth of current consumption as long as he is rewarded with an extra 10% of *consumption* in twelve months' time. However, an extra £10 will not be sufficient cash to buy this additional consumption, because of the presence of inflation.

In order to consume, in twelve months' time, the *same* amount of consumption as that given up now, the investor will need £100 (1 + 0.05) = £105, because of the rise in prices. But our investor has to be able to consume 10% *extra* in order to be persuaded to give up current consumption and so, in money terms, he will require £105 (1 + 0.10) = £115.50. This therefore represents a *money* interest rate of 15.5%: because of 5% inflation, 15.5% extra cash is required to purchase 10% extra consumption.

It follows from the analysis in Example 1 that, in inflationary conditions, two interest rates can be identified – a money (or nominal) interest rate and a consumption (or purchasing power) interest rate. In Example 1 these were 15.5% and 10% respectively. We shall refer to the former rate as the 'market' interest rate (as it would be the rate quoted on the capital market) and to the latter as the 'real' interest rate. (It is real in the sense that it represents the market interest rate, *deflated*, to take out the effects of inflation.) The general relationship, which is often referred to as the Fisher Effect, after the American economist who first developed it, is shown below:

$$\begin{pmatrix} \text{Real} \\ 1 + \text{interest} \\ \text{rate} \end{pmatrix} \begin{pmatrix} \text{General} \\ 1 + \text{rate of} \\ \text{inflation} \end{pmatrix} = \begin{pmatrix} \text{Market} \\ 1 + \text{interest} \\ \text{rate} \end{pmatrix}$$

Substituting in here the data from the example:

$$(1 + 0.10)(1 + 0.05) = (1 + 0.155)$$

Therefore, the real interest rate: $\dfrac{(1 + 0.155) - 1}{(1 + 0.05)}$ = 0.1 or 10%

the market interest rate: $(1.10)(1.05) - 1$ = 0.155 or 15.5%

and the general inflation rate: $\dfrac{(1 + 0.155) - 1}{(1 + 0.1)}$ = 0.05 or 5%.

Two possible approaches

The example used above shows that under inflationary conditions we can identify two possible interest or discount rates: the market interest rate and the real interest rate. The question that immediately arises is: which one should be used in an NPV investment appraisal analysis? The answer to this question is that either rate can be used, but they must each *only* be applied to an appropriate definition of the project cash flow. Specifically, we can state either:

1. *money* cash flows of the project can be discounted by the *market* interest rate to present value cash flows; or
2. *money* cash flows of the project can be discounted by the rate of general inflation to *current general purchasing power* cash flows, and then these current general purchasing power cash flows can be discounted by the *real* interest rate to present value cash flows.

Either approach will generate exactly the same NPV for the project.

In these statements the term 'money' cash flow can be defined as the physical quantity of money (i.e pound coins) that the project will generate at any particular point in time, and the term 'current general purchasing power' (CGPP) cash flow refers to the money cash flow, deflated by the *general* rate of inflation, so as to reflect the current general purchasing power of that future cash flow. Example 2 can clarify the definition and can also be used to show that these two alternative discounting approaches are entirely consistent with each other.

In Example 2 we should have expected the present values to be exactly the same for obvious reasons: in the first approach, the cash flow is being discounted by 15.5%, whereas in the second approach the cash flow is being discounted by 10% and 5%. Thus in each alternative the cash flow is being discounted by the same amount because:

$$(1 + 0.155) = (1 + 0.10)(1 + 0.05)$$

Example 2

Rhotacine plc wishes to evaluate a project. The company has taken great care to estimate how future rates of inflation will affect the prices charged for the project's output (and hence its revenue), and how inflation will affect the costs incurred in generating those revenues. The project's actual (money) cash flows have been estimated as:

Year	Cash flow (£)
0	−1000
1	+ 800
2	+ 600

The company believes that a 15.5% return is available elsewhere on the capital market for a similar risk project (i.e. the market rate of return) and that prices in general, as measured by the retail price index (RPI), will increase by 5% per year over the next two years.

Approach 1: Take the project's money cash flows and discount by the market rate of discount to NPV.

Year	Cash flow (£)	×	15.5% discount	=	PV c/f
0	−1000	×	1	=	−1000
1	+ 800	×	0.8658	=	+ 692.64
2	+ 600	×	0.7496	=	+ 449.76
					+ 142.40 NPV

Approach 2: Take the project's money cash flows and discount by the RPI to CGPP cash flow. Then discount the CGPP cash flow by the real discount rate to NPV.

Year	Cash flow (£)	×	5% discount	=	CGPP c/f
0	−1000	×	1	=	−1000
1	+ 800	×	0.9524	=	+ 761.92
2	+ 600	×	0.9070	=	+ 544.20

The real discount rate can be found from the Fisher Effect relationship:

$$\frac{(1+0.155)}{(1+0.05)} - 1 = 0.10 \text{ or } 10\%.$$

Year	CGPP c/f	×	10% discount	=	PV c/f
0	−1000	×	1	=	−1000
1	+ 761.92	×	0.9091	=	+ 692.66
2	+ 544.20	×	0.8264	=	+ 449.73
					+ 142.39 NPV

Notice that the two NPVs are (virtually) identical. (The fact that they are not identical simply arises from rounding errors because only four-figure discount factors were used.)

Therefore, it is for this reason that it was stated earlier that either the market discount rate or the real discount rate could be used in an investment appraisal analysis, *as long as each was applied to an appropriate definition of cash flow*.

The market discount rate is an interest rate expressed in money terms and so it is applied to the actual money cash flows that the project is expected to produce. The real discount rate is an interest rate expressed in consumption or purchasing power terms, and so it should be applied to the project cash flows that are similarly expressed; in other words it is applied to the money cash flows after they have had the inflationary element taken out. To illustrate this we can make use of the Year 2 cash flow from Example 2.

In Year 2 the project is expected to produce a physical cash flow of £600. Given an annual rate of general inflation of 5%, this money would buy the same 'basket of goods' that £544.20 would buy *today* (i.e. Year 0).

However, because of the time value of money of investors, £600 at Year 2 is not equivalent to £544.20 at Year 0. The present value of £600 at Year 2 (taking into account the time value of money, expressed in real terms, of 10%) is £449.73.

There are two further points to be noticed about this example. The first is that discounting the money cash flow by the general rate of inflation has nothing to do with the idea of the time value of money, it is simply a calculation to express the project cash flow – not in money terms, but in consumption/purchasing power terms. The idea of the time value of money is not taken into account until the discounting of these deflated cash flows by the *real* discount rate.

The second point to notice is that the project money cash flows are deflated (or discounted) by the general rate of inflation, *not* by the specific rate of inflation that applies to a particular cash flow. For example, suppose that although the general rate of inflation (as given by changes in the RPI) is 14%, the rate of *wage* inflation is 20%. The actual money cash flow paid out in wages would be discounted by 14% and not by 20%. This is because we wish to express the money cash flows of a project in terms of their ability to purchase a *general* range or collection of goods, not their ability to purchase any one *particular* good.

A final example

The above analysis shows that the two possible approaches to project appraisal are exactly equivalent. Both start with the actual 'money' cash flows that the project is expected to produce, and both result in an identical set of present value cash flows from which the net present value can be found.

Given this equivalence, it does not much matter which approach is used, although discounting the money cash flows by the market interest rate would appear more straightforward because it only involves a single set of discounting calculations and is the recommended approach to use. However, sometimes the easiest approach is to use a mixture of both, if there are some simplification benefits to be had through cancellations. Example 3 demonstrates the principle.

Example 3

Project A:	Outlay:	£1000
	Life:	30 years
	Scrap value:	£100
	Net revenues:	£20 per year in current (t_0) terms.

The net cash flow is expected to increase each year by 8%.

| | RPI: | 6% per year. |
| | Market discount rate: | 14.48% |

It would be possible to set out the project's money cash flows and discount by 14.48% to present value. However, 14.48% is a rather awkward discounting number to use, and thirty years of

---

cash flows would be hard work! Therefore we could instead discount the money cash flows by a combination of RPI (6%) and the real discount rate.

Using the Fisher Effect:

$$\frac{1.1448}{1.06} - 1 = 0.08 \text{ or } 8\% = \text{real discount rate.}$$

Therefore, the project's money cash flows can be expressed as:

Year	Outlay (£)	Scrap (£)	Net revs. (£)
0	−1000		
1			+120 $(1.08)^1$
2			+120 $(1.08)^2$
.			.
.			.
30		+100	+120 $(1.08)^{30}$

The outlay is already in present value terms and so does not require discounting. The scrap value can be discounted back either at 14.48% or at a combination of 6% and 8%:

$$\text{Year 30: } +100 \, (1.448)^{-30} = +100 \times 0.0173 = +1.73$$

or

$$\text{Year 30: } +100 \, (1.08)^{-30} (1.06)^{-30} = +100 \times 0.0994 \times 0.1741 = +1.73.$$

As far as the net revenue cash flows are concerned, it is convenient to discount them to present value using a combination of 8% and 6% in order to be able to simplify the calculation through cancellation:

Year	Net revs. (£)			Discount factors	
0					
1	+120 $(1.08)^1$	$\times$	$(1.08)^{-1}$	$(1.06)^{-1} =$	+120 $(1.06)^{-1}$
2	+120 $(1.08)^2$	$\times$	$(1.08)^{-2}$	$(1.06)^{-2} =$	+120 $(1.06)^{-2}$
.					.
.					.
30	+120 $(1.08)^{30}$	$\times$	$(1.08)^{-30}$	$(1.06)^{-30} =$	+120 $(1.06)^{-30}$

Therefore, we are left with a thirty-year annuity cash flow:

$$+120 \, A_{30-0.06} = 120 \times 13.7648 = +1651.78.$$

Hence, the project's NPV is:

$$-1000 + 1.73 + 1651.78 = +653.51 \text{ NPV.}$$

Inflation and the IRR rule

This discussion about allowing for inflation in investment appraisal has been conducted within the context of an NPV analysis. Nevertheless it is simple to transfer the conclusions into the context of an IRR calculation. Either the IRR of the money cash flows of the project can be compared against the hurdle rate of the market interest rate or, alternatively, the IRR of the project's current general purchasing power cash flows can be matched against the real interest rate. However, in order to be able to use the IRR successfully, it is important to remember that it is necessary to assume that either the market interest rate or the real interest rate will remain constant over the project's life.

Investment appraisal and taxation

Introduction

Taxation has an important role to play in investment appraisal, as it can have a substantial impact on the desirability, or otherwise, of an investment opportunity. Furthermore, taxation considerations affect virtually every area of financial decision making both in a practical and in a theoretical context. Indeed, the complexity of the tax system and the fact that its application to individual financial decision-making situations can sometimes be difficult to generalize mean that it causes problems for the development of a realistic theory of financial decision making.

In this section we shall deal briefly with only a relatively simple aspect of taxation – its impact on investment project cash flows and their subsequent evaluation. However, in many of the later chapters we will be returning to examine some of the more complex problems that the presence of taxation poses for financial decision making.

The impact of tax

The theory of financial decision making is developed on the basis of an important underlying assumption: management are taking decisions so as to maximize the wealth of the shareholders. It therefore follows that in the appraisal of an investment project, what is of importance is the cash flows that will be generated by the project, and *that are available for shareholders*. In other words, as far as investment appraisal is concerned, we would wish to evaluate the *after-tax cash flows* of a project.

In this analysis of the impact of tax on project appraisal, only a simplified version of the UK corporate tax system will be used. Furthermore it is assumed that the reader is aware – in outline – of this tax system but, for those who lack knowledge in this area, a brief appendix at the end of the chapter outlines the very basic elements. It should also be remembered that tax rates are set in the budget each year. Thus it is important to note that any tax rates used in this book may or may not be correct.

There are three ways in which the UK corporation tax regime impacts upon project appraisal:

1. Tax relief is available on capital expenditure through the system of *writing-down allowances*.
2. A tax liability will arise on any *taxable profit* generated by the project.
3. There will also be a tax impact caused by how the project is financed. If it is financed with the help of debt capital, then there will be *tax relief* available on the interest payments. Alternatively, if the project is financed with shareholders' funds (i.e. equity capital), then dividends will be paid on the equity, which in turn will give rise to a liability for advance corporation tax.

With these three factors in mind, the approach taken to project appraisal is to evaluate the *after-tax project cash flows* using the *after-tax discount rate*. The after-tax project cash flows take into account effects 1 and 2 above, and the after-tax discount rate takes into account effect 3.

Financing cash flows

Up to this stage of our analysis of investment appraisal, very little has been said about how a project should be financed and the effect of the financing method on the project appraisal. This is how the position will remain until the capital structure/financing decision is discussed in detail in later chapters.

However, the basic philosophy of the approach of investment appraisal – and the NPV technique in particular – will be outlined now. This approach is that the financing method, and hence *all* the cash flows associated with the financing method, including interest payments, divided payments and loan repayments, can be ignored. This is because, in effect, they are implicitly taken into account in the discount rate used in the NPV analysis. Example 4 attempts to show the underlying rationale to this advice using a very simple situation.

Example 4 shows why an NPV analysis can (apparently) ignore how a project is financed. The costs of finance are taken into account within the discount rate used. In a similar way – although this will not be explained in detail until a later chapter where the *cost of capital* is examined more fully – using an *after-tax* discount rate also takes into account the taxation impact on the financing cash flows.

Example 4

Suppose a company wishes to acquire a machine which costs £1000 and has a three-year life. The machine is expected to generate a net revenue (i.e. revenues less cash *operating* – not financing – costs) of £450 per year.

The company approaches its bank for a £1000 three-year term loan in order to buy the machine. The bank agrees to the loan, after examining the riskiness of the proposed investment, and sets an interest rate of 10%. (Notice that this interest rate, like any rate of return, reflects the risk of the investment involved.)

Normally the company would then evaluate the NPV of the project, *ignoring* how it was to be financed and the cash flows (interest payments and loan repayments) associated with the financing method. Using a 10% discount rate (as this reflects the project's risk – it is the return available elsewhere from a similar risk investment) the NPV is:

$$-1000 + 450A_{3-0.10} = +119.06 \text{ NPV.}$$

However, it *could* be argued that this does not represent the true company cash flow, as effectively the bank, not the company, buys the machine. Thus, from the company's standpoint the true cash flows associated with the project are:

Year	0	1	2	3
Interest		−100	−100	− 100
Loan repayment				−1000
Net revenue		+450	+450	+ 450
Net cash flow[1]	0	+350	+350	− 650

However, when this cash flow is discounted to NPV at 10%, the result is exactly as before:

$$+350A_{2-0.10} - 650 (1.10)^{-3} = +119.06 \text{ NPV.}[2]$$

The reason for this is important: it is that the present value of the financing cash flow always equals the amount of the finance. Hence the present value of the bank loan cash flow equals the amount of the bank loan:

$$-100A_{3\text{-}0.10} - 1000(1.10)^{-3} = -1000 \text{ PV.}^3$$

Therefore, in the original NPV analysis of the project, the financing method is not *really* being ignored, because the project's outlay represents the present value of the financing cash flows.

Finally, care should be taken in not being misled by this simple example. The NPV analysis would have been undertaken in exactly the same way (with exactly the same +119.06 NPV) if the project had been financed with (say) a £600 bank loan and £400 of retained earnings. The £1000 NPV analysis outlay would implicitly represent the present value of *all* the financing cash flows, *however* the project was financed.

Writing-down allowances

If a company spends money on capital equipment (such as a machine) the tax authorities do not usually allow that *whole* expense to be used to affect the tax liability in the year in which it is incurred. Instead, the expense – and so the tax relief – has to be spread over the project's life, in accordance with a specific schedule. That schedule is the system of 25% writing-down allowances on the reducing balance of the project's worth.

Just how many tranches of writing-down allowance (WDA) the company will receive depends upon when the project is bought. In our simplified tax world, we can set up two alternative scenarios:

1. The project is bought on the first day of the company's accounting year.
2. The project is bought on the last day of the *previous* accounting year.

In both cases the expenditure is effectively made at t_0, but it is made one day earlier in case 2. One day makes no significant difference as far as an NPV discounting analysis is concerned, but it can make a significant difference as far as writing-down allowances are concerned.

Therefore, in general, we can state that a project will have as many WDAs as there are years in its life in case 1, whilst there will be one *extra* WDA in case 2. Furthermore, assuming that corporation tax is paid twelve months after year end, in case 1 the first WDA tax relief is received by the firm in t_2, whilst in case 2 the first WDA is received by the firm in t_1. (This therefore is the advantage of case 2. By buying the machine one *day* earlier, the tax relief comes through one *year* earlier.) Example 5 shows the calculations.

Example 5

A machine costs £1000 and has a four-year life, at the end of which time it will be sold for £400 scrap. The corporation tax rate is 35%, payable twelve months in arrears and a system of 25% WDA, on the reducing balance, is in operation. The WDA tax relief is as follows.

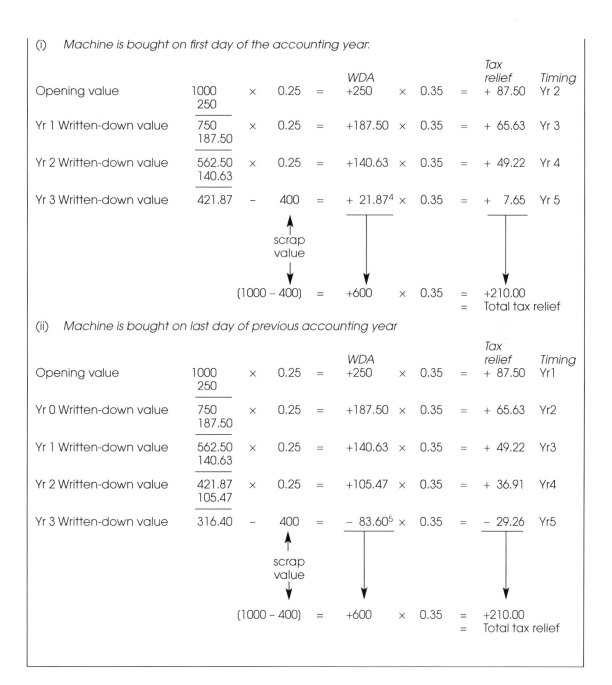

(i) *Machine is bought on first day of the accounting year.*

				WDA				Tax relief	Timing
Opening value	1000 250	×	0.25	=	+250	×	0.35	= + 87.50	Yr 2
Yr 1 Written-down value	750 187.50	×	0.25	=	+187.50	×	0.35	= + 65.63	Yr 3
Yr 2 Written-down value	562.50 140.63	×	0.25	=	+140.63	×	0.35	= + 49.22	Yr 4
Yr 3 Written-down value	421.87	–	400	=	+ 21.87[4]	× 0.35	=	+ 7.65	Yr 5

scrap value

$(1000 - 400) = +600 \times 0.35 = +210.00$
= Total tax relief

(ii) *Machine is bought on last day of previous accounting year*

				WDA				Tax relief	Timing
Opening value	1000 250	×	0.25	=	+250	×	0.35	= + 87.50	Yr1
Yr 0 Written-down value	750 187.50	×	0.25	=	+187.50	×	0.35	= + 65.63	Yr2
Yr 1 Written-down value	562.50 140.63	×	0.25	=	+140.63	×	0.35	= + 49.22	Yr3
Yr 2 Written-down value	421.87 105.47	×	0.25	=	+105.47	×	0.35	= + 36.91	Yr4
Yr 3 Written-down value	316.40	–	400	=	– 83.60[5]	× 0.35	=	– 29.26	Yr5

scrap value

$(1000 - 400) = +600 \times 0.35 = +210.00$
= Total tax relief

'Profit' tax charge

In our world of a simplified UK tax system, a straightforward tax charge, at whatever is the going rate, can be made on the project's net operating cash flow. (Depreciation is, of course, not an allowable expense against tax as it is substituted by the WDA system and, in any case, it is not a cash flow.) This tax liability then will be offset, to some extent, by the WDA tax relief. Example 6 shows a fully worked situation.

Example 6

Stanchion plc is considering investing in a project which will require a capital expenditure outlay of £250 000. It will have a four-year life and, at the end of that time, the equipment used will be sold off for £100 000.

In addition, £38 000 of working capital will be required from the start of the project, and this figure will have to be increased to £50 000 at the end of the second year. All the working capital will be recovered at the end of the project's life.

The project is expected to generate annual revenues of £200 000 and to incur annual cash operating costs of £80 000. The company believes that an after-tax discount rate of 10% would be appropriate.

The project would be bought on the last day of the company's previous financial year and would be financed with a three-year term loan of £250 000 at 3% over bank 'base rate'. Bank 'base rate' is currently 12%. The working capital would be financed out of Stanchion's own retained earnings.

Corporation tax is charged at 35%, payable twelve months after year end. 25% writing-down allowances on the reducing balance are available on capital expenditure. The company expects to have a substantial annual tax liability arising from other operations that it undertakes:

WDA calculations (£000s)

			WDA				Tax relief	Timing
250	×	0.25	=	+ 62.5	×	0.35	=	+ 21.9	Yr 1
62.5								
187.5	×	0.25	=	+ 46.9	×	0.35	=	+ 16.4	Yr 2
46.9								
140.6	×	0.25	=	+ 35.1	×	0.35	=	+ 12.3	Yr 3
35.1								
105.5	×	0.25	=	+ 26.4	×	0.35	=	+ 9.2	Yr 4
26.4								
79.1	−	100	=	− 20.9	×	0.35	=	− 7.3	Yr 5

Tax charge on project's profits (£000s)

Annual revenues	200
Less annual costs	80
Taxable 'profit'	120
Tax at 35%	£42

NPV calculation (£000s)

Year	0	1	2	3	4	5
Capital expenditure	− 250					
Scrap value					+ 100	
WDA tax relief		+ 21.9	+ 16.4	+ 12.3	+ 9.2	− 7.3
Working capital	− 38		− 12		+ 50	
Revenues		+ 200	+ 200	+ 200	+ 200	
Costs		− 80	− 80	− 80	− 80	
Corporation tax			− 42	− 42	− 42	− 42
Net cash flow	− 288	+ 141.9	+ 82.4	+ 90.3	+ 237.2	− 49.3
10% discount factor	× 1	× .9091	× .8264	× .7513	× .6830	× .6209
PV cash flow[6]	− 288	+ 129.0	+ 68.1	+ 67.8	+ 162.0	− 30.6

NPV: +£108 300

Notes
(i) Because of the company's substantial tax liability from other operations it is assumed that the company will be able to take the WDA tax relief that is available at Year 1. If not, this tax relief

would have to be carried over to Year 2 when there would be a sufficient tax liability from the project to offset against the WDA relief.

(ii) At the end of Year 2 an *additional* £12 000 has to be spent on working capital to raise the total expenditure up to the required £50 000.

(iii) All financing cash flows have been ignored for the reasons outlined earlier in this section.

Investment appraisal and the relevant cash flow

In an earlier chapter it was stated that in order properly to appraise an investment opportunity, we have to appraise all the cash flows that arise either directly or indirectly as a result of the project. Some of the cost or benefit cash flows that arise as a result of undertaking a project are both obvious and easy to identify. For example, if a project consists of buying a machine, operating it and selling its output, there are some 'obvious' cash flows involved, such as the cost of the machine and the revenue generated from the sale of the output. However, the identification of cash flow costs and benefits that are relevant to a project's appraisal are not always obvious.

Guiding rules

A set of 'guiding rules' will be used to outline the most important points and then a comprehensive example will be used to illustrate their application.

Rule 1: All costs incurred (and revenues generated) *prior* to the investment appraisal decision should be excluded. They are *sunk costs*, in that they are unaffected by the investment decision under appraisal. Example 7 illustrates this logic.

Rule 2: Ignore depreciation charges. Depreciation is a *non-cash flow* and so does not enter into the NPV *cash flow* analysis.

Rule 3: Ignore all financing cash flows (e.g. interest charges, loan repayments, dividends, etc.) and all their tax effects (e.g. interest tax relief and advance corporation tax (ACT)). This is because, as was seen in the previous section, these are all implicitly taken into account through the discounting process.7 The UK government has decided to phase out ACT.

Example 7

Suppose a company has spent £100 000 undertaking research (R&D) in order to develop a new product. They have now reached the stage where they need to take a decision on whether to invest in manufacturing facilities for the new product. In this investment appraisal, the £100 000 spent on R&D is a sunk cost and so is irrelevant to the decision to be made.

To see how misleading it could be to include the R&D expenditure, suppose the manufacturing equipment costs £500 000 and the product is expected to produce net revenues of £580 000. (For this simple example, we will ignore any discounting.) If the sunk costs were ignored, the decision would be to accept, but if the sunk costs were included in the analysis, the decision would be to reject:

Sunk cost excluded (£)		Sunk cost included (£)	
Cost	: − £500 000	Cost	: − £500 000
Net revenues	: + £580 000	R&D expenses	: − £100 000
		Net revenues	: + £580 000
'Profit'	: + £80 000	'Loss'	: − £20 000
Decision	: Accept	Decision	: Reject

The point here is that if the company accepts the project, at least they have the £80 000 'profit' to offset the £100 000 spent on R&D. If they reject the project, they are simply left with a £100 000 R&D expense.

Rule 4: Ignore all *non-incremental* cash flows. This is the more general case of Rule 1. Only those cash flows that arise because of the project should be included in an NPV analysis. Any cash flow that would arise *whether or not* the project was undertaken should be excluded.

An example of Rule 4's application would be *allocated* fixed costs. If a company normally allocated a particular proportion of its fixed Head Office costs to any new project, as part of its budgeting/costing process, these should be *excluded* from the investment appraisal. They would be cash flows that are non-incremental to the investment decision, in that the Head Office costs would still be incurred whether or not the project was accepted.

Rule 5: This concerns the cost, to the project, of using resources (usually raw materials) that the firm already holds in stock. Here there are three possible 'costs':

1. original purchase price/historic cost;
2. current replacement cost;
3. resale value or disposal cost.

The first of these is *never* relevant – the historic cost of the raw material stock is a sunk cost. However, which of the other two costs is relevant depends upon the particular circumstances.

Where the resources held in stock are used elsewhere in the company, then the cost to the project of using them is their replacement cost. This is because if the resources are used on the project, then those stocks will have to be replaced. Hence the current replacement cost is the *opportunity* cost[8] of their use.

If the resources already held in stock have no other use in the company than their use on the project, they will not be replaced. (Such a situation might arise through, say, the company using those particular resources in the past but no longer doing so, although some surplus stocks still remain.) Under these circumstances, if the stocks have a resale value then their resale value would be the (opportunity) cost to the project of their use. (The company, in using them on the project, forgoes the opportunity to sell them off.) If they only have a disposal cost, then their use on the project would *save* these costs. Hence the project would be credited with a benefit – or cash inflow – the saved disposal cost.

Rule 6: This concerns the use, by the project, of resources already in use with the company and where the company cannot obtain further supplies of those resources. In other words, this is the situation where the project utilizes 'scarce' or limited resources. The rule is that the cost of their use on the project is their *total* opportunity cost. Example 8 illustrates this situation.

Example 8

Suppose that there is a shortage of well-qualified mining engineers. A mining company at present employs 100 mining engineers and they are all fully utilized undertaking various projects. The company is now considering the development of an additional mine which would require five mining engineers. Because of the shortage of such staff, they cannot recruit any more, and so, if they undertook the new mining project, the engineers would have to be taken away from their existing tasks elsewhere in the company.

Suppose that each engineer is currently contributing £80 000 per year to the company's profits (i.e. revenue generated, less the engineer's salary, less the material and incremental costs incurred, equals £80 000). This will be lost if the company redeploys the engineer onto the new project: it would be the *internal* opportunity cost of using each engineer on the new project.

Thus the *total* cost of each engineer used on the new project would be the forgone contribution (the internal opportunity cost), *plus* the engineer's salary (the external opportunity cost, or *the market price* of the scarce resource).

These rules are now used together in Example 9.

Example 9

Radiometric plc has been offered a contract to manufacture six special communication systems for the government. Manufacture would take a total of three years at a rate of two machines per year. Payment would be in two instalments: £350 000 at the start of manufacture and another £350 000 upon completion.

The company is now evaluating the contract to see if it is worthwhile undertaking, and its management accounting department has produced the following estimates about the resources required to produce the special communication systems:

1 *Materials*

Type of material	Quantity per system (tonnes)	Amount in stock now (tonnes)	Original cost of stock per tonne (£)	Current purchase price per tonne (£)	Current realizable value per tonne (£)
Copper	20	60	700	1000	800
Radium	10	20	500	750	See below

Copper is used regularly by the company on many contracts. Radium is used rarely, and if the existing stock is not applied to this contract it will have to be disposed of immediately at a net cost of £100 per tonne. Materials required for the contract must be purchased and paid for annually in advance. Replacement costs of copper and radium and the realizable value of copper are expected to increase at an annual compound rate of 20%.

2 *Labour*
Each of the six systems will require 3000 hours of skilled electronic engineering and 5000 hours of unskilled labour. Current wage rates are £4 per hour for skilled electronic engineers and £3 per hour for unskilled labour.

Radiometric expects to suffer a shortage of skilled electronic engineers during the first year so that acceptance of the contract would make it necessary for the firm to give up other work on which a contribution of £7 per hour would be earned. (The 'other work' would require no unskilled labour.)

Again, in the contract's first year only, the company expects to have 20 000 surplus unskilled labour hours. Radiometric has an agreement with the in-house trade union whereby it lays off employees for whom there is no work and pays them two-thirds of their normal wages during the lay-off period.

All wage rates are expected to increase at an annual compound rate of 15%.

3 *Overheads*

Overhead costs are currently allocated to contracts at a rate of £14 per skilled electronic engineer, calculated as follows:

	£
Fixed overheads (including equipment depreciation of £5)	11.00
Variable overheads	3.00
	£14.00

Special equipment will be required to undertake this contract, and will be purchased at a cost of £200 000 payable immediately. It will be sold once the contract is completed for £50 000. Both fixed and variable overheads are expected to increase in line with the retail price index.

The special equipment will be financed with the first contract instalment paid by the government.

Radiometric have considerable experience in manufacturing this type of equipment and believe that a return of 20% would be available elsewhere on the capital market for a similar risk investment. The retail price index is expected to increase by 15% per year over the life of the contract.

It can be assumed that all current prices will hold for the next twelve months, before increasing in line with inflation. Therefore the material costs incurred for the second year's production will be 20% higher than the current market prices. Also it can be assumed that all cash flows arise on the last day of the year to which they relate, unless otherwise stated. Taxation should be ignored for the purposes of this evaluation (to simplify the analysis).

Project cash flows (£000s)

Year	0	1	2	3
Revenues	+ 350			+ 350
Equipment cost	− 200			
Scrap value				+ 50
Copper cost	− 40	− 48	− 57.6	
Radium cost	+ 2	− 18	− 21.6	
Elec. engin. cost		− 66	− 27.6	− 31.7
Unskilled labour		− 10	− 34.5	− 39.7
Variable o/hs.		− 18	− 20.7	− 23.0
Net cash flow	+ 112	− 160	− 162	+ 305.6
20% discount factor	× 1	× .8333	× .6944	× .5787
PV cash flow	+ 112	− 133.3	− 112.5	+ 176.8

Contract's NPV: +£43 000   Therefore it is worth undertaking.

Data calculations

1 Materials:

Copper	Year 1:	Use 40 tonnes from stock. As this will have to be replaced, its cost is the current purchase price of £1000 per tonne.
	Year 2:	Buy in 40 tonnes at £1000 (1.20) = £1200 per tonne.
	Year 3:	Buy in 40 tonnes at £1000 (1.20)^2 = £1440 per tonne.
Radium	Year 1:	Use 20 tonnes from stock. This will save a disposal cost of £100 per tonne. (Opportunity benefit.)
	Year 2:	Buy in 20 tonnes at £750 (1.20) = £900 per tonne.
	Year 3:	Buy in 20 tonnes at £750 (1.20)^2 = £1080 per tonne.

2	*Labour:*		6000 hours of skilled engineers required per year.

2   *Labour:*   6000 hours of skilled engineers required per year.
10 000 hours of unskilled labour required per year.

Skilled   Year 1:   6000 hours taken from elsewhere in the company. Cost is wage rate plus lost contribution: £4 + £7 = £11 per hour.

Year 2:   Hire 6000 hours at £4 (1.15) = £4.60 per hour.

Year 3:   Hire 6000 hours at £4 $(1.15)^2$ = £5.29 per hour.

Unskilled   Year 1:   Utilize 10 000 hours of surplus labour. Cost is the *incremental* wages paid: £1 per hour.

Year 2:   Hire 10 000 hours at £3 (1.15) = £3.45 per hour.

Year 3:   Hire 10 000 hours at £3 $(1.15)^2$ = £3.97 per hour.

3   *Overheads*

Fixed: Exclude as non-incremental.

Depreciation: Exclude as non-cash flow.

Variable: Year 1:   £3 per skilled labour hour.

Year 2:   £3 (1.15) = £3.45 per skilled labour hour.

Year 3:   £3 $(1.15)^2$ = £3.97 per skilled labour hour.

Summary

Having concluded in the previous chapter that of the four basic investment appraisal techniques, only one – the NPV – was satisfactory, this chapter then turned to examine some of the possible problems that may be encountered with the application of NPV: inflation, taxation and relevant project cash flows. The main points made are as follows:

- Inflation is not the cause of the time value of money, but it does affect its value through the Fisher Effect relationship.

- The simplest approach to take in an investment appraisal in an inflationary environment is to discount a project's actual *money* cash flows by the market (or money) discount rate to NPV.

- *Real* cash flows should not be confused with cash flows in *current* terms. 'Real' refers to expressing an actual money cash flow in current *general* purchasing power terms. This will only be the same as a cash flow in current terms if the latter is expected to inflate at the *general* rate of inflation.[9]

- With taxation, there are three impacts on project appraisal:
  — tax relief on capital expenditure;
  — tax charge on the project's profit;
  — tax effects on the project's financing method: tax relief on debt interest and/or ACT liability caused by dividends (ACT is however being phased out).

- The approach to use is to evaluate the after-tax project cash flows with the after-tax discount rate. The after-tax project cash flows take account of the capital expenditure tax relief and the tax charge on the project's profit. The third tax impact is taken into account through the after-tax discount rate.

- As far as the relevant project cash flows are concerned, an investment appraisal should only include the *incremental* cash flows. This is the key concept. Any cash flows that have already occurred prior to the investment decision, or any subsequent cash flows that will occur whether or not the project is undertaken, are irrelevant.

- In addition, use has to be made of the opportunity cost concept to ensure that the *full* costs and benefits of undertaking the project are captured in the investment appraisal.

Appendix: the UK corporate tax system

This appendix briefly outlines the basics of the UK corporate tax system as it affects investment appraisal. In no way does it purport to represent a complete analysis. However, some familiarity with the tax regime is necessary in order to be able to appreciate how it is likely to impact on project appraisal.

1. Company 'profits' are subject to a rate of tax – which can vary depending upon the situation – and the tax is paid approximately one year in arrears.
2. Profit can be defined as revenues less allowable costs. Within these costs, depreciation is not an allowable cost, nor are dividend payments or working capital expenses. However, interest payments are an allowable cost. Most normal business expenses such as labour, materials and overhead costs are allowable against tax.
3. As a substitute for depreciation, writing-down allowances are allowable costs. These are calculated annually at a rate of 25% of the reducing value of the capital expenditure. (Notice in the WDA calculations in Example 6, the tax relief was taken into account separately. It could have been incorporated into the 'taxable profit' calculations.)
4. If a company pays out a dividend, this has the effect of bringing forward part of the corporation tax payment. That part of the corporation tax liability that is brought forward for immediate payment is known as advance corporation tax (ACT) and that which remains payable twelve months after year end is known as mainstream corporation tax. However this is being phased out from 1998.

Notes

1. Alternatively, the cash flows could be shown as:

Year	0	1	2	3
Loan from bank	+ 1000			
Interest		– 100	– 100	– 100
Loan repayment				– 1000
Capital expenditure	– 1000			
Net revenue		+ 450	+ 450	+ 450
Net cash flow	0	+ 350	+ 350	– 650

but the net effect is the same.

2. Actually, using four-figure discount tables the NPV is + 119.08, but the difference between the two NPVs is solely brought about through rounding error.

3. Again, the two-pence difference is caused by rounding error in the discount factors used.

4. This value is referred to as the 'balancing allowance'.

5. This value is referred to as the 'balancing charge'.

6. Notice how tax produces a non-conventional cash flow and hence multiple IRRs.

7. There are two important possible exceptions to this rule. One is in a special investment appraisal situation: the lease versus purchase decision. The other is in the case of overseas project appraisal. Both topics will be covered at a later stage.

8. The concept of 'opportunity cost' is important in all forms of economic analysis. See the suggested reading.

9. An example might help to make this statement clear. Suppose the current wage rate is £5 per hour and we require 100 hours of labour at Year 2. Therefore the Year 2 labour cost in *current* terms is £500. This may or may not equal the Year 2 labour cost in *real* terms, depending upon the inflation rate of labour costs. If labour costs inflate at 10% per year and the RPI is also inflating at 10% per year, the current labour cost will equal the real cost. But if labour costs inflate up at a different rate from the RPI, then the two things are not equal:

(a) Labour inflates up at 10% per year.
RPI inflates up at 10% per year.
Actual Year 2 cash flow: £500 $(1.10)^2$ = £605.
Real Year 2 cash flow: £605 $(1.10)^{-2}$ = £500.
Current Year 2 labour cost = £500.

(b) Labour inflates up at 15% per year.
RPI inflates up at 10% per year.
Actual Year 2 cash flow: £500 $(1.15)^2$ = £661.25.
Real Year 2 cash flow: £661.25 $(1.10)^{-2}$ = £546.46.
Current Year 2 labour cost = £500.

Further reading

1. A good overview article on the problem of inflation and capital investment appraisal is: N.J. Coulthurst, 'Accounting for Inflation in Capital Investment: State of the Art and Science', *Accounting and Business Research*, Winter 1986.
2. Other interesting articles include: B. Carsberg and A. Hope, *Business Investment Decisions Under Inflation: Theory and Practice*, ICAEW 1976; A. Rappaport and R.A. Taggart, 'Evaluation of Capital Expenditure Proposals Under Inflation', *Financial Management*, Spring 1982; M.K. Kim, 'Inflationary Effects in the Capital Investment Process', *Journal of Finance*, September 1979; and S.N. Chan, 'Capital Budgeting and Uncertain Inflation', *Journal of Economics and Business*, August 1984.
3. Finally, on the whole area of relevant cash flows and opportunity costs see: L. Amey, 'On Opportunity Costs and Decision Making', *Accountancy*, July 1961; J.R. Gould, 'Opportunity Costs: the London Tradition', in *Debits, Credits,*

Finance and Profits, H.C. Edey and B.S. Yamey (eds), Sweet and Maxwell 1974; and N.J. Coulthurst. 'The Application of the Incremental Principle in Capital Investment Project Evaluation', *Accounting and Business Research*, Autumn 1986.

Quickie questions

1. If the market interest rate is 13% and the general rate of inflation is 4%, what is the real interest rate?
2. What approaches can be taken to an NPV investment appraisal in inflationary conditions?
3. What is a *real* cash flow?
4. Rent is paid each year. This year's rent – £10 000 – has just been paid. How much rent will need to be paid in two years' time if:
   (a) the rent remains constant in real terms;
   (b) the rent remains constant in money terms?
   In both of the above cases, what is the PV of the Year 2 rent? Assume that the market discount rate is 15.5% and the RPI is 5% per year.
5. A machine costs £500 and has a three-year life and a zero scrap value. It is bought on the first day of the accounting year. What are the amounts of WDA tax relief received if the corporation tax rate is 35%, paid twelve months in arrears, and the WDAs are calculated as 25% of the reducing balance?
6. A company owns a machine which is presently lying unused in the factory. The machine was bought five years ago at a cost of £60 000 and has now been depreciated down to a book value of £10 000. It could be sold now for £3000. Alternatively it could be rented out for a year at £2500. The company's chief engineer believes the machine will be totally obsolete in twelve months' time and would then have a scrap value of £800. The company is considering using the machine to undertake a one-year project. If it did, the machine's scrap value at the end of the year, net of dismantling costs, would be zero. Ignoring the time value of money, what is the cost of using the machine on the project?
7. What is the approach used to handling tax in investment appraisal?
8. Why should *allocated* fixed costs be excluded from project cash flows in an NPV analysis?
9. A company pays an annual rent of £20 000 for its factory of 10 000 m². All space is fully utilized and no more space is available for rent. Each square metre of space generates a contribution of £15. A project is being considered that would require 150 m² of factory space. What would be the cost, to the project, of that space?

Problems

1. Sanglo Radios plc is considering buying a machine to make printed circuit boards. The machine costs £1.2 million and will last for five years. Scrap value of these machines is £200 000. An investment of £150 000 in working capital will be needed initially. The accountant has prepared the following estimated annual trading account for the project:

	(£)
Sales	1 400 000
Materials	(300 000)
Labour	(500 000)
Depreciation	(200 000)
Allocated fixed overheads	(250 000)
Annual profit	£150 000

The machine would be financed with a four-year term loan from Barclays Bank at an interest rate of 3.5% over base. Currently, the bank base rate is 8%. The interest payments attract tax relief.

The machine would be bought on the last day of the company's previous fiscal year and would attract a 25% writing-down allowance. Corporation tax is payable at 40%, one year after year end.

The company believes that 10% would be the minimum after-tax return acceptable from a project with this level of risk and, if that return is achieved, then they will be able to increase dividends to shareholders by £50 000 a year over each of the next five years.

Required:
Calculate the project's net present value.

2. Sparrow Ltd is a construction company based in the southwest of England. Mr and Mrs Hawk each own 50% of the company's issued share capital. The company's latest accounts show a balance sheet value for share capital and reserves of £250 000 and an annual turnover of £1.25 million.

The company has recently been offered two contracts, both of which would commence almost immediately and last for two years. Neither contract can be delayed. The prices offered are £700 000 for contract 1 and £680 000 for contract 2, payable in each case at the contract's completion. The skilled labour force of Sparrow is committed during the coming year to the extent that sufficient skilled labour will be available to support only one of the two contracts. Due to a shortage in the area, the company will not be able to expand its skilled labour force in the foreseeable future. If necessary, Sparrow could subtract one entire contract, but not both, to a nearby company, Kestrel Ltd, which is of a similar size to Sparrow. If one contract were subcontracted, all work would be undertaken by Kestrel, subject to regular checks of progress and quality by Mr Hawk. Kestrel has quoted prices of £490 000 for contract 1 and £530 000 for contract 2, payable in either case by two equal instalments, half at the start of the contract and the remainder at the end of the first year.

Sparrow maintains a standard costing system and normally prices contracts on a cost-plus basis. Total cost is calculated by adding to direct costs 60% for overheads, this percentage being based on previous experience. A target price is then calculated by adding a 25% profit mark-up to total cost. Mrs Hawk has calculated the following target prices for the two contracts under consideration:

	Contract 1 (£)	Contract 2 (£)
Materials: Special materials (at original cost)	50 000	—
Other materials (at standard cost)	200 000	24 000
Labour: skilled (at standard cost)	80 000	80 000
Unskilled (at standard cost)	112 000	126 000
Direct costs	442 000	446 000
Overheads: 60% of direct costs	265 200	267 600
Total cost	707 200	713 600
Profit mark-up: 25% of total cost	176 800	178 400
Target price	884 000	892 000

The following additional information is available:

Materials: Contract 1 would require the immediate use of special materials which were purchased one year ago at a cost of £50 000 for a contract which was not completed because the customer went into liquidation. These special materials have a current purchase price of £60 000 and a current realizable value of £30 000. The company foresees no alternative use for these special materials. Usage of the other materials would be spread evenly between the two years of each contract's duration. These other materials are all used regularly by the company. Their standard costs reflect current purchase prices which are expected to continue at their present level for the next twelve months. In the following year, prices are expected to rise by 10%.

Labour: Skilled labour costs for each contract represent 8000 hours each year for two years at a standard cost of £5 per hour. Unskilled labour hours required are 16 000 hours per annum for contract 1 and 18 000 hours per annum for contract 2, in each case at a standard cost of £3.50 per hour. Standard costs are based on current wage rates. Hourly wage costs for both skilled and unskilled labour are expected to increase by 5% in the current year and then by a further 10% in the following year.

Overheads: An analysis of Sparrow's most recent accounts shows that total overheads may be categorized as follows:

Fixed administrative and office costs	60%
Depreciation of plant and equipment	30%
Costs which vary directly with direct costs	10%
	100%

Fixed administrative and office costs are expected to increase as a result of inflation by 5% in the current year, and by a further 10% in the following year. Sparrow expects to have sufficient surplus plant and equipment capacity during the next two years for either contract 1 or contract 2.

Sparrow has a money cost of capital of 10% per annum in the current year. Mr Hawk expects this to increase to 15% per annum in the second year of the contract.

Assume that all payments will arise on the last day of the year to which they relate, except where otherwise stated.

Required:
Provide calculations, on the basis of the estimates given, showing whether Sparrow should accept either or both contracts, and which one, if any, should be subcontracted to Kestrel.

3. Bailey plc is developing a new product, the Oakman, to replace an established product, the Shepard, which the company has marketed successfully for a number of years. Production of the Shepard will cease in one year, whether or not the Oakman is manufactured. Bailey plc has recently spent £75 000 on research and development relating to the Oakman. Production of the Oakman can start in one year's time.

Demand for the Oakman is expected to be 5000 units per annum for the first three years of production and 2500 units per annum for the subsequent two years. The product's total life is expected to be five years.

Estimated unit revenues and costs for the Oakman, at current prices, are as follows:

	(£)	(£)
Selling price per unit		35.00
less costs per unit:		
Materials and other consumables	8.00	
Labour (see (a) below)	6.00	
Machine depreciation and overhaul (see (b) below)	12.50	
Other overheads (see (c) below)	9.00	
		35.50
Loss per unit		0.50

(a) Each Oakman requires two hours of labour, paid at £3 per hour at current prices. The labour force required to produce Oakmans comprises six employees, who are at present employed to produce Shepards. If the Oakman is not produced, these employees will be made redundant when production of the Shepard ceases. If the Oakman is produced, three of the employees will be made redundant at the end of the third year of its life, when demand halves, but the company expects to be able to find work for the remaining three employees at the end of the Oakman's five-year life. Any employee who is made redundant will receive a redundancy payment equivalent to 1000 hours' wages, based on the most recent wage at the time of the redundancy.

(b) A special machine will be required to produce the Oakman. It will be purchased in one year's time (just before production begins). The current price of the machine is £190 000. It is expected to last for five years and to have no scrap or resale value at the end of that time. A major overhaul of the machine will be necessary at the end of the second year of its life. At current prices, the overhaul will cost £60 000. As the machine will not produce the same quality of Oakmans each year, the directors of Bailey plc have decided to spread its original cost and the cost of the overhaul equally between all Oakmans expected to be produced (i.e. 20 000 units). Hence the combined charge per unit for depreciation and overhaul is £12.50 ([£190 000 + £60 000] / 20 000 units).

(c) Other overheads at current prices comprise variable overheads of £4.00 per unit and head office fixed costs of £5.00 per unit, allotted on the basis of labour time.

All wage rates are expected to increase at an annual compound rate of 15%. Selling price per unit and all costs other than labour are expected to increase in line with the retail price index, which is expected to increase in the future at an annual compound rate of 10%.

Corporation tax at 35% on net cash income is payable in full one year after the income arises. A 25% writing-down allowance is available on the machine which will be bought on the first day of the company's accounting year. Bailey plc has a money cost of capital, net of corporation tax, of 20% per annum.

Assume that all receipts and payments will arise on the last day of the year to which they relate. Assume also that all 'current prices' given above have been operative for one year and are due to change shortly. Subsequently all prices will change annually.

Required:

(a) Prepare calculations, with explanations, showing whether Bailey should undertake production of the Oakman.

(b) Discuss the particular investment appraisal problems created by the existence of high rates of inflation.

8 Capital market imperfections

Capital rationing

In Chapter 4 we set up a single-period investment–consumption model to use as a guide to effective financial investment appraisal. The model was a crude and unrealistic simplification of the real world, but it was used so that the underlying principles of investment decisions could be examined, without becoming embroiled in elaborate complications (such as the existence of taxation, inflation and an uncertain future). In addition, a time horizon of only one time period was used so that the conclusions could be presented graphically rather than algebraically.

We saw that neither payback nor ROCE/ARR were satisfactory investment appraisal rules in terms of the Hirshleifer analysis, as they did not lead to the firm optimally locating onto the physical investment line. In contrast, both the DCF techniques – NPV and IRR – did lead the firm to locate optimally.

However, a closer examination of the IRR method uncovered a number of problems with its use and so, at the end of Chapter 6, we were able to conclude that the NPV decision rule was the only one of the four investment appraisal techniques which would consistently lead to investment decisions being taken that would help to maximize shareholder wealth. Even so, the NPV decision rule required the assumption of a perfect capital market.

In this chapter we are going to examine what happens to the NPV decision rule in the absence of a perfect capital market. In particular, we are going to examine the case where the company may not be able to undertake all the positive NPV projects it has discovered, because of a shortage of capital investment funds. This particular capital market imperfection is known as *capital rationing*.

Capital market borrowing

A great deal of attention, in both the applied and theoretical literature, has been paid to the problem of capital rationing but, even so, there is no general agreement on what precisely is meant by the term, and this has resulted in a certain amount of confusion. In an effort to avoid adding to this, it is important that we state from the outset what we shall take to be the meaning of capital rationing.

From the viewpoint of the making of investment decisions by financial management within companies, capital rationing is a *managerial* problem. It is, most certainly, a theoretical problem for our decision-making model but, more importantly, it is also a practical problem.

Up to this point, we have followed the NPV investment appraisal rule because it is most likely to indicate (in a practical sense) consistently good investment decisions. In its basic form the NPV decision rule is: accept all projects whose cash flows, when discounted by the market interest rate and then summated, have a positive or zero net present value. Such projects are acceptable because they yield a return that is either greater than (+ NPV), or at least equal to (zero NPV) the return that is available on the capital market for a similar-risk investment (which is defined by the rate of discount used).

Therefore, in terms of opportunity cost, the discount rule can be viewed as the minimum return that management must earn from investing shareholders' money in physical investment opportunities. It represents the minimum acceptable rate of return because it is the return that shareholders themselves can earn by placing their money in *financial* investment opportunities (i.e. investing on the capital market). Hence management should not invest shareholders' money to earn a lower rate of return than can be obtained on the capital market.

Implicit in the NPV decision rule is the idea that as long as a company's management can find investment opportunities that yield at least the capital market return (i.e. they satisfy the NPV decision rule), then capital will be available to finance them. This is because investing borrowed funds in projects with non-negative NPVs ensures that the project will yield a return that will at least be sufficient to repay the borrowed capital plus interest. In terms of the single-period investment–consumption diagram, this implies that if a company identifies so many acceptable projects (i.e. + or 0 NPV) that the company's existing resources at t_0 provide insufficient investment capital to undertake them all, then additional finance can be borrowed from the capital market.

In Fig. 8.1, OA represents the company's existing resources at t_0 and AB represents the physical investment line. The point of tangency between the physical and financial investment lines is at point C.

Therefore the company has identified acceptable projects that require a total investment outlay at t_0 of AD. As the company's existing resources only amount to OA, OD will have to be borrowed from the capital market.

The investment AD undertaken at t_0 will produce a cash inflow at t_1 of OE. The amount required to repay the loan, plus interest, is given by EF, leaving an amount OF for shareholders. Notice what the net result has been of borrowing on the capital market by the company. Without borrowing, the maximum amount of cash that could have been generated at t_1 would have been OG; but with borrowing (and hence undertaking additional

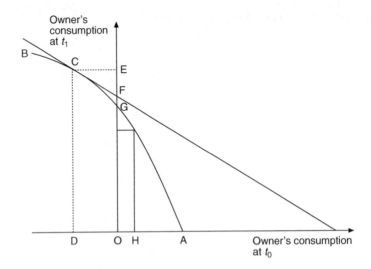

Fig. 8.1 *Capital market borrowing*

Owner's consumption at t_1

B
C
E
F
G
D   O H   A

Owner's consumption at t_0

physical investment), the company has been able to increase the t_1 cash flow available to the owner by the amount FG.

The term 'capital rationing' refers to the situation where the implicit assumption within the NPV decision rule, that capital will always be available to finance acceptable projects, *does not hold*. For example, using the situation as found in Fig. 8.1, suppose that the company was unable to raise OD on the capital market, then a situation of capital rationing would exist: acceptable projects requiring a total outlay of AD had been identified, but they cannot all be accepted because only OA of finance is available. Management have therefore to 'ration out' this limited amount of investment capital between the available projects.

It should be clear from the above that the existence of capital rationing need not only apply to externally raised funds. For example, not only may the company not be able to raise any capital market finance, but the shareholders (in the example used in Fig. 8.1) may be unwilling to allow the company to invest the *whole* of OA. Suppose that for some reason the maximum that shareholders will allow to be applied to physical investments is AH. Then the company has an even tighter capital constraint than before: only AH of capital available, although they have identified acceptable projects which require a total of AD of capital.

It should be clear from the above that the existence of capital rationing represents a capital market imperfection: investment funds are no longer freely available at the market rate of return. The reasons why such capital rationing may occur in practice are many and varied, but in the context of our analysis they are only of passing interest. The point that we wish to examine is, given a situation of capital rationing, how does it affect the efficiency of the investment decision advice given by the NPV appraisal technique, and can NPV be adapted to operate successfully in such situations?

Hard and soft capital rationing

Two types or classes of capital rationing are usually specified: 'hard' capital rationing (which has received the lion's share of attention in the literature but which is probably of little importance in practice, as far as investment decisions in companies are concerned), and 'soft' capital rationing.

Hard capital rationing describes the situation where forces external to the company, usually either the capital market itself or the government (which may or may not act through the capital market), will not supply unlimited amounts of investment capital to a company, even though the company has identified investment opportunities which would be able to produce the required return. Soft capital rationing arises from forces internal to a company, such as a capital budget, which limits the amount of capital available for investment. In certain situations and in certain cases, the distinction between hard and soft capital rationing and between the various different causes of hard rationing may be important for the analysis. Where they are, such a distinction shall be made, but for the moment we shall concentrate on the problems which capital rationing *per se* causes for investment appraisal.

An example

In a situation where capital rationing is non-existent (and hence we are assuming a perfect capital market), investment decision making involves a comparison between the investment funds being applied to the particular investment under consideration and their being applied to a similar-risk capital market investment, because this latter alternative reflects the opportunity cost of undertaking the investment. With the introduction of capital rationing, choice is still involved, but the alternative to the application of capital to a proposed investment project is not *necessarily* the capital market investment, but may instead be another of the firm's investment projects.

In other words, the opportunity cost of undertaking a particular investment is now not necessarily reflected in the capital market rate of return, but may be a higher value, represented by the return yielded by another project which could not be undertaken by the company because the supply of capital is limited. An example can help to illustrate the point.

Suppose a company has discovered two independent projects, A and B. Each requires £500 of investment capital, and Project A yields a return[1] of 12%, whereas B yields a return of 15%. If the company's cost of capital were 10% and funds were unlimited, both projects would be accepted because both would have positive NPVs. The acceptance procedure, using the NPV method, would involve the comparison of the return given by each project *in turn*, with the return available on the capital market.

However, if capital rationing exists, and the company's investment funds are limited to a *total* of £500, then a different decision process is required. The company must now choose, *not* between each project and the capital market return, but first between the two projects themselves and then, once it has decided which is the best project, must compare its return with the alternative given by the capital market. Thus in a non-rationing situation the company would be making two decisions: accept/reject Project A, accept/reject Project B; whilst in a rationing situation they would be making one, two-stage decision: select Project A or B, then accept/reject the selected project.

Single-period capital rationing

It appears at first sight that capital rationing involves little more than another type of the 'mutually exclusive projects' decision, which we dealt with earlier. In fact, as we shall see, the existence of capital rationing produces a much more difficult decision problem.

Most readers will be familiar with the idea of a budget as a means of planning and control[2] and so, for the sake of presenting a clear argument, we shall assume that for each decision period (say, a year), management have a capital budget within which to keep, i.e. total capital expenditure must not exceed some stated upper limit: the capital budget or (to avoid terminology confusion) the capital constraint. Therefore we shall assume a *soft* rationing situation, but the conclusions we derive will be equally applicable to hard rationing.

Let us begin with the most simple and straightforward capital rationing problem: a situation where capital is rationed at present (i.e. t_0) but will be freely available in the future – a rather unlikely situation in practice – or one where the collection of investment projects the company wishes to appraise involve capital outlays *only* in the current period (i.e. the capital outlay required for the project does not extend over more than one point in time). In addition, it is assumed that projects are infinitely divisible, so that fractions of projects may be undertaken, and that they exhibit constant returns to scale.

In such a situation, only a slight modification to the standard NPV decision rule is required. Each investment opportunity should have its expected future cash flows discounted to net present value by the appropriate market discount rate. This NPV is then expressed as a ratio of the capital outlay which the project requires in the rationed time period, and is often termed the *benefit–cost ratio*.

All projects which have a positive or zero benefit–cost ratio would normally be accepted in a non-rationed situation. However, because capital rationing exists and a choice has to be made between the alternative projects, they should be ranked in order of decreasing benefit–cost ratio. Starting with the project with the largest (positive) ratio, and working down the rankings, as many projects as possible (with positive or zero ratios) should be accepted, until all the available capital is allocated.

Examples of benefit–cost ratios

Example 1 shows this decision method in operation. It assumes that capital rationing will only exist in the current time period (Year 0), all the projects are independent and divisible, and exhibit constant returns to scale and none can be delayed.

Example 1

In a non-rationing situation all the projects in the table below would be accepted, except for Project F which has a negative NPV when discounted at the market interest rate. In order to undertake them all, the company would require a total of £460 of capital now (Year 0) and this would produce a total NPV of £283.09. Therefore acceptance of Projects A to E would cause shareholders' wealth to rise by £283.09.

Project			Year				NPV when discounted at 10%
	0	1	2	3	4		
A	− 100	+ 20	+ 40	+ 60	+ 80	⇒	+ 50.96
B	− 150	− 50	+ 100	+ 100	+ 140	⇒	+ 57.94
C	− 60	+ 20	+ 40	+ 40	–	⇒	+ 21.29
D	− 100	+ 60	+ 60	+ 100	–	⇒	+ 79.26
E	− 50	+ 20	+ 40	+ 60	+ 40	⇒	+ 73.64
F	− 100	+ 30	+ 30	+ 30	+ 30	⇒	− 4.91

Suppose that capital rationing exists at Year 0 (but not in Years 1 to 4) and as a result the company has only £300 of investment capital available. It therefore cannot undertake all of the five positive NPV projects. Which projects should be selected to be undertaken? The second table ranks the projects in decreasing order of benefit–cost ratio. (Note in particular, how project B's benefit–cost ratio is calculated. Although B requires two capital outlays, at Year 0 and Year 1, the ratio concerns the NPV and the outlay in the rationed time period only. Hence the denominator of the ratio is simply B's Year 0 outlay.)

Project	NPV / Yr 0 Outlay	=	Benefit-cost Ratio	Ranking
A	50.96/100	=	+ 0.51	3
B	57.94/150	=	+ 0.39	4
C	21.29/60	=	+ 0.35	5
D	79.26/100	=	+ 0.79	2
E	73.64/50	=	+ 1.47	1
F	− 4.91/100	=	− 0.05	6

Benefit-cost Project	Outlay ranking	Yr 0	
E	1	50	
D	2	100	
A	3	100	} Accept: E, D, A, ⅓B
B	4	150	
C	5	60	
F*	–	100	

* Note that in this simple type of rationing situation, Project F would never be accepted because it has a negative benefit–cost ratio.

$$\text{Total NPV} = £73.64 + £79.26 + £50.96 + 1/3\ (£57.94)$$
$$= £223.17$$

The table shows that the £300 of available capital should be applied to Projects E, D, A and one-third of Project B. This gives the company, for its £300 capital outlay, a total positive NPV of £223.17, which is the maximum possible total NPV, given the capital expenditure constraint. Therefore, because investment capital is scarce, shareholder wealth will only rise by £223.17 as a result of the investment decisions made, rather than by the possible total of £283.09. Thus, we can see that, as far as shareholders are concerned, there is a definite cost to capital rationing. In this case, because of the presence of capital rationing, shareholders' wealth will be approximately £60 below the value it would have otherwise attained.

However, given the situation specified, the process of selecting projects on the basis of their benefit–cost ratios ensures that the company will maximize the total amount of positive NPV gained from the available projects, assuming limited investment capital. This is because the terms in which the benefit–cost ratio focuses attention on the size of a project's NPV are not absolute, but *relative* to the scarce resources required to undertake it. In other words, projects are ranked in order of preference, in terms of the NPV they produce, for every unit (i.e. £1) of the limited investment capital which they require. In the example used above, Project A is preferred to Project B (even though B has the larger total NPV) because it produces 51p of (positive) NPV for every £1 of the scarce investment capital applied to its undertaking in Year 0, whereas Project B only produces 39p of NPV per £1 of investment outlay.

Example 2 is divided up into two separate single-period capital rationing situations. In the first situation there is straightforward Year 0 rationing. However in the second situation a further element is added to the analysis. This shows that the standard NPV decision rule for independent projects – accept all non-negative NPV projects – breaks down in capital rationing situations. This means that not only will some positive NPV projects (like Project C in Example 1) not be accepted, but there may also be circumstances where it is advantageous to accept a *negative* NPV project.

Example 2

The management accounting department of Septillion plc have identified six independent investment opportunities, codenamed G to L. The Year 0 and Year 1 cash flows of these projects, together with their NPVs, are as follows:

(£000s)

Year Project	0	1	....	NPV
G	− 100	− 500	....	+ 25
H	− 200	− 90	....	+ 36
I	− 150	− 220	....	+ 44
J	− 300	− 100	....	+ 30
K	− 50	+ 100	....	+ 10
L	− 100	+ 80	....	− 12

Under normal circumstances, Septillion plc would accept Projects G to K, as they all have positive NPVs, and Project L would be rejected. However, to undertake Projects G to K, a total of £800 000 would be required at Year 0, and an additional £910 000 at Year 1. (Notice that Project K does not require a further cash outlay at Year 1.)

In the first situation, Septillion's board of directors have stipulated that, although there will be no capital expenditure constraint at Year 1, the company is only willing to undertake £275 000 of capital expenditure at Year 0. Thus the company faces a single time-period capital rationing situation. In order to solve the problem, benefit–cost ratio rankings are used:

Project	NPV	÷	Year 0 outlay	=	Benefit–cost ratio	Rank
G	+ 25	÷	100	=	+ 0.25	2
H	+ 36	÷	200	=	+ 0.18	4
I	+ 44	÷	150	=	+ 0.293	1
J	+ 30	÷	300	=	+ 0.10	5
K	+ 10	÷	50	=	+ 0.20	3
L	− 12	÷	100	=	− 0.12	–

						NPV
Investment decision:	275	available				
	150	invested in I, producing		:		+ 44
	125	balance				
	100	invested in G, producing		:		+ 25
	25	balance				
	25	invested in 50% of K, producing		:		+ 5
	–	all funds invested				
			Total NPV			+ 74

Thus the company should undertake Projects I and G, and 50% of K. This will generate a total positive NPV of £74 000, which will be the maximum possible, given the expenditure constraint.

The second situation is somewhat contrived, but serves to show an important point. Suppose that, instead of constraining capital expenditure at Year 0, the board of directors decided that there is *no* constraint on expenditure at Year 0, but at *Year 1* there is only £290 000 of *external* finance available. However, this figure can be added to by any internally generated funds that arise from projects at Year 1.

Once again, the management face capital rationing and, although there is no constraint at Year 0, they must be careful at that time only to undertake projects for which there will be sufficient finance available at Year 1 for them to be continued. (It would be no good accepting every non-negative NPV project available at Year 0, only to find that many would subsequently have to be abandoned at Year 1 through insufficient finance.)

The revised set of benefit–cost ratios are now:

Project	NPV	÷	Year 1 outlay	=	Benefit–cost ratio	Rank
G	+ 25	÷	500	=	0.05	4
H	+ 36	÷	90	=	0.40	1
I	+ 44	÷	220	=	0.20	3
J	+ 30	÷	100	=	0.30	2
K	+ 10	÷	–			
L	– 12	÷	–			

Obviously Septillion will undertake Project K: it has a positive NPV and does not require any outlay in the rationed time-period. Furthermore, because it actually generates a cash *inflow* of £100 000 at Year 1, this amount can be added to the external funds available for capital expenditure. Thus the investment decision is:

	290	available				
plus	100	from investment in K, producing		:		+ 10
	390	balance				
	90	invested in H, producing		:		+ 36
	300	balance				
	100	invested in J, producing		:		+ 30
	200	balance				
	200	invested in 91% of I, producing		:		+ 40
	–	all funds invested				
			Total NPV			+ 116

However, this is not the end of the decision. Although the £390 000 of funds has been fully utilized, it is possible to obtain additional funds at Year 1 by investing in Project L. The question is: does the additional *positive* NPV generated from investing Project L's Year 1 cash inflow compensate for the *negative* NPV arising from Project L directly? The answer lies in examining Project L's *cost–benefit* (rather than benefit–cost) ratio and comparing it with the benefit–cost ratio of the 'marginal' project.

Project L has a cost–benefit ratio of –12/+80 = –0.15. In other words, every £1 generated at Year 1 from investing in Project L has a cost of 15 pence of negative NPV.

The 'marginal' project in Septillion's investment decision is I, because it was into Project I that the last £1 of the available expenditure was spent. Project I can have a total of £220 000 invested in it at Year 1. So far, only £200 000 has been invested and so, if any further investment funds are available – up to a maximum of £20 000 – they too would be invested in I. The benefit gain from a further investment in I is given by its benefit–cost ratio of 0.20. In other words, every £1 extra invested in I generates an additional 20 pence of positive NPV.

From this comparison of Projects I and L, it can be seen that the benefit generated from a further investment in I *does* exceed the cost arising from the investment in L (i.e. 0.2 > 0.15). Investing in the whole of L will produce £80 000 at Year 1, but as only a further £20 000 can be invested in I, for the moment, the decision will be to undertake just 25% of project L to produce the required cash flow:

		NPV
Invest in 25% L to yield 20, costing	:	–3
invest 20 in 9% of I, yielding	:	+4
Net gain		+1

Septillion has now undertaken the whole of Projects K, H, J *and* I, as well as 25% of L. On the benefit–cost ratio rankings, if any *more* investment funds were available, the next best project is G. Therefore is it worthwhile undertaking the remaining 75% of L – which would produce an extra £60 000 of funds at Year 1 – in order to invest in 12% of Project G (60 ÷ 500)?

Again comparison of the ratios provides the answer: every £1 generated from L costs 15 pence of negative NPV; every £1 invested in Project G produces 5 pence of positive NPV. Therefore further investment in L in order to invest in Project G is *not* worthwhile.

Thus the optimal investment decision is: undertake Projects K, H, J, I and 25% of L. This will yield a maximum total of positive NPV of: 10 + 36 + 30 + 44 – 3 = +£117 000 NPV.

Divisibility assumption

The benefit–cost ranking approach to the situation of single-period capital rationing depends heavily on the assumption that investment projects are divisible (i.e. that fractions of projects can be undertaken, such as 25% of Project L in the example). Where this assumption does not hold, benefit–cost ratios do not work and instead, the investment selection decision has to be undertaken by examining the total NPV values of all the feasible alternative combinations of whole projects (where the term 'feasible' refers to the fact that the total outlay required to undertake the combination does not exceed the amount available). Therefore using as an example the situation as in Example 1, if none of the investment projects were divisible, the combination of accepting Projects B, D and E would produce the greatest amount of NPV, keeping within the £300 capital expenditure limit.

Mutually exclusive investments

A variation on the infringement of the divisibility assumption occurs when projects are mutually exclusive. Suppose the same example is again taken, but now it is assumed that Projects A and E are mutually exclusive. Therefore either one or the other, or neither, can be accepted, but both *cannot* be accepted. In order to obtain the optimum selection of projects we would proceed as we did originally, going down the list of projects ranked by their benefit–cost ratios until all the capital is utilized, but now this process has to be undertaken *twice* – once excluding Project A from the list and then again, but now excluding Project E from the list:

Project	Benefit–cost rank	Outlay	
E	1	50	
D	2	100	Accept E, D, B:
B	3	150	Total NPV = £210.84
C	4	60	

Project	Benefit–cost rank	Outlay	
D	1	100	
A	2	100	Accept D, A, $\frac{2}{3}$B:
B	3	150	Total NPV = £168.84
C	4	60	

Preferred combination: Projects E, D and B.

Single-period rationing and the IRR

Before leaving the single-period rationing case, it is worth noting that the IRR investment appraisal technique cannot cope adequately with this situation. Ranking projects in terms of their IRRs is *not* the same as ranking via benefit–cost ratios. The reason why the IRR technique fails to adapt to capital rationing is because of the fact that the IRR is simply an absolute percentage rate of return, whereas what is required is a measure of project performance *relative* to the rationed investment outlay. Hence this is just one more example of the limitations of the IRR technique.

Multi-period capital rationing

Introduction

The problem of investment decision making in the face of capital rationing which extends over more than one period is both complex and, at present, not completely resolved. The complexity of the problem has not been helped by general confusion and differences in the literature over what precisely is meant by capital rationing and by the range of differing assumptions that have been made, both explicitly and implicitly. The main source of confusion over capital rationing, as far as the theory of corporate investment decision making is concerned, has occurred through a failure to isolate the problem from general capital market theory. As a result, a number of paradoxical problems have arisen.

In attempting to outline a normative theory of investment decision making, we shall try to be both as practical and realistic as possible. In doing so, we will assume that hard (or external) capital rationing, both for individuals and companies, is likely to be only a relatively short-run phenomenon which may well arise, in practice, out of poor forward planning.[3] It is certainly true to say that unlimited amounts of investment capital are not immediately available to companies, because capital-raising operations can take some time to arrange. Thus there can be a definite limit to capital supplies in the very short run. However, as long as a company plans its future operations carefully and well ahead of time, and its management appears competent, it is unlikely that it will be unable to raise the capital it requires for any planned project which is expected to be 'profitable', i.e. it is unlikely that it will run into any serious, externally imposed capital rationing. We are not assuming that hard capital rationing never occurs but that, in the majority of cases, for most of the time, it is an unlikely phenomenon.

Soft capital rationing

If we make the assumption that externally imposed constraints on the supply of capital to a company are unlikely to be anything but relatively short-term phenomena, we are left with the task of examining the effects of internally imposed or soft capital rationing on the investment decision-making process. We can define soft capital rationing as a capital expenditure constraint which is imposed on a company by its own internal management, rather than by external capital markets, and which limits the amount of capital investment funds available in any particular time period.

This capital limit will normally be imposed by a capital expenditure budget, of which, in a well-managed company, there are likely to be two: a short-term capital budget for the immediate twelve months ahead and a medium-term capital budget which covers the next three to five years ahead.[4] Both budgets are likely to impose relatively inflexible capital constraints upon management.

When looking at how the NPV appraisal method could be adapted to deal with the single-period rationing problem, we saw that when the capital constraint was binding (i.e. there was insufficient capital available to invest in all projects with positive NPVs), companies would have to forgo undertaking some projects which they would have otherwise undertaken. Such a situation is understandable when imposed from outside the company, but it seems ludicrous when imposed from within the company. Why should a company wish to constrain itself in this way?

The reason is that companies require to plan for the future and to monitor, control and evaluate the implementation of these plans, so that future planning and control can be further improved upon. A capital budget is just one part of these plans and of the controlling process. It requires the imposition of a ceiling on capital expenditure, because capital investment is not a simple operation but one which takes time and a range of resources.

For example, the decision to invest in a particular project does not consist simply of the evaluation and appraisal process. Capital may have to be raised for the project (an operation which cannot be carried out instantaneously), the company must have the trained manpower available to implement the project and monitor its performance (again, not an instantaneous process), and even the evaluation and decision procedure itself is likely to have its own manpower and resource constraints, as is the whole of the company's organizational structure. Thus, in order to plan carefully and to control efficiently, limits may quite properly have to be imposed – in the short and medium terms – on the level of capital investment expenditure that a company allows itself to undertake.[5]

The existence of capital budgets within companies is likely to mean that management is faced with the problem of decision making in a situation of multi-period capital rationing (i.e. where capital rationing extends over a number of future periods). In such circumstances, the simple benefit–cost ratio technique cannot be used to place investment opportunities in an order of preference. This is because, in the single-period rationing case, the problem was to allocate investment capital amongst competing projects in the face of a *single* constraint, in order to maximize the total amount of positive NPV gained. In the multi-period case, this allocation procedure has to be carried out simultaneously under more than one constraint, as each period's rationing forms a separate constraint. To assist in this simultaneous allocation problem, we employ the mathematical programming optimizing technique of linear programming (LP). It is assumed that the reader is familiar with the basic mechanics of this technique, which can be found in most introductory books on operational research methods. However, a brief outline of the technique is provided in an appendix to this chapter.

The opportunity cost of capital dilemma

The presence of multi-period capital rationing does not alter the objective of financial management decision making: the maximization of shareholder wealth. This, we know, can be achieved through making investment decisions so as to maximize the total amount of positive NPV generated. The NPV figure gains its significance from the fact that it represents the result of netting out project cash flows and comparing this net cash flow with the opportunity cost, which is embodied in the perfect capital market discount rate.

In examining how investment resources can be allocated to projects in a situation of multi-period capital rationing, we will assume that the *suppliers* of capital to a company do not themselves impose any form of capital rationing. It is self-imposed, rather than market-imposed capital rationing. This assumption releases the analysis from one of the major difficulties of the multi-period rationing problem: the choice of discount rate.

We know that the discount rate used in the NPV calculation represents the opportunity cost of cash which, in a perfect capital market, is reflected in the market rate of interest. Once a perfect capital market no longer exists, then the market interest rate no longer necessarily reflects the opportunity cost of capital. In such circumstances, as we saw when looking at the single-period rationing problem, the opportunity cost of investment capital is represented by the return gained from the marginal project in the rationed period. Therefore, in a multi-period rationing situation, the appropriate discount rate for any period is given by the return on the marginal project in that particular period. This is the dilemma.

The company needs to know the opportunity cost of cash in each period to use as the discount rate, in order to make the correct selection. Each period's opportunity cost of cash is represented by the return on the marginal project in that particular period, but this marginal project can only be identified *after* the correct project selection has been made. In other words, in order to make the correct investment project selection, the opportunity cost of capital in each rationed period needs to be known, but this can only be known once the correct selection of projects has been made. Thus, we are firmly on the horns of a dilemma, unless we assume that the company faces a perfect capital market and it is the company alone which imposes capital rationing. In such circumstances, the market interest rate still represents the opportunity cost of capital to shareholders and so can be used as the discount rate to aid project selection. Hence the need to assume soft capital rationing.

The LP solution to capital rationing

Example 3 illustrates how, in multi-period capital rationing, linear programming can help to allocate scarce investment capital to projects so as to maximize the total amount of positive NPV.

Example 3

A company has found the following independent investment opportunities (all figures in £000s):

Project	Year					
	0	1	2	3	4	5
A	− 100	− 50	− 25	+ 100	+ 100	+ 100
B	− 50	− 70	+ 100	+ 100		
C		− 100	− 30	+ 150	+ 200	
D	− 10	− 20	+ 50	− 100	+ 100	+ 100
E	− 100	− 100	+ 200	+ 100	+ 50	
F			− 200	+ 300	+ 100	+ 100

We shall assume that none of these projects can have the timing of its cash flow brought forward or delayed, and none can be undertaken more than once. Furthermore, we shall again assume that all projects exhibit constant returns to scale. Finally, the perfect capital market rate of interest is 10% and this rate is expected to remain constant over the next five years, and can be assumed to reflect the capital suppliers' opportunity cost.

Calculating the NPVs of the projects, using a 10% discount rate, we can see that the company would normally undertake them all, because each has a positive NPV:

Project	NPV (£)
A	+ 39.4
B	+ 44.1
C	+ 133.6
D	+ 68.4
E	+ 83.6
F	+ 190.5

In order to do so, however, the company would require the expenditure of £260 000, £340 000, £255 000 and £100 000 of investment capital in the next four time periods (Years 0–3) respectively.

Suppose that the company has an internally imposed capital constraint, such that external finance raised in any one period must not exceed £150 000. In addition, internally generated finance (from projects) cannot be used to increase the amount of capital expenditure. Clearly, in these circumstances the company cannot undertake all six projects, and so which should be selected to be undertaken and which should be rejected?

There are several ways in which this problem could be formulated into a linear programme, but each alternative formulation would produce a solution giving exactly the same selection of investment projects to undertake. One approach, which fits directly into our NPV approach, is to take as the LP's objective function the maximization of the total amount of NPV which the company can generate over the next five years, given the imposed constraints. Thus, taking a, b, c ... f to represent the proportion of Projects A, B, C ... F undertaken:

Objective function:
$$39.4a + 44.1b + 133.6c + 68.4d + 83.6e + 190.5f \quad \text{Max.}$$

The assumptions behind LP

In using linear programming to solve this type of capital rationing problem, a number of assumptions and limitations are involved, one of which we have already touched upon: the specification of the rate of discount to be used. In addition, the technique assumes that all the relationships expressed in the model are linear (for example, all the projects are assumed to exhibit constant returns to scale) and that the variables are infinitely divisible. There is also an assumption that the project cash flows are known with certainty because, as yet, no way has been found of satisfactorily adjusting the technique to take account of risk.

The first of these three assumptions does not necessarily cause too much trouble because, where non-linear relationships are involved, they can often be adequately described in the LP formulation as a number of linear approximations. Similarly, the second assumption also may not be too troublesome, especially if the LP is being applied to the solution of the capital rationing problem within a company operating in a process industry (e.g. oil or chemicals), because the output is (approximately) infinitely divisible. (Integer programming – another type of allocation technique – avoids this assumption, but in doing so involves a number of new, and often more difficult, problems.) However, what really is a serious practical drawback to the use of LP in capital rationing situations, is the inability of the technique to handle uncertainty. There have been some attempts to allow for uncertainty,[8] but by and large they represent mathematical solutions to mathematical, rather than practical problems.

The dual values

In Example 3, where the objective was to maximize the total amount of positive NPV generated, the solution involved the company undertaking the whole of Projects C and D, together with 30% of Project E and 60% of Project F. The reader will be able to confirm from the project cash flow information that this solution results in the utilization of only £40 000 of the £150 000 available for investment in Year 0, and of only £100 000 of the £150 000 available in Year 3. Therefore, although the company's capital expenditure is constrained in these two periods, the constraints are 'non-binding', i.e. they do not bind or constrain the company in its efforts to achieve its objective. For this reason, there is no *additional* opportunity cost of the cash used for capital expenditure in these two periods (i.e. there is no opportunity cost incurred in addition to that opportunity cost already allowed for in the discounting process used to convert the project cash flows to NPVs), because the company does not forgo any of its investment project opportunities as a result of these two constraints.

The situation is different in respect of the Year 1 and Year 2 capital expenditure constraints. In these periods, the linear programme's project selection results in the £150 000 available (in both Years 1 and 2) being *fully* utilized and therefore the constraints are said to be *binding*: their existence limits the company's freedom of action in pursuit of its objective of NPV maximization because it limits the amount of investment the company can undertake. As a result, there is an additional opportunity cost attached to the use of investment cash in each of these two periods.

These additional opportunity costs are represented by the 'dual' values produced by the linear programme. In the example used above, the LP solution produced the following dual values for the four capital expenditure constraints:

Year	Dual value (£)
0	0
1	0.837
2	0.952
3	0

The dual values which are produced from LP with a maximizing objective function represent the increase (decrease) in the total value of the objective function that would arise if a binding constraint were marginally – i.e. by one unit – slackened (tightened). Thus, in the example, the investment capital constraints result in the company achieving a total NPV value (i.e. the objective function's value) of £341 400. If £150 001 were available for investment in Year 1 (keeping the £150 000 limit in force in each of the three other periods), then the value of the objective function would rise by £0.837 to £341 400.837.

In this very simple example this increase in the objective function would be achieved by increasing the level of investment in Project E (the marginal project in Year 1) from 30% of E to 30.001%.[9] Also, because the use of LP assumes linear relationships, a *reduction* in the amount of capital available in Year 1 to £149 999 would result in the value of the objective function *falling* by £0.837.

A similar analysis can be made in terms of the Year 2 capital constraint dual value of £0.952 which is caused by a 0.0005% change in the level of investment in Project F. Because the capital constraints in Years 0 and 3 are non-binding their dual values are both zero: a marginal change in either constraint will leave both the original project selection and the value of the objective function unaltered.

There are a number of points to be made here. The first is that the example used is a highly simplified one and the practical application of the use of LP to solve capital rationing problems is far more complex and problematical. We have only outlined the approach and specified the main theoretical difficulties. Second, if we accept that Projects E and F are the marginal projects in Years 1 and 2 respectively (i.e. investment levels in these two projects change in response to marginal changes in available investment capital in these two years), it is important to realize that the relative IRRs of these two projects do *not* produce their dual values, because the IRR represents a project's *average* return over the *whole* of its life, whilst the dual value refers to a project's *marginal* return in *just* the period specified.

A third point of importance is that dual values apply only to incremental/marginal changes in binding constraint values. To identify the effect of any non-marginal change – i.e. a substantial change – the LP has to be reformulated accordingly and re-solved. Finally, dual values apply only to individual marginal changes in binding constraints, i.e. they operate under a *ceteris paribus* assumption that all other variables in the formulation remain unchanged. Thus, in the example used, if an extra £1 of investment capital is available in both Years 1 *and* 2, the resulting change in the value of the objective function is not necessarily the sum of the two individual dual values. Therefore we can see that dual values can be informative in that they represent part of the opportunity cost of investment capital, but their usefulness is relatively limited because of their marginal nature.

A more complex example

Example 4 deals with a more complex multi-period capital rationing problem.

Example 4

Butyrin Ltd is the subsidiary of a large holding company. It is formulating capital investment plans. The company has identified the following independent projects (all figures in £000s):

Project	Year 0	1	2	3
A	– 100	– 50	– 60	+ 300
B	– 80	+ 40	+ 50	
C	– 200	– 100	+ 400	

The company judges that 10% is the correct discount rate to use, which produces the following NPVs:

Project	NPV
A	+ 30.35
B	– 2.36
C	+ 39.65

However, the company finds itself in a capital rationing situation imposed by its parent and there is only £170 000 available at Year 0 and £65 000 available at Year 1.

In addition, the following facts are relevant:
1. Projects A and C each use a particular type of raw material which is in short supply. Project A requires 32 tonnes and Project C requires 17 tonnes. Butyrin can only purchase 25 tonnes in total.
2. Any surplus funds the company has can be placed on deposit from Year 0 to Year 1 at 8% interest. However, all surplus funds available at the end of any subsequent year must be returned to the parent company.
3. Butyrin's bank has indicated that it is willing to give a two-year term loan of any amount up to £120 000. Interest would be payable at each year end at 15%, and the loan would have to be repaid at Year 2.
4. The parent company will allow Butyrin to reinvest any project-generated cash flows.

Before this problem can be formulated into an LP, points 2 and 3 above have first to be dealt with. Placing money on deposit can be viewed as a mini-project and so, like Projects A, B and C, we need to calculate its NPV:

NPV of £1 placed on deposit

	Year	
	0	1
Cash flow	− 1	+ 1.08
10% discount factor	× 1	× 0.9091
	− 1	+ 0.98 = − 0.02 NPV

Similarly with the bank loan:

NPV of £1 bank loan

	Year		
	0	1	2
Cash flow	+ 1	+ 0.15	− 1.15
10% discount factor	× 1	× 0.9091	× 0.8264
	+ 1	+ 0.14	− 0.95 = − 0.09 NPV

We are now ready to formulate the LP:

Let *a* equal the *proportion* of Project A undertaken.
Let *b* equal the *proportion* of Project B undertaken.
Let *c* equal the *proportion* of Project C undertaken.
Let *d* equal the *amount* of cash placed on deposit: Yr 0 to Yr 1.
Let *L* equal the *amount* of cash borrowed: Yr 0 to Yr 2.

The *objective function* is:

$$30.35a - 2.36b + 39.65c - 0.02d - 0.09L \quad \text{Max.}$$

Notice that the negative, as well as the positive NPV variables are included. It should be left to the LP to decide the investment plan and, as we saw with single-period capital rationing, negative NPV projects can sometimes be acceptable.

The set of *capital expenditure constraints* are:

$$
\begin{aligned}
100a + 80b + 200c + d &\leq 170 + L \\
50a + 100c + 0.15L &\leq 65 + 40b + 1.08d \\
L &\leq 120 \\
a, b, c &\leq 1
\end{aligned}
$$

Notice that *only* the cash flows in the rationed time periods need be specified in the LP. Hence the LP doesn't need to know explicitly about the loan repayment because it occurs in Year 2 when there is not expected to be any capital expenditure constraint. The LP implicitly is aware of the *overall* effect of the loan because it knows what its NPV is.

Finally, there is the raw material constraint and the non-negativity conditions:

$$
\begin{aligned}
32a + 17c &\leq 25 \\
a, b, c, d, L &\geq 0
\end{aligned}
$$

With the raw material constraint, there is no need to enquire when the constraint will occur. Time is only important in the LP as far as money flows are concerned because of the differing capital expenditure constraints. Also, notice that the non-negativity conditions not only prevent negative projects, but they also prevent a negative deposit account and bank loan.

Therefore, the complete LP formulation, ready for solution via a computer package, is:

$$
\begin{aligned}
30.35a - 2.36b + 39.65c - 0.02d - 0.09L && \text{Max.} \\
100a + 80b + 200c + d &\leq 170 + L \\
50a + 100c + 0.15L &\leq 65 + 40b + 1.08d \\
L &\leq 120 \\
a, b, c &\leq 1 \\
32a + 17c &\leq 25 \\
a, b, c, d, L &\geq 0
\end{aligned}
$$

Two applications of dual values

Two Examples, 5 and 6, of possible applications of dual values will serve to indicate their usefulness and will also help to demonstrate the different procedures required. The first example concerns the evaluation of an additional investment, and the second shows how to determine the value of additional sources of cash.

In order to do so, use will be made of our original multi-period example in this section, involving six independent projects (A to F), where the LP's solution to the multi-period capital rationing problem was:

Investment plan:	Project A: reject
	Project B: reject
	Project C: undertake 100%
	Project D: undertake 100%
	Project E: undertake 30%
	Project F: undertake 60%
Dual values:	Cash at Year 0: 0
	Cash at Year 1: £0.837
	Cash at Year 2: £0.952
	Cash at Year 3: 0

Example 5

Suppose that, before the investment plan can be undertaken, a new project is identified: Project W. This project involves the following cash flows (all figures in £000s):

Year	Cash flow
0	−100
1	+ 20
2	+ 90

The dual values can be used to indicate either that the project is *not* worth considering or that it *is* worth considering and so the LP should be reformulated to include Project W's cash flows, and then re-solved.

If the original LP formulation dual values are to be used, the project's NPV has first to be determined and then the opportunity cost of its cash flows. If the *net* effect is positive, the project is worth considering and the LP should be reformulated and re-solved. If the net effect is negative, the project can be discarded without further analysis. The calculations are as follows:

Year	Cash flow		10% discount rate		PV cash flows
0	− 100	×	1	=	− 100
1	+ 20	×	0.9091	=	+ 18.18
2	+ 90	×	0.8264	=	+ 74.38
			NPV	=	£ − 7.44

Year	Cash flow		Dual value		Opp. cost cash flows
0	− 100	×	0	=	0
1	+ 20	×	0.837	=	+ 16.74
2	+ 90	×	0.952	=	+ 85.68
			Opportunity cost		+102.42

Net effect of project: NPV + opportunity cost = − £7.44 + £102.42 = + £94.98.

As the overall net effect of the project is positive, this indicates that the project is worthwhile considering further and the LP should be reformulated (now including Project W's cash flows) and re-solved. This analysis is in fact very similar to the analysis made in Chapter 7 when looking at relevant cash flows. There we saw that the cost of utilizing a scarce resource was equal to its *total* opportunity cost: the internal opportunity cost, plus the external opportunity cost (the market price of the resource).

That is exactly the approach used to evaluate Project W. The NPV analysis evaluates the project's use of cash in terms of the market 'price' of cash (the discount rate); and then the subsequent analysis evaluates the project in terms of its impact on the firm's capital rationing problem – the internal opportunity cost.

On this basis, therefore, Project W could have been evaluated directly on the total opportunity costs involved:

	10% discount rate	+	Dual value of cash	=	Total opportunity cost of cash
Year 0	1	+	0	=	1
Year 1	0.9091	+	0.837	=	1.7461
Year 2	0.8264	+	0.952	=	1.7784
Year 3	0.7513	+	0	=	0.7513

Project W

Year	Cash flow		Opportunity cost		
0	– 100	×	1	=	– 100
1	+ 20	×	1.7461	=	+ 34.92
2	+ 90	×	1.7784	=	+ 160.06
					+ 94.98

Thus, if Project W is accepted, it should enable the total NPV generated by the projects under consideration to be increased.

<hr>

Example 6

Now suppose that the company, having formulated its production plan from the original six available projects, is then offered an opportunity to borrow additional cash at Year 2 as long as it is repaid (with interest) at Year 3. What is the maximum interest rate that the company would be willing to pay to take out such a loan?

The maximum interest rate represents the point of indifference or *equality* between what would be *gained* (in terms of the objective function) by borrowing (say) £1 at Year 2 and what would be *lost* from the resulting repayment of capital plus interest at Year 3. Using the *total* opportunity cost figures calculated in Example 5 makes for a simple solution to the problem:

$$£1 \times \text{opportunity cost of cash at Year 2} = £1(1 + i) \times \text{opportunity cost of cash at Year 3}$$

$$£1 \times 1.7784 = £1(1 + i) \times 0.7513$$
$$1.7784 = 0.7513 + 0.7513i$$

$$\frac{1.7784 - 0.7513}{0.7513} = i = 1.367 \text{ or } 136.7\%$$

This very high rate of interest should not come as a surprise. The firm should be willing to pay such a rate of interest (at a maximum) for the sake of gaining extra cash in a time period when cash is constrained, and repaying in a time period when it is unconstrained.

Introduction

Up to this point in the chapter, we have been examining the investment decision in the face of one particular capital market imperfection, that of soft capital rationing. Let us now turn to examine another common imperfection: the existence of a gap between the borrowing and the lending interest rate, caused by the presence of market transaction costs, where the borrowing rate is somewhat higher than the lending rate. Perhaps the best way to lay bare the problem here is to make use of the single-period investment–consumption diagram.

Identification of the opportunity cost

In the basic model we saw that, because of the so-called 'separation theorem', it made little difference to the appraisal of physical investment opportunities whether a company had one or several owners and, if it had several owners, whether their indifference curve sets were similar or dissimilar; in fact the company did not even require knowledge of its owners' indifference curve sets.

In the face of a perfect capital market, a company would invest in physical investment opportunities until the return from the marginal project equated with the market rate of interest (i.e. it would invest in all projects which had positive or zero NPVs). This investment decision rule determined the dividend flow pattern which the individual shareholder could adjust, if he wished, by using the capital market. The company used the market interest rate as the investment appraisal discount rate because it reflected the opportunity cost of cash to the shareholders.

Let us now start with the simple case of a single-owner company and a perfect capital market, except that transaction costs result in the borrowing interest rate being higher than the lending interest rate. In such a case the separation theorem (i.e. separation between management investment decisions and shareholder consumption decisions) breaks down, as there is no longer a single opportunity cost of cash because there are now two market interest rates.

Fig. 8.2 illustrates this situation with the steeper of the two financial investment lines (BC) representing the borrowing rate and the other (DF) representing the lending rate. In these circumstances the shareholder's indifference curve may be tangential at any point along the non-linear boundary BCDF. We can specify three separate cases:

1. If a point of tangency occurs on the BC segment then, at time t_0, the company should undertake physical investments up to point C, and then the shareholder should add to his received dividend by borrowing on the capital market. For the company to locate itself correctly at point C on the physical investment line, the market *borrowing* rate should be used as the NPV discount rate because it would represent the opportunity cost of cash. The borrowing rate reflects the opportunity cost in these circumstances because the shape and location of the shareholder's indifference curve set is such that preference

emphasis is placed on consumption at time t_0. Thus, if cash is to be invested rather than consumed at time t_0, the investment should earn a return at least equal to the borrowing rate, because the shareholder will be borrowing to replace (at least in part) the investment outlay undertaken.

2. If a point of tangency occurs along segment DF, then the company should locate itself at point D on the physical investment line and the shareholder should then lend out some part of his received dividend on the capital market. In this case, the company can ensure optimally locating at point D by undertaking all physical investments which produce positive or zero NPVs when discounted at the market *lending* rate. This rate represents the shareholder's opportunity cost of cash for reasons analogous to those cited in the previous case, except that his indifference curve set is now shaped so as to bias preference towards consumption at time t_1. Thus the company should undertake physical investments as long as they earn a return which is at least equal to that which the shareholder could earn by lending on the capital market.

3. If the point of tangency between the shareholder's indifference curve set and the boundary curve BCDF occurs along the segment CD, then this also represents the optimal point of location for the company on its physical investment line. In such circumstances, the opportunity cost of cash is represented by the slope of the shareholder's indifference curve at the point of tangency (his *personal* time value of money) and it is also represented by the return on the marginal investment at the point of tangency on the physical investment line. Therefore, this is the rate of discount which the company should use in its investment appraisal, to ensure that it locates itself at the optimal point on the physical investment line.

In practical terms, the company's management is unlikely to be aware of the location of its shareholder's indifference curve set in relation to the boundary BCDF and so will not know whether to use the borrowing rate (case 1),

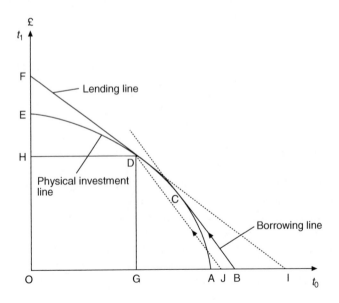

Fig. 8.2 *Lending and borrowing*

the lending rate (case 2) or some intermediate rate between the borrowing and lending rates (case 3) as the investment appraisal discount rate. However, even if the company were aware of its single shareholder's indifference map and so could optimally locate on the physical investment line, in the more realistic case where there are several shareholders, their indifference curve sets are unlikely to be the same, which may well lead to a direct conflict over the value at which the discount rate should be set in order to reflect the opportunity cost of cash.

Quite simply, then, the real-world solution to the problem is indeterminate, and all that a company can hope to do is to use a single discount rate both consistently and publicly, so that it attracts shareholders whose opportunity cost of cash approximates to this rate.

Three further points

There are three further points worth noticing in this analysis. First, suppose that the company is aware of the indifference curve set of shareholders and, as a result, uses the lending rate for discounting and so locates at point D in Fig. 8.2. The total net *present* value of the company's investments (given by AI) does not have any real meaning in the sense that the dividend flow produced of OG at t_0 and OH at t_1 cannot be converted by the shareholder into a cash flow of zero at t_1 and OI at t_0. Such a dividend flow can only have a present value of OJ.

This presents an interesting problem in terms of management's objective function, which we have stated as the maximization of the stock market's current valuation of the company. To do this – and assuming the stock market valuation is based on the present value summation of the future dividend flow – it could be argued that the company should use the borrowing rate as the discount rate, because this is the only meaningful way a 'present value' could be stated, but then in this example, maximization of the market value of the company's equity capital would not bring maximum benefit to the shareholders, in terms of assisting them to obtain the highest possible indifference curve.

A second point is that, if the company selects a discount rate between the market borrowing and lending rates (inclusively) and it makes an *incorrect* selection, the smaller the gap between the borrowing and lending rate, the less serious (in terms of lost utility) will be the mistake.

Finally, it is interesting to speculate upon the situation of a company which was either totally ignorant of its shareholders' indifference curve sets or which had shareholders with widely different indifference maps. In these circumstances, and still using a one-period analysis, the most conservative action for the company to take would be to use the borrowing rate for discounting when evaluating projects.

If that is the correct rate (i.e. case 1) then there is no problem. If either the lending rate or some intermediate rate is correct, then, although shareholders will not maximize their utility, the utility level achieved will *always* be higher than if the company did not undertake any investment at all. If either the lending rate or an intermediate rate is chosen to evaluate investment possibilities and this chosen rate proves to be incorrect, then shareholders *may* find themselves at a *lower* utility level than if the company had undertaken no investment at all, but instead had liquidated itself at time t_0.[10] Taking immediate corporate liquidation as the ultimate alternative, investing in projects with positive NPVs when discounted at the borrowing rate will always raise the shareholders' utility level. The use of a discount rate above the borrowing rate *may* reduce the utility level to below that achieved through immediate liquidation.

In conclusion

We have seen that the presence of different lending and borrowing interest rates can cause an insurmountable difficulty to investment appraisal (or at least to the theory). However, if we can conclude that in the real world the difference between lending and borrowing rates is likely to be relatively small, then the problem does not disappear, but it does take on considerably less significance. In such circumstances the detrimental effect on the owners' wealth and utility is likely to be fairly small. We shall touch upon this problem once again at a later stage.

Summary

Principally, this chapter has covered the capital rationing problem; but, in addition, another capital market imperfection, that of differential interest rates for lending and borrowing, has also been examined. The main points made are as follows:

- Capital rationing refers to a situation where a company cannot undertake all positive NPV projects it has identified, because of a shortage of capital.

- Two different types of capital rationing situation can be identified, distinguished by the source of the capital expenditure constraint. Hard capital rationing occurs when the constraint is externally imposed on the firm by the capital market. Soft capital rationing occurs when the constraint is internally imposed on the firm, by its own management.

- In a situation of capital rationing the standard NPV decision rule for independent projects no longer holds and so has to be modified.

- In the single-period capital rationing situation, the NPV decision rule is replaced with a benefit–cost ratio analysis which evaluates the project's NPV relative to the required outlay in the rationed time period.

- In multi-period capital rationing, the optimal investment solution can only be obtained through solving the individual capital rationing constraints simultaneously via linear programming.

- The solution to a multi-period capital rationing LP not only provides advice on the capital investment decision (the LP's primal solution), but it also provides a dual solution. The dual solution indicates the (internal) opportunity cost of the scarce resources which, in this type of situation, is principally cash.

- The usefulness of the dual values is limited because of their marginal nature. However, they can be used to help evaluate some decisions that arise after the capital rationing LP has been solved.

- Finally the problem of differential lending and borrowing rates of interest was examined. It was concluded that, in such circumstances, the optimal investment decision is indeterminate because of lack of knowledge as to which market interest rate (lend or borrow) should be used to evaluate projects. However, it was judged that, in the real world, the sub-optimal decisions that might arise as a result would be likely to have only a small impact on shareholder wealth.

Appendix: linear programming

A company has identified two independent projects with the following cash flows:

Project	Year 0	Year 1	Year 2
A	−100	−50	+200
B	− 80	−60	+170

Assuming a discount rate of 10% correctly reflects the return available elsewhere on the capital market, their NPVs are approximately:

Project	NPV
A	+20
B	+ 6

However, to undertake both projects requires an outlay of £180 at Year 0 and 110 at Year 1. The company has imposed a capital expenditure constraint of £65 at Year 0 and £90 at Year 1. This problem can be formed into a linear programme (LP) in order to solve the investment decision, where a equals the proportion of Project A undertaken and b equals the proportion of Project B undertaken.

a and b can take on values between 0 (where *none* of the project would be undertaken), and 1 (where the whole of the project would be undertaken). Thus if the solution turns out to be $a = 0.25$ and $b = 0.80$, it means 25% of Project A should be undertaken and 80% of Project B.

Every LP consists of just *three* elements: an objective function, a set of constraints and a set of non-negativity conditions. Here, the objective is to make an investment decision (that is select values for a and b) in order to maximize the total NPV generated. Therefore, the objective function will be:

$$20a + 6b \quad \text{Max.}$$

where $20a$ is the amount of positive NPV generated from the investment in A (i.e. if $a = 0.40$, then $20a$ equals: $20 \times 0.40 = 8$; undertaking 40% of Project A produces a positive NPV of 8), and similarly with $6b$.

There are two constraints on the investment decision: the fact that capital is limited in Year 0 and in Year 1. The formulation of the Year 0 capital expenditure constraint would be:

$$100a + 80b \leq 65$$

where $100a$ is the capital invested in Project A at Year 0 (i.e. if $a = 0.40$, then $100a$ equals: $100 \times 0.40 = 40$; undertaking 40% of Project A will require a Year 0 outlay of 40), and similarly for Project B. Thus this constraint simply indicates that the amount of cash spent on undertaking Project A at Year 0 ($100a$), plus the cash spent on undertaking B at Year 0 ($80b$) must not exceed ($\leq$) the £65 of investment finance available at Year 0.

The Year 1 capital expenditure constraint is similarly:

$$50a + 60b \leq 90.$$

In addition, to prevent the LP from suggesting that any project should be undertaken more than once, the values that can be placed on a and b are limited to a maximum of 1 (i.e. 100%). Therefore:

$$a, b \leq 1.$$

The non-negativity condition is simply there to prevent nonsensical negative values being assigned to a and b:

$$a, b \geq 0.$$

Thus the complete LP formulation is:

$20a + 6b$		Max.
$100a + 80b$	$\leq$	65
$50a + 60b$	$\leq$	90
a, b	$\leq$	1
a, b	$\geq$	0

There are many computer packages available which will solve this LP. What is being solved is the values of a and b in a pair of simultaneous equations (the two constraints), so as to maximize the total NPV generated. The solution to this particular, very simple, problem is

$$a = 0.65$$
$$b = 0$$

In other words, 65% of Project A should be undertaken and Project B should be rejected. This produces a total NPV of 13, the maximum possible amount, given the constraints.

Notes

1. This return would be the project's IRR. For simplicity, we are abstracting from the problems which may arise in calculating or using an IRR.

2. If not, any book on management accounting will outline the basic principles. For example, see C. Drury, *Management and Cost Accounting*, 5th Edition, Thomson Learning 2000.

3. We will shortly discuss the reason for making this assumption.

4. In addition, there may be a very much longer-term capital budget which might stretch as far as 20–25 years ahead, depending upon the company and the industry in which it operates and upon the gestation period of its major capital investment projects.

5.   It could be argued that even this internally imposed capital rationing is, in reality, produced by external – but not exclusively financial – market inefficiencies, in that there is a time-lag between demand signals and the subsequent supply.

6.   The primal solution reads: $a = 0$, $b = 0$, $c = 1$, $d = 1$, $e = 0.3$, $f = 0.6$.

7.   If it *were* possible to relieve the capital expenditure constraint through the use of internally generated funds (from projects), then the LP formulation would have to be revised and a different solution would result:

$$39.4a + 44.1b + 133.6c + 68.4d + 83.6e + 190.5f \text{ Max.}$$
$$100a + 50b + 10d + 100e \leq 150$$
$$50a + 70b + 100c + 20d + 100e \leq 150$$
$$25a + 30c + 200f \leq 150 + 100b + 50d + 200e$$
$$100d \leq 150 + 100a + 100b + 150c + 100e + 300f$$
$$a, b, c, d, e, f \leq 1$$
$$a, b, c, d, e, f \geq 0$$

8.   By including 'chance' constraints into the LP formulation, whereby some level of cash flow must be provided by the solution, with a given level of probability.

9.   Project E produces a total NPV of + £83 700, and 0.001% of this amount is £0.837, the dual value for Year 1. This information on how the dual value arises is supplied by the computer solution to the problem. In a more complex example the source of the dual value is likely to involve more than merely an adjustment to the level of investment in a single project.

10. We are assuming here that liquidation can be achieved without incurring costs.

Further reading

1.   For a good starting point on the literature of capital rationing, see J.H. Lorie, L.J. Savage, 'Three Problems in Rationing Capital', *Journal of Business*, October 1955, and H.R. Fogler, 'Ranking Techniques and Capital Budgeting', *Accounting Review*, January 1972.
2.   For an approach equating with the Hirshleifer analysis, see F.D. Arditti, R.C. Grinold, H. Levy, 'The Investment–Consumption Decision under Capital Rationing', *Review of Economic Studies*, July 1973.
3.   For application of LP to multi-period capital rationing, see two articles by K.N. Bhaskar, 'Linear Programming and Capital Budgeting: a Reappraisal', *Journal of Business Finance and Accounting*, Autumn 1976, and 'Linear Programming in Capital Budgeting: the Financing Problem', *Journal of Business Finance and Accounting*, Spring 1983.
4.   Perhaps the most thoughtful article of all on the subject is H.M. Weingartner, 'Capital Rationing: Authors in Search of a Plot', *Journal of Finance*, December 1977; whilst also of interest is G.W. Trivol and W.R. McDaniel, 'Uncertainty, Capital Immobility and Capital Rationing in Investment Decision', *Journal of Business Finance and Accounting*, Summer 1987.

Quickie questions

1. What are the two types or classes of capital rationing?
2. Why does capital rationing cause problems for the NPV decision rule?
3. Given these projects:

	t_0	t_1	....	NPV
A	-100	-50	....	$+60$
B	-200	-200	....	$+90$
C	-40	-150	....	$+20$
D	-100	$+20$	....	-10

   If only 200 is available at t_0, which projects should be selected?
4. Given the projects in question 3, if only 240 external capital was available at t_1 (no capital rationing at t_0), which projects should be selected?
5. Given these projects:

	t_0	....	NPV
A	-100	....	$+40$
B	-100	....	$+30$
C	-200	....	$+50$
D	-100	....	$+10$
E	-50	....	$+4$

   Only 300 is available at t_0 and Projects B and C are mutually exclusive. Which projects should the firm accept?
6. Given the projects:

	t_0	t_1	t_2	....	NPV
A	-100	-200	$+50$	....	$+40$
B	-150	$+70$	$+70$	....	$+20$
C	-200	-120	-30	....	$+50$

   External capital is limited to 190 at t_0, 110 at t_1 and zero at t_2. Formulate the problem into an LP.
7. A capital rationing LP produces the following dual values for cash:

t_0	1.86
t_1	0.73
t_2	0.64
t_3	1.21

   A bank loan is available at t_1, repayable at t_2. What is the maximum rate of interest you would be willing to pay, given the firm uses a 10% discount rate for project appraisal?
8. Given the dual values in question 7, the firm now discovers an additional project:

Year	Cash flow
0	-100
1	$+40$
2	$+90$

   What action should be taken?

Problems

1. Sporangium plc is a large bakery company with other interests including ice-cream manufacture and specialized catering. For investment appraisal purposes, it uses a 15% rate of discount.

The management are considering the company's capital investment plans for the coming year. One project under consideration is the purchase of a fleet of delivery vans. Two alternative proposals have been put forward. One is to purchase a fleet of petrol-powered vans; the other is to purchase electrically-powered vans.

Investment in the petrol-powered fleet would yield an internal rate of return (IRR) of 25% whilst the electrically-powered fleet would only yield a return of 20%. However, when the two alternatives are evaluated using net present value (NPV), the electrically-powered fleet has the larger positive NPV.

In addition to the above, the company has identified four other projects (all independent). Their outlays and NPVs are shown below:

Project	Outlay (t_0) (£000)	NPV (£000)
A	50	+ 60
B	80	+ 40
C	140	+ 84
D	80	+ 32
Petrol fleet	100	+ 80
Electric fleet	170	+ 110.5

All projects require only a single outlay at t_0, except Project A which requires a further £70 000 one year later at t_1.

The company has only £290 000 available for capital investment projects at t_0. Capital is expected to be freely available from t_1 onwards. None of the above projects can have their starts delayed. All projects are divisible, exhibit constant returns to scale and have the same level of risk, which is the same as that of the projects already being undertaken by the company.

Required:
(a) Carefully explain the reasons for the conflict in the investment advice about the fleet of delivery vans. In the absence of capital rationing which vehicle fleet should be purchased and why?
(b) When faced with capital rationing which projects should the company undertake at t_0? Explain the reasons for your decision.
(c) How would your advice in (b) above be modified if the start of the delivery fleet project could be delayed until t_1? What would be the resulting gain in shareholder wealth?

2. Hyalophane plc has identified the following investment projects:

Project	t_0 Immediate outlay (£000)	t_1 Year 1 (£000)	t_2 Year 2 (£000)
A	− 100	− 100	+ 302
B	− 50	− 100	+ 218
C	− 200	+ 100	+ 107
D	− 100	− 50	+ 308
E	− 200	− 50	+ 344

Required:
(a) The company faces a perfect capital market, where the appropriate discount rate is 10%. All projects are independent and divisible. Which projects should the firm accept?
(b) The company faces capital rationing at t_0. There is only £225 000 of finance available. None of the projects can be delayed. Which projects should the firm accept?
(c) The situation is as in (b) above, except that you are now informed that Projects A and B are mutually exclusive. Which projects should now be accepted?

(d) All projects are now independent but indivisible. Which projects should be accepted? What will be the maximum NPV available to the company?

(e) All projects are independent and divisible. There is capital rationing at t_1 only. No project can be delayed or brought forward. There is only £150 000 of external finance available at t_1. Which projects should be accepted?

(f) Given the information as in (e) above, except that there is capital rationing at both t_0 (£225 000 available) and t_1 (£150 000 available), formulate the linear programme to solve the problem, so as to maximize the total NPV generated.

(g) Suppose that the solution to the above linear programme produces the following dual values for cash:

t_0	0.92
t_1	0.84
t_2	0

If money can be transferred from t_0 to t_1, via a deposit account, under what circumstances would it be worthwhile?

(h) Given the circumstances in (g) above, what minimum rate of interest would be required to make the linear programme transfer cash from t_1 to t_2?

In all the above questions, none of the projects can be accepted more than once.

3. Raiders Ltd is a private limited company which is financed entirely by ordinary shares. Its effective cost of capital, net of tax, is 10% per annum. The directors of Raiders are considering the company's capital investment programme for the next two years, and have reduced their initial list of projects to four. Details of the projects are as follows:

Cash flows (net of tax)

Project	Immediately (£000)	After one year (£000)	After two years (£000)	After three years (£000)	Net present value (at 10%) (£000)	Internal rate of return (to nearest 1%)
A	− 400	+ 50	+ 300	+ 350	+ 157.00	26%
B	− 300	− 200	+ 400	+ 400	+ 150.0	25%
C	− 300	+ 150	+ 150	+ 150	+ 73.5	23%
D	0	− 300	+ 250	+ 300	+ 159.5	50%

None of the projects can be delayed. All projects are divisible; outlays may be reduced by any proportion and net inflows will then be reduced in the same proportion. No project can be undertaken more than once. Raiders Ltd is able to invest surplus funds in a bank deposit account yielding a return of 7% per annum, net of tax.

Required:
(a) Prepare calculations showing which projects Raiders should undertake if capital for immediate investment is limited to £500 000, but is expected to be available without limit at a cost of 10% per annum thereafter.

(b) Provide a linear programming formulation to assist the directors of Raiders Ltd in choosing investment projects if capital available immediately is limited to £500 000, capital available after one year is limited to £300 000 and capital is available thereafter without limit at a cost of 10% per annum.

(c) Outline the limitations of the formulation you have provided in (b).

(d) Comment briefly on the view that in practice capital is rarely limited absolutely, provided that the borrower is willing to pay a sufficiently high price, and in consequence a technique for selecting investment projects which assumes that capital is limited absolutely, is of no use.

9 Uncertainty, risk, diversification and returns

Introduction to uncertainty

This chapter considers some of the methods that have been developed to aid investment decision making in a world where the future is largely unknown and those decisions have to be carried out on the basis of *expectations*. In other words, in an uncertain world, capital investment decisions have to be taken on the basis of *expected* project cash flows, which may or may not turn out to be the same as the cash flows that *actually* arise.

So, in the real world, investment decision making involves taking a risk: the risk that the actual outcomes will almost certainly differ from what was expected. In our analysis of the handling of uncertainty in decision making we use the two terms 'risk' and 'uncertainty' interchangeably. Although it is possible to distinguish between the two terms, there is little purpose in doing so for our present needs. Thus when reference is made to a risky investment decision, we are concerned with a situation where we are uncertain about that investment's *actual* future outcome.

The more complete version of this text, *Investment Appraisal and Financial Decisions* (Lumby and Jones 1999), devotes seven chapters to risk with a further five chapters concerning the related issue of capital structure and cost of capital. These are complex issues and the aim of this chapter is to provide an overview of the problems and some of the suggested solutions that are grounded in economic theory. The next chapter considers some of the more traditional and technological approaches that might be adopted.

We will first look at the nature of risks associated with investments in companies. From there we move on to the relationship between investment in companies and the investment by those companies in specific assets and how we can use market data to determine appropriate returns for investments. Finally we will consider the use of historical data within the company.

Accepting more risks means expecting better returns

We start our examination of the problem of investment decision making in an uncertain world with the assertion that investors are averse to uncertainty – in other words they dislike risk. Therefore, in order to be persuaded to take on an investment for which the outcome is uncertain, they have to be offered the expectation of a higher return from the investment as a *reward*, or as *compensation* for taking on the risk involved. Further, it follows that the greater the degree of uncertainty surrounding an investment's outcome, the greater will have to be the level of expected return in order to make the investment attractive to investors.

In a perfect world, the capital market would not display just a single rate of interest, but a whole continuum of interest rates – one for each level of risk: the higher the risk, the higher the interest rate. We could therefore adapt the NPV appraisal technique by using as the discount rate for any particular project's appraisal, the perfect capital market discount rate which related to that particular project's level of risk.

In such a way the discount rate would still correctly reflect the opportunity cost of undertaking the investment: the investment should only be undertaken if it produces a return that is at least equal to the return that could be obtained on the capital market, *for a similar level of risk*. (The IRR appraisal technique could be similarly adapted. The perfect capital market interest rate appropriate for the project's level of risk would be used at the hurdle/cut-off rate.)

However, this simple analysis – although fundamentally and conceptually correct – does beg two rather problematic questions: how are we to identity the degree of risk associated with a particular investment project and, given that we can measure a project's risk level, how are we then to identify the corresponding perfect capital market interest rate? These two questions will form the basis for much of the following discussion.

A caution

The impact of uncertainty has a fundamental and pervasive impact on the whole of financial decision making. It is often useful to assume away its existence in order to clarify the basic analysis of investment decision making; however, if our theory is to have any real-world validity then we must come to grips with the problems it poses.

When we look at the research work that is currently being undertaken, we find that a very substantial proportion of it is concerned with the presence of risk in decision making, because it is our lack of understanding about risk – its nature, measurement and investor's attitude towards it – that causes the greatest number of problems and unanswered questions. Perhaps some of the most important questions are beyond answer but the more traditional approaches to risk are not seen as providing satisfactory solutions and so recent years have seen the development of different approaches such as chaos theory. Despite this, it is worthwhile developing an appreciation of some of the techniques that have been developed over the past 25 years or so.

Individuals attitudes to risk and the concept of utility

Utility is an economic concept that describes the benefit an individual perceives from his or her wealth. It is based on the truth that for most people the value they perceive of an increase in wealth is a function not only of the absolute size of that increase but also how it relates to their existing wealth.

Figure 9.1 is a graphical representation of possible attitudes to utility but it should be pointed out that it is unlikely that an individual should be any thing other than risk averse, an issue we return to below. Figure 9.1 describes three possible attitudes towards wealth. The risk-neutral function describes a situation where the individual perceives a directly proportional relationship between their wealth and the benefit they derive from it. So, an increase in wealth of 25% results in a 25% increase in the perceived benefits produced by that wealth. A risk-averse function describes a situation where the individual perceives diminishing benefit from each increase in wealth so that the £10 increase from wealth of £100 to wealth of £110 would be seen as being more significant than the £10 increase in wealth from £1000 to £1010. The risk seeking function describes a situation where individual perceives increasing benefit from each increase in wealth so that the £10 increase from wealth of £100 to wealth of £110 would be seen as being *less* significant than the £10 increase in wealth from £1000 to £1010.

A 'risk-neutral' person would require no compensation for undertaking a risky project whilst a 'risk-seeker' should be willing to pay a premium in order to be allowed to bear a risk! It is difficult to imagine why any investor should be indifferent towards risk, let alone why they should actively seek it without reward. If we ignore the 'buzz' that some individuals might get from gambling, there are good reasons why investors should be risk averse. Indeed, even gamblers will generally be prepared to pay insurance premiums, which might seem a little inconsistent.

So why should investors be risk averse? The answer is that other things being equal, each £1 we stand to lose in a gamble is worth more to us in relative terms than each £1 we stand to gain. Let us take a simple example. If

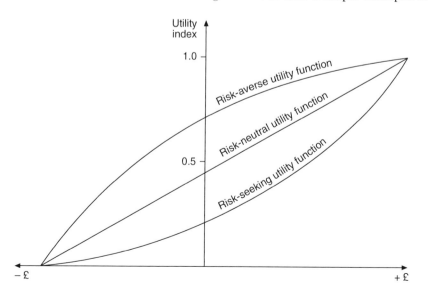

I was to give a destitute person £10 it would probably represent quite a significant amount of money to them. If I was to give £10 to somebody who already had £100, it would still be fairly significant to them. However, if I was to give £10 to a millionaire it would make no practical difference to their financial position. In other words, although each individual experiences the same absolute increase in their wealth, their perception of the increase is very different. We can see that this is to do with the increase in wealth relative to existing wealth. We can take this a stage further and consider the situation where I am offered an even chance bet that I will win or lose £5. Should I take it? The answer is no. Let us say I start from the position where I have £100. The relative difference between £95 and £100 is greater than the relative difference between £100 and £105 (it is 5.26% compared to 5%) so, relatively speaking, the £5 I stand to lose is worth more than the £5 I stand to gain. Buying a lottery ticket is not really the same thing as the risks involved in investment since the purchaser compares the possible £millions to be won with the £1 spent on the ticket and whilst the odds against winning are huge, they see that the amount to be won can change their life whilst the £1 risked will not.

Returning to Figure 9.1, which illustrates the possible utility functions for the three categories of attitudes to risk, it follows that the greater the aversion or attraction to risk, the more pronounced will be the concavity and convexity respectively of the utility functions, and vice versa. However as we have already pointed out, we can effectively ignore risk seeking and even risk-neutral attitudes as being illogical.

The implications of this for investment decision making are, at first sight, profound. Even if we assume that all investors are risk averse, it means that they are likely to have different attitudes towards the risks that they take and hence different people will require different rates of return for the same level of risk. It also means that relatively simple measures of expected return and risk such as the arithmetic mean and the variance of predicted returns will be inadequate in terms of their ability to predict decisions. Indeed, attitudes to downside risk (i.e. the risk of loss) may be such that even the possibility of huge returns will not compensate for the possibility of relatively modest losses. It has been suggested that corporate decision makers may well be more risk averse than the investors in companies.

Dealing with risk

Given the above, it would seem that it is impossible to define risk return relationships that are universally appropriate. Whilst it is true that different individuals require different levels of return before they are willing to take risks, in practice this means that there will be an equilibrium position where the returns on risky investments are such that they are sufficiently high that there will be just enough investment money available to satisfy the need for investment funds. We shall see later that, in fact, the return for the risk that matters is actually defined by the function of supply and demand in financial markets.

Diversification

The best solutions we have for arriving at appropriate discount rates, relating risk and return, are based on the concept of diversification. The nineteenth century Scottish–American millionaire philanthropist, Andrew Carnegie, is reported to have said 'The way to make a fortune is to put all your eggs into one basket and then watch the basket very carefully'. In fact, as we shall see, this is a high risk strategy. Choosing the right basket might indeed lead to the making of a fortune but choosing the wrong basket could turn out to be the way to lose one! As we will demonstrate, a more logical approach to investment is to diversify and thus spread our risks. It is beyond the scope of this text to go into the mathematics of diversification (see Lumby and Jones 1999 chapter 11 for this) however, it is important to have a feel for the significance of this. Putting our money in a number of different investments means that we can reduce the risks to which we are exposed without suffering a corresponding reduction in the returns we enjoy. Taken at its simplest level, a kiosk selling both ice cream and hot drinks might be expected to experience more stable patterns of sales and hence income, than one that only sells ice cream. This is because the weather is a significant, non-controllable factor in determining the level of sales for each group of goods and we can expect the demand for ice cream and hot drinks to be negatively correlated in terms of weather conditions. Developing this idea further, we find that as the number of different investments (or business activities) increases, so the significance of the risks associated with each individual activity diminishes and the risks arising from the relationships between the investments become more significant. In technical terms, the variance of the returns of the individual investments become less significant whilst the covariances of the returns become more significant. If the covariances are high it means that the investments have a high level of correlation of returns (i.e. a change in return in one investment will be expected to be accompanied by a similar change in the others) and the benefits of diversification will be limited.

Unique and market risk

The study of diversification or, as it is more commonly referred to, portfolio theory has resulted in the identification of two types of company risk.

The first, unique or non-systematic risk, is specific to the business. For instance, the business might have a particularly charismatic chief executive who makes a really significant contribution to the prosperity of the company. If something were to happen to this person, we might expect the company's performance to suffer. So, if Bill Gates or Richard Branson were to be forced to retire through ill health or a ballooning accident, the profitability of Microsoft and Virgin might be expected to suffer in the medium to long term. A good example of this would seem to be the case of Laura Ashley. Other examples of unique risk would be things like a food company being responsible for a serious outbreak of food-poisoning, or (slightly less uniquely!) the tobacco industry being hit by very large compensation claims for the damage done to its customers over the years.

The important thing about unique or non-systematic risk is that to all intents and purposes it can be diversified away. Studies have shown that investment in around 20 companies is sufficient to ensure that unique risk has virtually no impact on the returns enjoyed by the investor. Taken at its simplest, an evenly weighted portfolio of 20 shares would mean that each share accounts for 5% of the total investment. Even if a business in which we had invested lost 50% of its value in one year (which is unusual but not impossible) we have only suffered a 2.5% loss and it might be expected that there is a fair chance of something good happening to one of the other companies in the portfolio. In other words, the effect of diversification is that the risks specific to the individual companies are evened out. Given that we can diversify away this unique risk, it follows that we should not be too worried about it and we should not be looking for returns to compensate us for taking it.

There is, however, a second type of risk that we cannot diversify away. This is the risk related to the economy as a whole and it is this risk that, in the end, determines the appropriate rate of return on shares and physical investments. This risk is called market or systematic risk. Different businesses display differing levels of systematic risk and it is this that determines the level of return that is appropriate for each one.

So, what determines the degree to which a particular firm's shares are exposed to systematic risk? In other words, why do some companies have high systematic risk and other companies low systematic risk?

If we define systematic risk as being the extent to which a company's cash flow is affected by economy wide or non-company-specific factors, then there are likely to be three main determinants of that systematic risk exposure:

1. the sensitivity of the company's revenues to the general level of economic activity in the economy and other macro-economic factors;
2. the proportion of fixed to variable costs (i.e. the degree of cost sensitivity);
3. the level of financial gearing or leverage (i.e. the amount of interest bearing debt compared to shareholder equity).

In other words, in the first instance, what makes a company risky in systematic risk terms is the degree to which the company's revenues are determined by macro economic factors largely outside the control of its management. This risk can then be either increased or reduced by the proportions of fixed and variable costs involved and further increased by exposure to debt.

A company manufacturing machine tools might be seen as an example of high revenue sensitivity. If the economy is booming and wage levels are rising demand for all kinds of products will increase. Manufacturers will take this opportunity to buy new machines either to replace old ones or to increase capacity. However, if the economy is depressed then demand for many products will decline and it may not be necessary for manufacturers to buy any machinery at all, preferring to make do with existing machines until the economy begins to pick up. Thus the cash flows for a machine tool manufacturer can be expected particularly volatile, being especially sensitive to general economic conditions, and these general economic conditions cannot be diversified away in a portfolio.

On the other hand, a food retailer, such as Tesco or Sainsburys, might be taken as an example of a business with a low degree of revenue sensitivity. Generally speaking, in both good times and bad, the supermarket's revenue is likely to be little changed. In bad times people have still got to eat to live, while in good times spare cash will probably be spent on other things (such as holidays and cars), rather than increasing the consumption of food.

The second factor is related to fixed costs. Fixed costs are those costs that do not change with the level of business activity such as rent, rates and a significant part of salaries. This is contrasted with variable costs such as raw materials and salespersons which do change according to the level of sales. Where a company has a high level of fixed costs relative to total costs its net cash flows will be more volatile than would otherwise be the case. This is because it will still have to pay the fixed costs, no matter how high or low its income might be.

The final factor, the relationship of debt to equity is similar in that the company will still have to pay interest on the debt no matter what its level of cash flows before interest.

These secondary factors are particularly important for companies that have relatively volatile income flows. However for firms with low revenue sensitivity, the proportion of fixed to variable costs will make little difference to its riskiness. As its revenues are relatively stable, it should at all times be able to cover its operating and financing costs, whether they are fixed or variable.

Given the foregoing, and assuming that managers – like investors – are risk averse, it should not surprise us to find that firms with high revenue sensitivity try to minimize the proportion of both fixed financing and fixed operating costs. On the other hand, the management of firms with low revenue sensitivity can afford to be more relaxed about such issues.

The significance of systematic risk is that because it is unavoidable for the company, it is this that will determine the appropriate rate of return for the investor.

The Capital Asset Pricing Model and Beta

Given the ideas concerning systematic risk described in the previous section, it should come as no surprise that there is a measure of the volatility of the returns on the shares of companies. This has been given the symbol β i.e. the Greek letter beta. It is a measure of the volatility of the returns of a specific share compared to the market.

This raises the question as to just what 'the market' might be. In theory it is a perfectly weighted portfolio of all economic assets in the world but such a portfolio would be impossible to identify for many reasons. So, in practice, an approximation is used. This will normally be the stock exchange for the country in which the company is based. This raises yet another difficulty in that we are still in the position of having to assume that these markets set appropriate prices, and hence returns, for shares. Whether they do are not has been the most researched area in the whole of the social sciences since the identification of systematic errors in price setting would result in the ability of the researcher to make large if not vast amounts of money.[1] Since we have no real evidence to the contrary, we will assume that financial markets set the most appropriate prices for shares available but it should be recognized that the prices and returns can only be described as 'appropriate given the available information' and not 'correct'.

The measure β is calculated on past market data and is actually the covariance of the returns of a share with the market divided by the variance of the market. As the covariance of a series with itself is the same as its variance, the β of the market is 1.

There is a valuation system based on the idea of β. This is called the capital asset pricing model. This defines the expected return on a share j as:

$$E(r_j) = r_F + [E(r_M) - r_F] \, b_j$$

Where r_F is an appropriate risk free rate of return,

$[E(r_M) - r_F]$ is the difference between the expected return on the market and the risk free rate, in other words the market risk premium

and b_j is the β of the share.

So, if we estimate the most likely relevant risk free rate to be 8%, we expect the market risk premium to be 7% and we calculate that the investment with which we are concerned is slightly more risky than average and has a beta of 1.2 we would calculate its appropriate return to be 8% + (15% – 8%)1.2 = 16.4%.

Of course, the beta has been calculated by reference to past market data and the expected return on the market and the risk free rate are forward looking but it is possible to identify reasonable estimates of medium to long term risk free returns and, historically, the market risk premium has been somewhere around 6–8%. The appendix to this chapter provides an introduction to the techniques involved in this type of analysis.

It is not normally necessary to calculate β as estimates for quoted companies are available from a number of sources such as the London Business School Risk Management Service.

Beta and project risk

The analysis we have discussed above is based on market and share prices and returns but it can be adapted to provide discount rates for individual projects. The β of a business is the weighted average of the βs of its individual sources of finance but it is also the beta of its assets. There are many differing capital instruments issued by companies but all of these can be said to be based on the two pure forms of instrument which is to say, equity (ordinary shares) and debt. For the purposes of our analysis we will limit ourselves to the consideration of these two but most of the other variants can be accommodated by this approach without too much difficulty. We will also assume that debt is riskless in the sense that the interest on debt is not correlated with the required return on the market. This being so, the β of debt will be zero.

Example 1

$$\beta \text{ company (assets)} = \beta \text{ equity} \times \frac{E}{E+D} + \beta \text{ debt} \times \frac{D}{E+D}$$

Where E = value of equity and D = value of debt

But β debt = zero so:

$$\beta \text{ company (assets)} = \beta \text{ equity} \times \frac{E}{D+E}$$

You find that the equity β for a company is 1.2 and that its debt is 20% of the total value of the company. The average β for the assets (or projects) is thus:

$$1.2 \times 80\% = .96$$

Once the project β has been estimated, we can use this to calculate the appropriate return on a new (similar) project through the CAPM. However, as always, this assumes that we can define an appropriate risk free rate and also a market rate.

The example we have looked at assumes that there is no tax effect but in the real world it is likely that interest on debt will be a tax allowable expense. This alters the equation somewhat (for a detailed explanation see Lumby and Jones 1999 page 504 on).

Example 2

Asset β taking tax into account

$$\beta \text{ company (assets)} = \beta \text{ equity} \times \frac{E}{E+D(1-Tc)} + \beta \text{ debt} \times \frac{D}{E+D(1-Tc)}$$

Where E = value of equity D = value of debt and Tc is the tax relief on debt interest

But β debt = zero so:

$$\beta \text{ company (assets)} = \beta \text{ equity} \times \frac{E}{E+D(1-Tc)}$$

You find that the equity β for a company is 1.4 and that its debt is 40% of the total value of the company. Tax relief on debt interest is 25%. The average β for the assets (or projects) is thus:

$$1.4 \times \frac{60}{60+40(1-.25)} = .93$$

It should be noted that the effect of debt interest being tax deductible is that increased borrowing has less effect on the risk of equity than would otherwise be the case.

Weighted average cost of capital

Another way of looking at the appropriate return for a company is to calculate its weighted average cost of capital (WACC). This is really only possible for a company that has a share price quoted and, as we shall see, the technique has certain limitations. However, under certain circumstances it can provide useful guidance as to an appropriate discount rate to use in investment decisions.

The cost of capital for a company will be the weighted average of the component parts of its long term capital. Again we will assume that this is debt and equity. To estimate the proportions debt and equity we use market values and not figures taken from financial statements. So if a company has a market capitalization of £75m (i.e. the total value of its shares on the stock exchange) and long term debt of £25m it would be 75% equity and 25% debt. If the return on equity is 20% and the average after tax cost of debt is 8% than we can identify the company's cost of capital as being:

$$(.75 \times 20\%) + (.25 \times 8\%) = 17\%$$

If a new project is available that is broadly similar in risk terms to the company's existing projects (or, at least, the average risk of existing projects) then 17% will be an appropriate rate of return to use in assessing that project. It is possible that the company will borrow at 8% to fund the project and at first sight it would appear that 8% is the appropriate rate to use. However, this is not the case because borrowing will change the level of shareholder risk (upwards) and will thus increase the required return on the equity of the company. The net effect of this is that the project will still need to generate at least 17% to be worthwhile.

It is generally not too difficult to estimate the cost of borrowing of a company but the calculation of the cost of equity is more difficult. It has to recognized that the price that the market sets for shares is based on expectations rather than past performance and this has a significant effect on the implied returns on shares. The market is actually attempting to value the cash flows that are expected to be paid back to shareholders over the whole of the rest of the company's existence. In practice this will be dividends. However we are concerned with all future dividends and we are forced to assume that these will continue infinitely (otherwise we would have to identify the point at which they would stop!). However, because dividends will normally increase over time, we cannot use the simple formula for a perpetuity ($V = C/R$). We do not actually know what will happen in the future so we are forced to assume that the future will be broadly similar to the past. This is no different from any other forecasting system but it does raise significant questions as to the likely accuracy of our results. Lumby and Jones 1999 pp 376–389 discusses this issue but it is sufficient for our purposes to know that there is a mathematical formula for estimating the cost of equity. This is known as the dividend valuation model or the Gordon Constant Growth Model after its inventor. This states that:

$$P_E = \frac{d1}{K_E - g}$$

Where P_E is the price of a share E
              d1 is the dividend to be received in twelve months' time
              K_E is return on the share
              g is the estimated growth rate of dividends

Our normal assumption is that the growth in future dividends will be the same as the historic growth in dividends and the figure that we will normally know is the share price.

Example 3

A company's share price is £1.10 and it has paid out the following dividends

Year	Dividend per share (pence)
t_{-4}	8.0
t_{-3}	9.0
t_{-2}	9.5
t_{-1}	10.5
t_0	12.0

The dividends have grown from 8.0 to 12.0 over 4 years. Average growth is g

$$8.0\,(1+g)^4 = 12$$
$$1 + g = (12/8)^{1/4} = 1.1067$$
$$g = 1.1067 - 1 = 0.1067 \text{ or } 10.67\%$$

We can now calculate a cost of equity by rearranging the formula above so that

$$K_E = \frac{d_0\,(1+g)}{P_E} + g$$

$$K_E = \frac{12\,(1.067)}{110} + .1067$$

$$K_E = .1207 + .1067 = 22.74\%$$

Of course we have made some rather heroic assumptions here. In particular we have assumed that the future will be like the past but, without evidence to the contrary, it is difficult to see what else we can assume. We are implicitly assuming that the business will be able to find new projects to produce the cash flows to pay out the dividends ad infinitum but again, it is difficult to see what else we might assume. We are thus not suggesting that the figure calculated is completely correct but it is at least an indication of the company's existing cost of capital. As one academic put it, 'there's bad news and worse news . . . we can't prove that it works but we haven't got anything else!'

A comparison of Beta and WACC

Neither of the two techniques discussed above is guaranteed to provide the correct discount rate for all projects. They are calculated at a single point in time and are then applied to a decision that may live with the business for many years, over which time things will invariably change. However, both techniques provide us with some indication of what the required rate of return should be. In fact there is really no inconsistency between the two approaches from a theoretical point of view even though there might be in their application. WACC is really only valid as a measure of required return so long as the project in question is of the same risk class as the existing 'average' project. If anything different were to be considered, it would be necessary to identify another appropriate WACC, perhaps by looking at another business. In a similar way, the existing β of the business should only be used to assess a project when it is similar to the risk class of existing projects and also when the financial risk of the business has been allowed for. If the former is not the case, it is possible to estimate an appropriate β by reference to businesses that are considered to operate in the appropriate area and it is also possible to make allowances for differing capital structures. The use of β in investment decision making would not seem to be very widespread, perhaps because of its perceived complexity. However, it does provide us with a way of looking at risk and it should emphasise that the appropriate return on a project will indeed depend upon its risk.

Summary

The decision techniques discussed in previous chapters assumed that we had firm data to work with but this is very rarely true in the real world. We recognized that individual investors are likely to be unhappy about taking risks unless they are rewarded for doing so.

- It is not possible to identify the attitudes to risk of the investors in a company and hence the simplest measures of risk and return are inadequate as ways of determining risk return trade offs.

- Diversification provides a mechanism for reducing risk without necessarily reducing returns.

- There are two distinct types of risk, systematic and non-systematic. Whilst non-systematic risk can be diversified away, systematic risk cannot. It follows that exposure to systematic risk will require a return to compensate.

- The higher the systematic risk, the higher the required return. This applies to both companies and the individual projects in which they invest.

- Beta (β) is a measure of systematic risk that can be used to determine an appropriate rate of return for both companies and projects.

- Weighted average cost of capital (WACC) can also be used to determine rates of return but care must be taken to ensure that this is used appropriately.

- There are no techniques that are guaranteed to provide the 'right' answer but the techniques we have discussed do at least provide us with some indication as to what the right answer might look like.

Appendix

The β of a share is calculated by dividing the covariance of its returns with those of the market by the variance of the returns of the market. This would normally be calculated over a large number of observations but we will illustrate the calculation by calculating β based on only six observations.

Time	Return of market for period	Return of share j for period
1	14%	16%
2	18%	11%
3	8%	12%
4	16%	19%
5	12%	10%
6	16%	16%

We calculate variance as:

$$\frac{(Rt - \text{Mean Return})^2}{\text{number of time periods}}$$

Where Rt is the return in time period t.

The mean return is the sum of all the returns divided by the number of time periods so the mean return on the market for the period in question is

$$(14 + 18 + 8 + 16 + 12 + 16) \div 6 = 14\%$$

So the variance of the return on the market is :

$$
\begin{aligned}
(14 - 14)^2 &= 0 \\
(18 - 14)^2 &= 16 \\
(8 - 14)^2 &= 36 \\
(16 - 14)^2 &= 4 \\
(12 - 14)^2 &= 4 \\
(16 - 14)^2 &= 4 \\
\text{Total} &= 64 \div 6 = 10.667
\end{aligned}
$$

Covariance is

$$\frac{(Rt \text{ market} - \text{mean return market}) (Rt \text{ share } j - \text{mean return share } j)}{\text{number of time periods}}$$

The mean return for share j over the six time periods is

$$(16 + 11 + 12 + 19 + 10 + 16) \div 6 = 14 \%$$

The covariance is thus calculated as

$$(14 - 14) \times (16 - 14) = 0$$
$$(18 - 14) \times (11 - 14) = -12$$
$$(\ 8 - 14) \times (12 - 14) = +12$$
$$(16 - 14) \times (19 - 14) = +10$$
$$(12 - 14) \times (10 - 14) = +\ 8$$
$$(16 - 14) \times (16 - 14) = +\ 4$$
$$\text{Total} \qquad\qquad\qquad = 22 \div 6 = 3.667$$

So the β of share j is 3.667 / 10.667 = .34

In other words, in terms of market related risk, the risk of this share is well below the average for the market.

Note

1. It appeared that an investment hedge fund in the USA called Long Term Capital Management had found such an opportunity. Amongst its partners were two Nobel Prize winning academics called Robert Merton and Myron Scholes who had (with Fisher Black) devised the option pricing model. The *Washington Post* of September 24th 1998 reported that LTCM had lost more than $4 billion and had to be bailed out by a group of banks at the request of the US Federal Reserve

Further reading

1. For a much fuller explanation of the issues raised here see S. Lumby and C.J. Jones *Investment Appraisal and Financial Decisions* International Thomson Press 1999, particularly chapters 11, 12, 16, 17 and 21.
2. K. Peasnell, 'The Capital Asset pricing Model', in M. Firth and S. Keane (eds) *Issues in Finance*, Philip Allen 1986 provides a very good review of this topic.
3. J. M. Stern and D.H. Chew (eds) *The Revolution in Corporate Finance* Blackwell 1992 contains a number of very good articles including J MacQueen 'Beta is Dead! Long live beta!' and B. Rosenberg and A. Rudd 'The Corporate Uses of Beta'.
4. There are a number of interesting articles which are, in the main, critical of the use of the WACC as an NPV discount rate. For example, see: F.D. Arditti, 'The Weighted Average Cost of Capital: Some Questions on its Definition, Interpretation and Use', *Journal of Finance*, September 1973, and M.J. Brennan, 'A New Look at the Weighted Average Cost of Capital', *Journal of Business Finance*, Summer 1973.
5. Particularly good, in this context, are: S.M. Keane, 'The Cost of Capital as a Financial Decision Tool', *Journal of Business Finance and Accounting*, Autumn 1978; H.P. Lanser, 'Valuation, Gains from Leverage and the Weighted Average Cost of Capital as a Cut-off Rate', *Engineering Economist*, Fall 1983; and E.F. Brigham and T.C. Tapley, 'Financial Leverage and the Use of the NPV Criterion: A Re-examination', *Financial Management*, Summer 1985.

Quickie questions

1. Why is it likely that investors will be risk averse?
2. How does diversification reduce the risks of investment?
3. What is the difference between systematic and unsystematic risk?
4. What factors determine the exposure of a company to systematic risk?
5. Write down the standard CAPM expression for the expected return on a share X.
6. If the risk free rate of return is 6% and the market rate of return is 13%, what would be the expected return on a share with a beta of 1.3?
7. If the return on the shares of a company are 20%, it borrows at 8%, tax is 25% and the company is made up of 80% equity and 20% debt, what will its weighted average cost of capital be?
8. Despite the fact that the two approaches are not inconsistent, it would seem likely that the use of β will be more reliable in determining appropriate discount rates than WACC. Why should this be so?

Problems

1. The returns on the stock exchange and on the shares for Divco over five periods are as follows:

Period	Return of market for period	Return of share in Divco for period
1	12%	14%
2	16%	16%
3	18%	17%
4	14%	14%
5	16%	15%
6	8%	10%

Required
(a) Calculate the β (beta) of shares in Divco.
(b) The current market capitalisation of shares in the company is £25m and the company has debt of £5m. Interest on debt is tax deductible and company tax is paid at 30%. What is the average β for the projects undertaken by the company?
(c) If the expected risk free rate of return is 8% calculate an appropriate discount for Divco to use to assess a new project, assuming that the project is of the same risk class as average and that the capital structure of the business will not change as the result of the investment.

2. Stanley Park plc has a share price of £1.85 and there are 20m shares in issue. In addition the company has debt of £8.2m on which it pays interest of 12%. Interest is a tax allowable expense and the company pays tax at the rate of 30%. It has just paid a dividend of 14 pence per share and the dividends for the past six years are as follows:

t_{-6}	t_{-5}	t_{-4}	t_{-3}	t_{-2}	t_{-1}
7.5p	8p	9p	10p	11p	12.5p

Required:

(a) Calculate the weighted average cost of capital for Stanley Park plc.

(b) Discuss the assumptions underlying the calculation you have carried out and how reliable the figure for cost of equity might be.

(c) Discuss the applicability of WACC as a discount rate for a new project to be undertaken by the company.

10 Traditional and technological approaches to risk

Introduction

In this chapter we examine some of the more traditional approaches that management use to cope with the problem of risk in capital investment decision making. We will also, briefly, consider an alternative approach to risk, utilising the power of desktop computers.

We have already introduced the concept of risk and the idea that investors are risk-averse and so require a reward for taking on risk. The last chapter introduced two different but related approaches to setting a risk adjusted discount rate that are based on economic theory. However, there are other techniques that are used to allow for risk in decision making.

Expected net present value

In an uncertain world, even assuming the presence of perfect capital markets, use of the NPV method of investment appraisal cannot be said necessarily to lead to optimal investment decisions or to the maximization of shareholder wealth. All it can lead to is the *expected* maximization of wealth. Hindsight, that is knowledge about the actual outcome of past events, may suggest different advice from that given by the NPV appraisal rule, because the latter is based only upon estimates of the future.

When we examined the rationale and operation of the NPV appraisal method, we paid very little attention to how the estimates of a project's future net cash flows were derived. In practice, many decision-makers do not produce a series of 'point' (i.e., single figure) estimates of each year's net cash flow but instead construct a *range* of estimates.

For example, a project may have an initial cost of £1000 and a life of three years, but the level of the net cash flows may be uncertain, depending, say, on the general state of the industry in which the company operates.

Example 1 shows a simple illustration of the estimated annual net cash flows based on three economic states: boom, normal and depressed conditions. From these data the project's NPV is calculated in each state and a figure is attached expressing the probability or likelihood of each state actually occurring. These NPVs are combined to produce the arithmetic mean (i.e., average) NPV of the project: the *expected* NPV of the project, given the different estimates and their probabilities of occurrence. It is upon the value (and more importantly, the sign) of this expected net present value (ENPV) that the normal investment appraisal decision rule is applied.

Example 1

Paraiso PLC is considering whether to purchase a machine to produce glue for ceramic tiles. The machine costs £1000 and is expected to have a productive life of three years. However, the estimate of the annual net revenue from the machine is uncertain and depends on the state of the house-building industry. The company's management have produced the following estimates:

	State of industry	0	1	2	3
(I)	Boom	− 1000	+ 500	+ 700	+ 980
(II)	Normal	− 1000	+ 500	+ 600	+ 700
(III)	Depressed	− 1000	+ 300	+ 300	+ 250

Paraiso normally use a 10% discount rate in project appraisal, believing that this correctly reflects the risk of the project. On this basis, the project NPVs have been calculated as follows:

State	NPV
I	+ 769
II	+ 477
III	− 291

Latest figures from the Building Trades Research Institute suggest the following probabilities for the industry's future prospects:

State	Probability
Boom	0.20
Normal	0.60
Depressed	0.20

On this basis, Paraiso PLC estimate the project's expected (i.e., arithmetic mean) NPV:

State	Prob.		NPV		
I	0.20	×	+ 769	=	+ 153.8
II	0.60	×	+ 477	=	+ 286.2
III	0.20	×	− 291	=	− 52.2
					+ 387.8 ENPV

As the project has a positive expected net present value (ENPV), it is accepted.

It is important to notice that, as this example shows, management not only has the task of estimating the project's annual net cash flow in each of the different states of the industry, but must also estimate the probability of the occurrence of each state. (Strictly, these are *subjective* probabilities, because they are based upon management's subjective judgement, rather than on past observations of similar events.)

In addition, it is also assumed in Example 1 that, whichever state of the industry occurs, the industry will remain fixed in that state over the duration of the project. If this assumption is unrealistic, further adjustments will need to be made to the ENPV calculation. Example 2 illustrates this more complex type of situation.

Example 2

Maravista PLC design and manufacture clothes for the 13–15 years segment of the fashion industry. The success or otherwise of their products depends upon whether they are in fashion in any particular year.

The company's management are considering investing £40 000 to produce a range of leather belts which, they believe, will have a two-year fashion life. However, the outcome of the project is dependent upon whether the belt design turns out to be in fashion and hence, successful (State I) or out of fashion and so a relative failure (State II), or a marketing disaster (State III).

Maravista's marketing analysts have studied the situation carefully and have estimated the following net revenue figures for the project (£000s):

Year 1 State	Prob	Net rev.	Year 2 State	Prob.	Net rev.
I	0.5	+ 80	I	0.6	+ 100
			II	0.3	+ 80
			III	0.1	+ 20
II	0.3	+ 30	I	0.4	+ 80
			II	0.3	+ 40
			III	0.3	+ 10
III	0.2	+ 10	I	0.1	+ 70
			II	0.4	+ 40
			III	0.5	+ 5

For example, as Maravista's marketing analyst explained to the chief executive, we believe that in the first year of the product's life it has a 50% chance of being in fashion and, hence, a success. Given it is successful in the first year, then there is a 60% chance of being similarly successful in its second year, a 30% chance of it then being a relative failure and, finally, a 10% chance of turning into a marketing disaster.

On this basis, the analysis can be simplified by estimating the expected (i.e., arithmetic mean) revenue in the second year, for each possible first year state:

Year 1 state	Year 2 rev.		Prob.		
I	+ 100	×	0.6	=	+ 60
	+ 80	×	0.3	=	+ 24
	+ 20	×	0.1	=	+ 2
					+ 86 Expected Yr 2 net revenue
II	+ 80	×	0.4	=	+ 32
	+ 40	×	0.3	=	+ 12
	+ 10	×	0.3	=	+ 3
					+ 47 Expected Yr 2 net revenue

	+ 70	×	0.1	=	+ 7
III	+ 40	×	0.4	=	+ 16
	+ 5	×	0.5	=	+ 2.5
					+ 25.5 Expected Yr 2 net revenue

Now, the project's expected cash flows have been simplified to:

Year 1 state	Prob.	Year 0 outlay	Year 1 net rev.	Year 2 expected rev.
I	0.5	− 40	+ 80	+ 86
II	0.3	− 40	+ 30	+ 47
III	0.2	− 40	+ 10	+ 25.5

Maravista usually uses a 20% discount rate to reflect the high-risk nature of the fashion industry and, on this basis, the project's expected NPV can be calculated:

Year 1 state	Prob.		NPV		
I	0.5	×	+ 86.4	=	+ 43.2
II	0.3	×	+ 17.6	=	+ 5.3
III	0.2	×	− 14.0	=	− 2.8
					+ 45.7 ENPV

As the project has a positive expected net present value of approximately £45 700, Maravista PLC decides to proceed with production.

Limitations of ENPV

The concept of *expected* NPV (indeed an expected IRR could be similarly calculated) has been found by management to be useful for project appraisal in an uncertain world because it provides an average value of the proposed project's performance. However, it is important to realize that it *cannot* be said to take account of risk, because all that the ENPV calculation provides is a measure of the investment's *expected* performance, whereas risk is concerned with the likelihood that the *actual* performance may diverge from what is expected.

Example 3 illustrates this point very simply. Two mutually exclusive projects have identical expected NPVs. Therefore on the basis of the ENPV decision rule, the management should be indifferent between them – they are both expected to make a positive NPV of £8.5m.

However, almost certainly, the management of Armacao PLC will *not* be indifferent, but instead will strongly prefer the silicon chip project. The reason for this is that this project is likely to be viewed as being less risky than the semi-conductor project.

Example 3

Armacao PLC wants to enter the electronics industry and is considering two possible projects. Both projects require the same outlay of £10m and both have the same expected net present value. However, because this is a venture into a new area of business, Armacao only want to undertake *one* of the projects. The figures are as follows (£m.):

State of world	Prob.	Semi-conductor project NPV	Silicon chip project NPV
Strong growth	0.20	+ 30.6	+ 13.0
Slow growth	0.60	+ 8.5	+ 8.5
Recession	0.20	− 13.6	+ 4.0

Semi-conductor project:	0.2	×	+ 30.6	=	+ 6.12
	0.6	×	+ 8.5	=	+ 5.10
	0.2	×	− 13.6	=	− 2.72
					+ 8.5 ENPV

Silicon chip project:	0.2	×	+ 13.0	=	+ 2.6
	0.6	×	+ 8.5	=	+ 5.1
	0.2	×	+ 4.0	=	+ 0.8
					+ 8.5 ENPV

Risk is to do with the fact that the project's actual outcome can vary from what is expected. In this respect the actual outcome can either be better (the *upside potential*) or worse (the *downside risk*) than the expected outcome. A 'gambling' investor will focus most of his attention on the upside potential, but a 'risk-averse' investor will be more concerned with looking at the expected outcome and the downside risk.

Given the assumption (which is generally correct) that investors *dislike* risk – they are *risk averse*, the managers of Armacao PLC are likely to view the silicon chip project as less risky because, even in the *worst* state of the world, it is still expected to produce a small positive NPV. In contrast, the semi-conductor project will produce a large negative NPV of £13.6m if the economy moves into recession.

There is however one set of circumstances in which the ENPV approach does 'allow' for risk. That is to say, there is one set of circumstances when, if faced by the two alternative projects in Example 3, it would be correct to conclude that the company would be indifferent between them because they produce the same ENPV.

Those circumstances would be where the company intended to undertake a *large number* of similar or identical projects. In that case the ENPV indicates (quite correctly) the average outcome of each individual investment. Thus if the company were to undertake (say) 100 semi-conductor projects, then twenty of them would produce an NPV of 1 £30.6m, sixty would produce an NPV of 1 £8.5m and the remaining twenty would produce negative NPVs of £13.6m. Thus the *average* outcome *per project* would be a positive NPV of £8.5m.

Similarly, the average outcome of 100 silicon chip projects would be a + £8.5m NPV per project. Twenty of the projects would produce an NPV of + £13m, and so on. Therefore, in these circumstances, the company would be indifferent between the two projects, given they have the same ENPV.

Unfortunately, most capital investment projects are *not* undertaken a great number of times, but are unique, one-off investments. It therefore follows that the idea of ENPV remains as an inadequate way of 'allowing for' or 'indicating' a project's risk.

Value of additional information

One interesting use of the ENPV technique is that it can help to indicate the value of additional information. Example 4 illustrates such a situation.

Example 4

Alvor PLC has developed a new product and has now reached the stage of making a decision whether or not to undertake manufacture. The manufacturing machinery would cost £90 000 and the project is expected to have a life of six years. However, the performance of the product in the market place is uncertain.

Alvor's marketing director has indicated that there are four possible outcomes (states I, II, III or IV): very successful, moderately successful, disappointing and complete failure. On this basis, the company's management accountants have estimated the possible NPVs and the project's overall expected NPV (£000s):

State of world	Prob.		NPV		
I	0.2	×	+ 110	=	+ 22
II	0.5	×	+ 70	=	+ 35
III	0.2	×	+ 5	=	+ 1
IV	0.1	×	− 25	=	− 2.5
				ENPV	+ 55.5

As the ENPV is positive, the company decides to go ahead with production but, just before this decision is implemented, Carvalho Intelligence PLC, a market research company, offers to undertake a survey of the new product which will indicate, *in advance of production*, what outcome is likely to occur. The cost of the survey would be £2000 and the management of Alvor PLC are now trying to decide what should be done.

The approach to take is to examine what action the company would take in response to the various possible outcomes of the market research. Clearly, if the market research indicated that either states I, II or III would occur, the company would undertake manufacture, as to do so would generate a positive NPV. However, if the market research indicated that state IV would occur, the company would not proceed with manufacture, as manufacture would lead to a negative NPV of £25 000.

Survey indicates: State	Company's investment decision	Prob. of survey result		NPV outcome of decision		
I	Accept	0.2	×	+ 110	=	+ 22
II	Accept	0.5	×	+ 70	=	+ 35
III	Accept	0.2	×	+ 5	=	+ 1
IV	Reject	0.1	×	0	=	0
					ENPV	+ 58

Therefore:

	£
ENPV of project *with* market research survey	58 000
ENPV of project *without* market research survey	55 500
Maximum worth of survey	2500
Cost of survey	2000
Net benefit of survey to Alvor PLC	£+ 500

On the basis of this analysis, the survey is worthwhile. The company should undertake the survey prior to manufacture and only proceed to manufacture if the survey indicates that either states, I, II or III will occur.

In Example 4 the additional information was always correct. A more complex analysis involving the opportunity cost concept is required if the additional information may be incorrect. This situation is illustrated in Example 5.

Example 5

Centianes PLC is considering undertaking a project as follows:

Outcome	Prob.				NPV	
Success	0.6	×	+ 100	=	+ 60	
Failure	0.4	×	− 40	=	− 16	
				ENPV	+ 44	

A market research survey will indicate *with 90% accuracy* which outcome will actually occur. The maximum worth of the survey can be estimated as follows:
There are four possible states of the world:

State	
A:	Survey indicates 'success' and is correct.
B:	Survey indicates 'success' and is wrong.
C:	Survey indicates 'failure' and is correct.
D:	Survey indicates 'failure' and is wrong.

There is a 60% chance the survey will indicate 'success' and a 40% that it will indicate 'failure'. There is a 90% chance that the survey result will be correct and a 10% chance that it will be wrong. The probabilities of each of the four 'states of the world' will be given by the product of the individual probabilities:

State					Prob.
A	0.6	×	0.9	=	0.54
B	0.6	×	0.1	=	0.06
C	0.4	×	0.9	=	0.36
D	0.4	×	0.1	=	0.04

Therefore:

State	Decision	Prob.		Outcome		
A	Accept	0.54	×	+ 100 NPV	=	+ 54.0
B	Accept	0.06	×	− 40 NPV	=	− 2.4
C	Reject	0.36	×	0 NPV	=	0
D	Reject	0.04	×	− 100 NPV*	=	− 4.0
				ENPV	=	+ 47.6

ENPV with survey	:	+ 47.6	
ENPV without survey	:	+ 44.0	
Max worth of survey	:	+ 3.6	

*Notice that this is an opportunity cost. If the survey incorrectly forecasts 'failure' and we act on the survey's advice, we forgo the opportunity of gaining an NPV of +100.

The abandonment decision

Another 'special case' of the ENPV decision is the evaluation of an option to abandon a project before it reaches the end of its life. Such an analysis is illustrated in Example 6.

However, the limitations of the abandonment analysis should be noted. The first is that when *multiple* abandonment points are available – such as at the end of Years 1, 2 and 3 of a project with a life of four years – there is a real-world information problem as to how reliable future abandonment values are to be estimated. The second problem is that the analysis of a multiple abandonment point decision is much more complex than that of Example 6. A *dynamic programming* analysis is required. The problem here is that the more complex the analysis required, often the more reluctant are management to accept its advice as they lack an understanding as to how the advice was generated.

Example 6

Irmaos PLC operates a series of photocopier shops in which customers can walk off the street and have their photocopying done immediately. The company normally only keeps its machines for two years before disposing of them on the second-hand market.

They have recently been approached by a photocopier manufacturer who is trying to break into the UK market. Each machine will cost £10 000.

Irmaos believe that the crucial factor is the reliability of the new photocopiers. On past experience they believe that there is only a 60% chance that they will prove to be reliable.

On this basis they have estimated the following net cash flows produced by an individual photocopier:

Photocopier	Yr 1	Yr 2	Scrap
Reliable	+ 8000	+ 6000	+ 400
Unreliable	+ 4000	+ 3000	+ 200

A 15% discount rate is used to reflect the risk of the photocopying business and, on this basis, the project's NPV and ENPV is calculated:

					NPV		Prob.		
Reliable	− 10 000	+ 8000(1.15)$^{-1}$	+ 6400(1.15)$^{-2}$	=	+ 1796	×	0.6	=	+ 1078
Unreliable	− 10 000	+ 4000(1.15)$^{-1}$	+ 3200(1.15)$^{-2}$	=	− 4102	×	0.4	=	− 1641
							ENPV		− 563

On this basis, Irmaos declines to purchase the machines. However, in order to try to get the company to change their mind, the photocopier manufacturer offers to buy back the machines at the end of the first year for 50% of their purchase cost. In other words, Irmaos are being offered an abandonment option. This decision can be analysed as follows:

Assuming that the company purchases a photocopy machine and then, at the end of the first year, decides not to abandon, the resulting NPVs of the decision are as follows:

Photocopier	Yr 1	Yr 2		NPV	Decision taken
Reliable	− 5000(1.15)$^{-1}$	+ 6400(1.15)$^{-2}$	=	+ 491	Don't abandon
Unreliable	− 5000(1.15)$^{-1}$	+ 3200(1.15)$^{-2}$	=	− 1928	Abandon

In each case, the negative cash outflow at Year 1 is an opportunity cost. If the photocopier is not abandoned, the company forgo the opportunity to sell it back to the manufacturer for £5000.

This analysis allows the abandonment decision (at Year 1) to be made. If the photocopier turns out to be reliable, the machine should not be abandoned, as this generates a positive NPV outcome. However, if the photocopier turns out to be unreliable then the company *should* abandon the project at the end of Year 1, because not to do so would incur a negative NPV of £1928.

Having made the abandonment decision, the overall investment decision can then be made:

Photocopier reliable:

Outlay	:	$-$ 10 000			
Net revs	:		+ 8000	+ 6000	
Scrap	:			+ 400	
Net cash flow	:	$-$ 10 000	+ 8000$(1.15)^{-1}$	+ 6400$(1.15)^{-2}$	= + 1796 NPV

Photocopier unreliable:

Outlay	:	$-$ 10 000			
Net revs	:		+ 4000		
Abandon value	:		+ 5000		
Net cash flow	:	$-$ 10 000	+ 9000$(1.15)^{-1}$		= $-$ 2174 NPV

Photocopier	Prob.		NPV		
Reliable	0.6	$\times$	+ 1796	=	+ 1078
Unreliable	0.4	$\times$	$-$ 2174	=	$-$ 870
			ENPV		+ 208

As the project has a positive ENPV, Irmaos should go ahead and purchase the photocopiers, but should abandon the project by selling them back to the manufacturer at the end of the first year if they prove to be unreliable.

Example 7 works through a more complex expected net present value question (which includes a little inflation for added interest!). It is designed to illustrate how the basic principles outlined in some of the earlier, simple examples may be applied in a more complex situation.

Example 7

The directors of Starlite PLC are considering the purchase and exploitation of a disused tin mine which is being offered for sale for £50 000. A review of the mine's history shows that the total amount of pure tin that can be extracted depends upon the type of rock formations in the area and that only the following three possibilities exist:

Rock type	Total tin output	Probability
A	240 tonnes	0.4
B	120 tonnes	0.4
C	72 tonnes	0.2

If Starlite purchases the mine, the first year of ownership will be spent in making the mine and associated smelting plants operational, at a cost of £95 000 payable at the end of the year. Production will start at the beginning of the second year of ownership, when the output of pure tin will be 2 tonnes per month, whatever the type of rock formation. This production rate will remain unchanged until the mine is exhausted. During the first year of production, the directors expect that the resale value of the tin will be £9900 per tonne and that labour and other production costs will be £187 000. These revenues and costs are expected to rise by 10% per annum in subsequent years. These cash flows can be assumed to occur at the end of the year in which they arise.

Special mining equipment will also be purchased at the beginning of the first year of production at a cost of £48 000. This equipment will be sold immediately on the cessation of production, at an amount expected to equal its purchase price, less £200 for every tonne of tin produced during its life. Other revenues from the sale of the mine at the end of production are expected to equal the closure costs exactly.

The company has received permission from the present owners of the mine to carry out a geological survey of the area. The survey would cost £10 000 and would reveal for certain the type of rock formations in the area and hence how much tin could be produced from the mine.

Starlite PLC has a money discount take of 21% per annum for this type of project.

The ENPV of the project – without the geological survey – can be calculated as follows.

If the output of tin per month is constant, whatever the rock type, then the different rock types simply affect the *life* of the mining operation:

$$\text{Annual rate of production: 2 tonnes} \times 12 = 24 \text{ tonnes}$$

Life of mine:

Rock type A:	$\dfrac{240}{24}$	$=$	10 years
Rock type B:	$\dfrac{120}{24}$	$=$	5 years
Rock type C:	$\dfrac{72}{24}$	$=$	3 years

Whatever the rock type, the following cash flows will be incurred:

t_0	$-$ £50 000		purchase cost	
t_1	$-$ £95 000		plant purchase	
t_1	$-$ £48 000		equipment purchase	
t_2	$24 \times$ £9900	$=$	$+$ 237 600	1st year's revenue
			$-$ 187 000	1st year's costs
			$+$ £50 600	1st year's net revenue

The net revenue increases 10% per year

Disposal value of mining equipment:

Rock type A:	£48 000	$-$	(240×200)	$=$	£	0
Rock type B:	£48 000	$-$	(120×200)	$=$	£	24 000
Rock type C:	£48 000	$-$	(72×200)	$=$	£	33 600

The discount factor is $(1.21)^{-n} \equiv (1.1)^{-n}(1.1)^{-n}$

Rock type A
PV of mine, plant and equipment purchase costs:

						£
t_0	$-$ £50 000	$\times$	1		$=$	$-$ 50 000
t_1	$-$ £143 000	$\times$	$(1.21)^{-1}$		$=$	$-$ 118 182
					£ $-$	168 182

PV of net revenue flows: (£000)

t_2	t_3	t_4	t_{11}
$\dfrac{50.6}{(1.1)^2(1.1)^2}$	$\dfrac{50.6\,(1.1)}{(1.1)^3(1.1)^2}$	$\dfrac{50.6\,(1.1)^2}{(1.1)^4(1.1)^2}$ $\cdots$	$\dfrac{50.6\,(1.1)^9}{(1.1)^{11}(1.1)^2}$

$$50.6\,(1.1)^{-2}\,A_{10\neg10} \times (1.1)^{-1}$$

$$50.6 \times 0.83 \times 6.14 \times 0.91 \;=\; £+234\,660$$

Net present value: £ $+$ 66 478

Rock type B
PV of mine, plant and equipment purchase costs: £− 168 182
PV of net revenue flows: (£000)

$$50.6(1.1)^{-2} \, A5_{20.10} \times (1.1)^{-1}$$
$$50.6 \times 0.83 \times 3.79 \times 0.91 \;=\; £+144\,847$$

PV of disposal of mining equipment:

$$24\,000\,(1.21)^{-6} \quad=\quad 24\,000\,(1.1)^{-6}\,(1.1)^{-6}$$
$$=\quad 24\,000 \times 0.56 \times 0.56 \;=\; £+7526$$

Net present value: £− 15 809.

Rock type C
PV of mine, plant and equipment purchase costs: £− 168 182
PV of net revenue flows: (£000)

$$50.6\,(1.1)^{-2} \, A_{3\neg 0.10} \times (1.1)^{-1}$$
$$50.6 \times 0.83 \times 2.49 \times 0.91 \;=\; £+95\,163$$

PV of disposal of mining equipment:

$$33\,600\,(1.21)^{-4} \quad=\quad 33\,600\,(1.1)^{-4}\,(1.1)^{-4}$$
$$=\quad 33\,600 \times 0.68 \times 0.68 \;=\; £+15\,537$$

Net present value: £− 57 482

Expected net present value:

				£
+ 66 478	×	0.4	=	+ 26 591
− 15 809	×	0.4	=	− 6324
− 57 482	×	0.2	=	− 11 496
		ENPV	=	£+ 8771

Hence, on the basis of the expected NPV, the project is worthwhile undertaking without the survey.
   We can now move on to examine whether or not the survey is worthwhile. From the previous set of calculations, it can be seen that the project would not go ahead if the company knew, ex ante, that either rock type B or rock type C existed. This is because both would involve negative net present values. Thus the company would only go ahead with the mine if rock type A was indicated. Hence, assuming a survey is undertaken, the expected value of the outcome would be:

Rock type	NPV		Probability		£
A	+ 66478	×	0.4	=	+26 591
B	0	×	0.4	=	0
C	0	×	0.2	=	0
					£+26 591

The expected net present value of the mine project, without the survey is approximately + £8800; whilst if the survey is undertaken, this rises to + £16 500[1] approximately. Therefore, on this basis, it would suggest that the survey is worthwhile undertaking. Although the expected net present value approach is a rather unsatisfactory method of selecting between alternative financial opportunities as it takes no account of the risk involved, inspection of the alternative NPVs that might occur under the two options does support the initial advice that the survey should be undertaken:

	Survey NPV	No survey NPV
Rock type A	+ £ 56 478	+ £ 66 478
Rock type B	− £10 000	− £ 15 809
Rock type C	− £10 000	− £ 57 482

Sensitivity analysis

The appraisal of almost any investment project in the real world will involve the making of a great number of estimates. For example, the outlay required to undertake the project, its life, the annual cash inflows and out-flows it will generate, the scrap value it will have, and even the correct rate of discount to reduce the cash flows to present values. Estimates will be made for all these factors and the project will then be appraised by calcu-lating an expected net present value.

If this NPV is positive then the appraisal is in favour of acceptance. But, in terms of down-side risk, the decision maker is also interested in how sen-sitive the advice is to changes in the estimates made about the project. In other words, he is likely to be interested in the *margin of error* that there can be in the estimates made about the individual components of the project (i.e., outlay, life, etc.) *before* the advice that the appraisal gives (in this case to accept) becomes incorrect.

The decision pivot point

The decision whether to accept or reject a particular project *pivots* around the zero NPV. If the NPV is greater than zero, then the advice is to accept. On the other hand, if the NPV is negative, then the advice is to reject. Thus a zero NPV becomes the decision *pivot point*.

Sensitivity analysis is the term used to describe the process where each estimated element of a project's cash flow is taken in turn (with a *ceteris paribus* assumption holding all other estimates constant) to see the extent to which it can vary before the project's positive NPV is reduced to a zero value. Therefore if the estimated element varies by *more* than this amount, then the decision advice given by the original estimate of the project's NPV will be incorrect. These sensitivity calculations are illustrated in Example 8.

Example 8

Suppose the following estimates have been made about an investment proposal:

Outlay:	£ 1000
Life:	3 years
Annual revenues:	£2000
Annual costs:	£1500
Appropriate discount rate:	10%

On the basis of these estimates, the NPV can be calculated as follows:

	Year			
	0	1	2	3
Capital outlay	−£1000			
Revenues		+£2000	+£2000	+£2000
Costs		−£1500	−£1500	−£1500
Net expected cash flows	−£1000	+ £500	+ £500	+ £500

$$\text{ENPV} = -1000 + 500\ A_{3\neg 0.10} = +£243$$

Taking each of the five estimated factors in turn (and holding all the others constant at their initial estimated values), we shall examine the degree of variation necessary to reduce the +£243 NPV to zero.

Outlay: Let the outlay value be x.

$$-x + 500\,A_{3\neg 0.10} = 0$$
$$\therefore x = 500\,A_{3\neg 0.10} = 1243$$

The outlay can be as high as £1243 before the appraisal advice to invest (i.e. + NPV) becomes incorrect; in other words the original estimate can increase by £243 or by $(243/1{,}000) = 0.243$ or 24.3%

Life: Let the life be x years.

$$-1000 + 500\,A_{x\neg 0.10} = 0$$

Thus the value for x that produces a zero NPV lies between 2 and 3:

$$x = 2 + \left[\frac{132}{243+132} \times (3-2)\right] = 2.35 \text{ years.}$$

The project life can be as short as 2.35 years before the advice of the original investment appraisal is incorrect; i.e. the original estimate can decrease by 0.65 year or by $0.65/3 = 0.217$ or 21.7%.

Revenues: Let the annual revenue be x.

$$-1000 + x\,A_{3\neg 0.10} - 1500\,A_{3\neg 0.10} = 0$$

$$x = \frac{1000 + 1500\,A_{3\neg 0.10}}{A_{3\neg 0.10}} = £1902.$$

Thus the annual revenues can be as low as £1902, over the three years, before the original advice is incorrect; i.e., the original estimate can decrease by £98 per year or $98/2000 = 0.049$ or 4.9%.

Costs: Let the annual costs be x.

$$-1000 + x\,A_{3\neg 0.10} - 1500\,A_{3\neg 0.10} = 0$$

$$x = \frac{1000 + 2000\,A_{3\neg 0.10}}{A_{3\neg 0.10}} = £1598.$$

The annual costs can be as high as £1598 in each of the three years before the original investment advice is incorrect, i.e., the original estimate can increase by £98 per year or $98/1500 = 0.065$ or 6.5%

Discount rate: Let the discount rate be x (i.e. the project's IRR)

$$-1000 + 500\,A_{3\neg x} = 0$$

$$A_{3\neg x} = \frac{1000}{500} = 2.0.$$

Using linear interpolation, $A_{3\neg 0.20} = 2.11$ and $A_{3\neg 0.25} = 1.95$

$$x = 0.20 + \left[\frac{2.11-2.0}{2.11-1.95} \times (0.25-0.20)\right] = 0.234.$$

Thus the estimate for the discount rate can be as high as 23.4% before the original investment advice is incorrect; i.e. the original estimate can be increased by 13.4% or $0.134/0.10 = 134\%$

Variable	Original estimate	Sensitivity table Maximum value	Maximum change	% Change
Outlay	1000	1243	+ 243	+ 24.3%
Life	3	2.35	− 0.65	− 21.7%
Revenues	2000	1902	− 98	− 4.9%
Costs	1500	1598	+ 98	+ 6.5%
Discount rate	10%	23.4%	+ 13.4%	+ 134%

Using linear interpolation, we know that when $x = 3$ the NPV equals $+£243$. Trying when $x = 2$:

$$-1000 + 500\, A_{2\neg 0.10} = -132 \text{ NPV}$$

The sensitivity table in Example 8 shows that the decision to invest is most sensitive to the estimates of annual cash flows (where an actual outcome of only 4.9% below estimate would cause the NPV decision advice to be incorrect) and the annual cash outflows (a decision sensitivity of 6.5%). The decision advice is fairly insensitive to all the other estimates. We would conclude from this that management should review both of these decision-sensitive estimates to ensure that they are as accurate as possible.

Example 8 outlines the general approach of the sensitivity analysis technique, which is a good working tool in that it makes the decision maker more aware of the possible effects of uncertainty on his investment decisions. In addition, it can also help to direct attention to those particular estimates which require a special forecasting effort on account of their effect on the decision's sensitivity.

Non-annuity cash flows

However, Example 8 is rather unrealistic, because most of its cash flows are annuities. It was this characteristic that allowed us to take the approach that we did. Example 9 illustrates the approach to be taken when there are only non-annuity cash flows.

Example 9

Benagil PLC is considering undertaking a project and has made the following estimates:

Outlay:	£2300						
Life:	3 years						
Discount rate:	10%						
Revenues:	Yr 1	:	+£ 2000	Costs:	Yr 1	:	−£ 900
	2	:	+£ 2400		2	:	−£ 1100
	3	:	+£ 1600		3	:	−£ 800

On this basis, the project's NPV has been estimated at + £375.
The management of Benagil now wish to analyse how sensitive is the NPV's decision advice to accept, to changes in the estimates:

Outlay: Let outlay = x

$$-x + 1100(1.10)^{-1} + 1300(1.10)^{-2} + 800(1.10)^{-3} = 0 \text{ NPV}$$
$$-x + 2675 = 0$$
$$x = 2675$$

Therefore the outlay can increase by as much as £375 (or 375 ÷ 2300 = 16.3%) before the original decision advice is changed.

Life: Let life = x
When $x = 3$, the project's NPV is + 375
When $x = 2$, the project's NPV is:
$$-2300 + 1100(1.10)^{-1} + 1300(1.10)^{-2} = -226$$

Using linear interpolation to estimate a value for x that gives a zero NPV:

$$x = 2 + \left[\frac{-226}{226 - (+375)}(3-2)\right] = 2.38 \text{ years.}$$

Therefore the project's life can be shortened by up to 0.62 year (approximately 7.5 months) or 0.62 ÷ 3 = 20.7% before the original decision advice is incorrect.

Discount rate: Let the discount rate = x
When $x = 10\%$, the project's NPV is + 375
When $x = 20\%$, the project's NPV is:

$$-2300 + 1100(1.20)^{-1} + 1300(1.20)^{-2} + 800(1.20)^{-3} = -18$$

Using linear interpolation to estimate a value for x that gives a zero NPV:

$$x = 10\% + \left[\frac{375}{375 + 18}(20\% - 10\%)\right] = 19.5\%.$$

Thus the correct discount rate for the project can be as high as 19.5%, an increase of 9.5% (or 9.5% ÷ 10% = 95% on the original estimate), before the NPV's decision advice to accept is incorrect.

Revenues
If the revenues were to decrease by 5% per year, they would become:

Yr 1	+ 1900
2	+ 2280
3	+ 1520

and the NPV would become:

$$-2300 + 1000(1.10)^{-1} + 1180(1.10)^{-2} + 720(1.10)^{-3} = +125$$

If the revenues were to decrease by 10% per year, then the project's NPV would become:

$$-2300 + 900(1.10)^{-1} + 1160(1.10)^{-2} + 640(1.10)^{-3} = -125$$

Costs
If the costs were to increase by 5% per year, they would become:

Yr 1	− 945
2	− 1155
3	− 840

and the NPV would become:

$$-2300 + 1055(1.10)^{-1} + 1245(1.10)^{-2} + 760(1.10)^{-3} = +259$$

If the costs were to increase by 10% per year, then the project's NPV would become:

$$-2300 + 1010(1.10)^{-1} + 1190(1.10)^{-2} + 720(1.10)^{-3} = +142$$

		Sensitivity table		
Variable	Original estimate	Maximum value	Maximum change	% change
Outlay	2300	6675	+ 375	+ 16.3%
Life	3	2.38	− 0.62	− 20.7%
Discount rate	10%	19.5%	+ 9.4%	+ 95%

Revenues : Decision advice *not* sensitive at the 5% level, but *is* sensitive at the 10% level.

Costs : Decision advice *not* sensitive at either the 5% or the 10% level.

Therefore, the advice to management is that the decision given by the NPV calculation is insensitive to changes in most of the estimated variables. However, if the revenues were to fall by 10% of their estimated value the original decision advice would turn out to be incorrect. Hence it may be worthwhile to re-examine the estimates of annual revenues to see if the company's confidence in their accuracy can be improved.

Limitations of sensitivity analysis

The technique suffers, in particular, from an obvious and important drawback: the fact that each estimated component is varied *in turn* whilst all the others are held constant. Thus, in Example 9, the discount rate can be as high as 19.5% (approximately) before the NPV calculation advises rejection of the project, but this degree of sensitivity only holds (except through a chance ordering of factors) if all the other estimates turn out to be accurate. In other words, the technique ignores the possible effects on the decision of two or more of the estimated components varying simultaneously.[2]

Even if this problem with sensitivity analysis is set to one side, it can also be criticized on the basis that it makes no attempt to analyse risk in any formal way. Nor does it give any indication as to what the decision maker's reaction should be to the data presented in a sensitivity table.

In the examples set out above, the original NPV calculations indicated a decision to accept. Sensitivity analysis provides no rules to guide the decision maker as to whether the initial appraisal advice should or should not be amended in the light of the sensitivity data. With these limitations in mind, let us now look at other approaches which may be used to deal with the problem of uncertainty in investment appraisal.

The risk-adjusted discount rate

Risk and return

The risk-adjusted discount rate approach attempts to handle the problem of risk in a more direct and thoughtful way. As we know, investors are risk adverse and so require a reward for undertaking a risky investment in the form of the rate of return that it is expected to produce. The more risky the investment, the greater must be its expected return if investors are going to be persuaded to undertake it.

It is this idea – the relationship between risk and return – that the risk-adjusted discount rate approach picks up on. We have seen from our analysis of the NPV decision rule that a positive NPV means that the project produces a return greater than the discount rate – which itself represents the minimum acceptable rate of return. Thus the risk-adjusted discount rate idea takes the commonsense approach to handling risk in investment appraisal of adjusting the *level* of the minimum acceptable return to reflect the project's level of risk.

The approach taken is usually to add a risk *premium* to the 'risk-free' rate of return. The greater the project's perceived level of risk, the greater is the risk premium. The risk-free rate of return is usually taken to be the going rate of return on long-term government bonds (on the basis that such bonds have no *default-risk*: a situation is never realistically going to occur where the government defaults on its loan obligations – after all, governments are allowed to print money!).

For example, suppose that the current rate of return on government long-term bonds is 8%. Management may decide to classify investment proposals into three broad categories, low, medium and high-risk, and assign risk premiums of 3%, 5% and 9% respectively. Therefore the cash flows of low-risk projects would be discounted to present value using a discount rate of 8% + 3% = 11%, whilst projects of medium or high risk would be evaluated by discounting their cash flows to present value using 13% and 17% discount rates respectively.

In one very important way, the risk-adjusted discount rate approach to the problem of uncertainty is much more useful to the decision maker than sensitivity analysis, in that it does actually produce decision *advice*, in the form of a risk-adjusted net present value. In addition, the method is easily understandable and appears to be intuitively correct: investors *do* require a higher expected return on riskier investments. However, we can identify several drawbacks in this essentially correct (but too casual) analysis.

The problems

The two main problems are the allocation of projects into risk classes and the identification of the risk premiums. In addition there is a technical problem with this approach to allowing for risk, in that it implicitly implies that risk increases over time (which may or may not be the case).

The problems of the risk class and the risk premiums simply arise from the casual nature of the analysis. Thus the allocation of a project to a particular risk class and the premia assigned to each class will be based on the *manager's* own personal attitude towards risk, and on the manager's personal perception as to the nature of risk and the reward required for accepting risk. Our earlier discussion on objectives is sufficient for us to realize that the manager's view of risk – and the required rewards – may not be the same as those of the shareholders. (This whole area will be examined much more closely in the three chapters which follow.)

Certainty-equivalents

The 'technical' problem is easy to illustrate, as is shown in Example 10. The problem is that a constant risk premium implies *increasing* risk over time. In Example 10 a risk-adjusted discount rate of 8% implies that a project's cash flows become more risky over time. It is debatable whether the riskiness of a project's cash flows do correspond with this assumption.

Example 10

An investment produces an uncertain cash flow at Year 1 which is expected to be £100. If you would be willing to accept £90 for certain at Year 1, instead of the uncertain £100, then £90 is said to be the 'certainty-equivalent'.

Given that you are indifferent between the two amounts, the certainty-equivalent factor at Year 1 – a_1 – can be identified by:

$$£90 = a_1 \times £100$$

$$a_1 = \frac{£90}{£100} = 0.90$$

What this certainty-equivalent factor of 0.90 means is that at Year 1, every £100 of uncertain cash flow is valued as being equivalent to £90 of certain cash flow. Therefore the smaller the certainty-equivalent factor, the more *risky* is the uncertain cash flow and the less valuable it is. For example, if the certainty equivalent factor was 0.70 this implies that investors would be willing to accept £70 for certain for every uncertain £100: the less you are willing to accept for certain, the more risky is your perception of the equivalent uncertain cash flow.

Furthermore, given that these two amounts are seen as equivalents, their *present values* should also be the same. Therefore the present value of the *certain* £90, discounted at the risk-free interest rate, should be the same as the present value of the *uncertain* £100, discounted at a rate which has been adjusted to reflect the risk involved.

If we let the risk-free interest rate be R_f and the risk-adjusted discount rate be R, then, in our example:

$$\frac{£90}{(1+r_F)^1} = \frac{£100}{(1+r)}$$

and given that £90 = $a_1 \times$ £100
then

$$a_1 \times \frac{£100}{(1+r_F)^1} = \frac{£100}{(1+r)^1}.$$

This can be rearranged to give:

$$a_1 = \frac{(1+r_F)^1}{(1+r)^1}.$$

More generally, the certainty-equivalent factor at any time period *t* is:

$$a_t = \frac{(1+r_F)^t}{(1+r)^t}.$$

To see what this implies, let's put in some numbers. Suppose the risk-free interest rate is 5% and you judge that a satisfactory *risk-adjusted* discount rate is 8%, (i.e. there is a 3% risk premium being added to the risk-free rate of return).

The certainty-equivalent factors will be as follows:

Year 1	:	$(1.05/1.08)^1$	=	0.9722
Year 2	:	$(1.05/1.08)^2$	=	0.9452
Year 3	:	$(1.05/1.08)^3$	=	0.9190
		etc.		etc.

As can be seen, over time the certainty-equivalent factor is getting *smaller*. In other words, the implicit assumption is that, over time, the project's cash flows are getting more risky and so less valuable.

Use of the normal distribution

Another attempt to take a more analytical approach to the problem of risk makes use of the properties of normal probability distributions. The approach starts from the premise that if a project's risk can be defined as the degree of possible variability between its expected outcome and its actual outcome, then what is of prime importance to the risk-averse decision maker (or more correctly, the risk-averse owner on whose behalf the decision is being made) is just *one* side of this variability: the risk of project underperformance. Therefore, what would be of interest to the decision maker is the probability of the project actually producing a negative NPV, even though the *expected* result was a positive NPV. On the assumption that the range of possible outcomes for the project are normally distributed, then the properties of the normal curve can be used to provide the required probability.

The discount rate

A problem arises, however, in the choice of the discount rate to be used to calculate the possible NPVs of the project being appraised. One possibility is to use the risk-free discount rate. The investment decision advice is then based on whether or not the probability of a negative NPV exceeds some maximum acceptable probability, in much the same way as a risk-premium is utilized when using the risk-adjusted discount rate. If the probability of a negative NPV were sufficiently small, the project would be acceptable.

An alternative approach is to discount the project cash flows using an appropriate *risk-adjusted* discount rate in order to calculate the expected NPV and then use the properties of the normal curve to estimate the probability of a negative NPV. This latter approach uses the probability of a negative NPV as an *additional* piece of decision information, almost as an extension of the sensitivity analysis concept. By contrast, the former approach attempts to use the properties of the normal curve to allow directly for risk in investment decision making. In doing so it avoids the element of 'double-counting' risk which occurs when using a risk-adjusted discount rate to calculate the range of possible NPVs.

A simple illustration, such as that set out in Example 11, can be used to explain the mechanics of both approaches. From the results of this example it can be seen that when using a risk-free discount rate, the decision advice is based on whether a 13.8% probability of the project actually producing a return below the riskless return is acceptable for the perceived level of risk of the project concerned. Alternatively, the second approach informs the decision maker that the project can be expected to produce a positive NPV of £492 when discounted at a rate thought appropriate for its degree of risk, but that if a decision is made to accept the project there is an 18.4% probability that this decision will turn out to be incorrect (i.e., that the project actually produces a negative NPV).

Example 11

A project under evaluation is thought to involve a medium degree of risk. The risk-free discount rate is 4% and the appropriate risk premium is believed to be 6%. The project has the following estimated cash flows:

Cash outlay (year 0):   £1000

Cash inflows:

		Year			
		1	2	3	Prob.
	Good	+ 1000	+ 1000	+ 1000	0.10
	Med./good	+ 800	+ 800	+ 800	0.20
Market conditions:	Medium	+ 600	+ 600	+ 600	0.40
	Med./poor	+ 400	+ 400	+ 400	0.20
	Poor	+ 200	+ 200	+ 200	0.10

(a) Using the risk-free discount rate of 4%:

Market conditions	NPV		Prob.			$(NPV - ENPV)^2$	×	Prob.		
Good	+ 1775	×	0.10	=	+ 177.5	$(1775 - 665)^2$	×	0.10	=	123 210
Medium good	+ 1220	×	0.20	=	+ 244.0	$(1220 - 665)^2$	×	0.20	=	61 605
Medium	+ 665	×	0.40	=	+ 266.0	$(665 - 665)^2$	×	0.40	=	0
Medium Poor	+ 110	×	0.20	=	+ 22.0	$(110 - 665)^2$	×	0.20	=	61 605
Poor	− 445	×	0.10	=	− 45.5	$(-445 - 665)^2$	×	0.10	=	123 210
			ENPV		+ 665.0			Var	=	369 630

Whilst the ENPV = + 665, the standard deviation = $\sqrt{369\,630}$ = 608 NPV

Probability of a negative NPV: $\dfrac{0-665}{608}$ = 1.094 Std. units

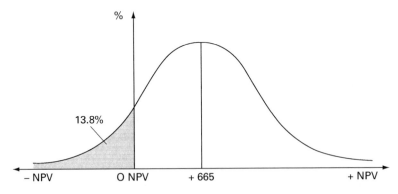

Using area under the normal curve tables (page 255) this gives a value for the shaded area (-NPV) of 0.1379

Therefore there is a 13.8% probability that the project will produce less than the risk-free return of 4%.

(b) Using the risk-adjusted discount rate of 4% + 6% = 10%:

Market conditions	NPV		Prob.			$(NPV - ENPV)^2$	×	Prob.		
Good	+ 1487	×	0.10	=	+ 148.7	$(1487 - 492)^2$	×	0.10	=	99 002.4
Medium good	+ 989	×	0.20	=	+ 197.8	$(989 - 492)^2$	×	0.20	=	49 401.8
Medium	+ 492	×	0.40	=	+ 196.8	$(492 - 492)^2$	×	0.40	=	0
Medium Poor	× 5	×	0.20	=	+ 1.0	$(-5 - 492)^2$	×	0.20	=	49 401.8
Poor	− 503	×	0.10	=	− 50.3	$(-503 - 492)^2$	×	0.10	=	99 002.4
			ENPV		+ 492.0			Var	=	296 808.4

ENPV = + 492
Standard deviation = √296 808.4 = 545 NPV

Probability of a negative NPV: $\frac{0-492}{545}$ = 0.903 Std. units

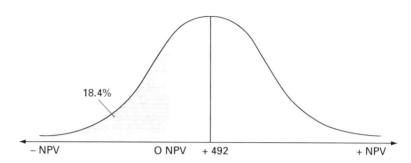

Using area under the normal curve tables this gives a value for the shaded area (−NPV) of: 0.1841.
Therefore there is an 18.4% probability that the project will produce less than the required return of 10%.

Simulation

Over the past ten years or so there has been a massive expansion in the accessibility of computer software designed for simulation. The idea of simulation is to create a computer model that will allow for the variables in a model to be related to each other in any way that might be required and also to allow them to be varied singly or together in almost infinite combinations. By doing this it is possible to form a view as to what the possible outcomes of a decision might be. Of course, it will still be necessary to to make predictions but the predictions should be more reliable in nature. For example, a mining company might be making a decision about the exploitation of a new mine and wishes to calculate its NPV. Traditionally a best estimate of the variables would have been used in the model and, eventually a single value would have been arrived at for the NPV of the project. However, by using a simulation package it is possible to enter ranges of values in the cells of the spreadsheetand and the packages allow for the inputting of most statistical distributions into individual spreadsheet cells. In the case of the mining company, they might well have access to scientific data that will tell them (for instance) that the expected yield of ore from rock is normally distributed with a mean of 150 grammes per kilogramme and a standard deviation of 40 grammes.

Once the spreadsheet has been written the simulation goes ahead. This involves the generation of the distributions in the spreadsheet in random or structured combinations with the NPV of the project being calculated each time. The more iterations of the model that are run, the more reliable will be the distributions generated. The only limit to the number of iterations in practical terms is the power and capacity of the computer being used. Let us assume that it has been decided that it is appropriate to run 2500 iterations.

The spreadsheet model would be recalculated 2500 times and the distributions for the various cells would be generated in a random manner. Each run will generate a value for the NPV of the project which is stored. By the end of the process there will be 2500 possible values for NPV and these will be reported. This might be in the form of a graph or it might be in the form of statistical information that discloses the possibility of differing levels of return (including, perhaps, the possibility of negative returns).

The results of such a process are likely to be far more reliable than those resulting from guesswork as to a single most likely outcome. However, they are still dependent upon the availability of information about possible future outcomes. There is also the problem of the 'black box' syndrome. The whole approach has the very strong feel of science about it and, generally speaking, the results are presented in a way that is extremely plausible. This might have the effect of removing some of the healthy scepticism that all decision makers should have. In other words, this is still an approach based on predictions and whilst its results might be rather more reliable than those produced by other approaches, this should never be forgotten.

A particular strength of the approach is that it encourages decision makers to pay attention to the underlying factors that are likely to have a significant impact on the outcome of the project.

A comparison of the approaches

The last two chapters have examined a number of approaches to risk in investment decision making. Whilst there is no doubt that the future orientation of decisions means that it will never be possible to ensure that every decision is the correct one, ignoring risk is simply not an option. In the end, the investment decisions made by managers will determine a number of significant issues including:

- the cash flows generated by the company;
- the dividends paid out by the company;
- the market value of the company;
- the survival of the company.

They will influence not only the size but also the variability of cash flows. For instance, a decision might be made to replace labour intensive production methods with new capital intensive methods. Amongst other effects, this is likely to mean that the cost structure of the business will be altered so that it has a relatively higher proportion of fixed costs. As we saw in the last chapter, this might be expected to produce a higher beta for the company's shares because returns should become more volatile. So we can argue that, whether or not a manager believes in the validity of β as a determinant of the discount rate is irrelevant. Assuming financial markets to be reasonably efficient at setting prices, the discount rate calculated by the use of β will indeed be the best indicator of an appropriate return for a project because the project will contribute to the returns and the β of the company as a whole.

Many managers would claim that there is no substitute for judgement in making investment decisions. This is, in a sense, a truism but generally those making this claim are suggesting that the techniques we have described are not particularly relevant to their decision-making processes. We would claim that the use of the techniques described in this book allow for much more informed judgement with the caveat that their application does become more problematical in a period of rapid technological and economic change. Mostly, our techniques are based on an examination of the the past, so we have a problem if we do not expect the future to be like the past. In such a situation, it may well be that some form of computer based simulation approach may well turn out to be of great practical use.

Summary

This chapter has looked at some of the approaches used to cope with the problem of risk in capital investment appraisal that are not based on market data. None of these can be said really to tackle the issue except in a rather intuitive, rule-of-thumb way. However, it could be argued that their use in practice is better than ignoring the presence of risk completely. The major points made were as follows:

- The expected net present value (ENPV) approach examines the *average* outcome of a project. However, because of this it fails to capture what is the essence of risk, by ignoring *variability* of outcome.

- However, the analysis can be useful for examining the value of additional information to a company.

- The abandonment decision analysis can help to evaluate investment appraisal situations where an option is available to abandon the project before it reaches the end of its life.

- The abandonment decision analysis suffers from the difficulty of obtaining reliable abandonment value data and requires a complex mathematical analysis in all but the simplest problems.

- Sensitivity analysis examines the degree to which the various estimates made about a project can change, before the decision advice given by NPV is overturned.

- There are two main advantages. The first is that it highlights those estimates to which the decision advice is most sensitive. Management can then go back and take more time and trouble to ensure those particular estimates are as accurate as possible. The second advantage is that it gives the decision maker more information to use in deciding whether or not to accept the advice of the original NPV analysis.

- There are two disadvantages of sensitivity analysis. The first is the more serious: it only looks at the effect of changing one estimate at a time. It doesn't examine the effects of simultaneous changes in two or more estimates. The second disadvantage is it gives no indication as to *how* the decision maker should evaluate and make use of the sensitivity data.

- The risk-adjusted discount rate approach described in this chapter represents an intuitive attempt to recognize the relationship between risk and return.

- It can be faulted on a number of grounds. First, on the basis of how the risk premiums are derived and the project's risk category is determined. Secondly, we saw that using a risk-adjusted discount rate makes an assumption about implicit project risk which may not be justified.

- The use of the normal probability distribution was examined. This is an interesting approach to the handling of risk in decision making, although little used in practice. The most sensible approach is to obtain a probability that the investment project will produce a return that is less than the *risk-free* return. The alternative approach, looking at the probability of a negative NPV calculated on the basis of a discounted rate assumed to reflect the project's risk, is simply a variation on sensitivity analysis.

- Finally we described the use of computer simulation. This is rather more sophisticated than most of the other options and whilst it is still not used very extensively, its use is becoming more common. It is likely that it will become much easier to use this approach as software improves and it is probable that it will improve the quality of decision making.

Notes

1. £26 591 minus the cost of the survey.

2. In theory this problem can be overcome by use of the operational research technique of simulation; in practice, however, this does little to enhance or clarify the decision maker's view of the effects of uncertainty on a project's desirability.

Further reading

1. The articles in this general area of the more traditional approaches to handling risk are not particularly rewarding. However, two interesting pieces are: G.J. Grayson, 'The Use of Statistical Techniques in Capital Budgeting', in *Financial Research and Management Decisions*, ed. A.A. Robicheck, 1967, which looks at the use of sensitivity analysis; and A.A. Robicheck and S.C. Myers, 'Conceptual Problems in the Use of the Risk Adjusted Discount Rate', *Journal of Finance*, December 1966.
2. Other articles of interest are: D.B. Hertz, 'Risk Analysis in Capital Investment', *Harvard Business Review*, January–February 1964; J.F. Magee, 'How to Use Decision Trees in Capital Investment', *Harvard Business Review*, September–October 1964; A. Rappaport, 'Sensitivity Analysis in Decision Making', *Accounting Review*, July 1967; and E.F. Brigham, D.F. Shone and S.R. Vinson, 'The Risk Premium Approach to Measuring a Utility's Cost of Equity', *Financial Management*, Spring 1985.

3. On the abandonment decision, see J.E. Jarrett, 'An Abandonment Decision Model', *Engineering Economist*, Autumn 1973.
4. Finally, on certainty-equivalents, see A.A. Robicheck and S.C. Myers, 'Conceptual problems with the use of risk-adjusted discount rates', *Journal of Finance*, December 1966, and G.A. Sick, A Certainty-Equivalent Approach to Capital Budgeting, *Financial Management*, Winter 1986.

Quickie questions

1. A machine costs £1000 and has a life of three years. It can either be a success or a failure. If it is successful – and it has a probability of 45% – then it will produce an annual net cash flow of £500. If it is a failure, the annual net cash flow will be only £350. The discount rate is 10%. What is its ENPV?
2. What is the maximum worth of a survey that would tell you, in advance of the decision, whether the machine in question 1 would be a success or failure?
3. What would be the maximum worth of the survey in question 2 if it was only 75% accurate?
4. Given the following information:

State	Prob.	£NPV
I	0.3	+ 100
II	0.5	+ 50
III	0.2	− 300

    What would be the maximum worth of a survey which could tell you, in advance, which state of the world would occur?
5. A machine costs £140. It has a two-year life and a 15% discount rate correctly reflects its risk. Its performance depends upon the state of the world:

State	Yr 1	Yr 2	Prob.
I	+ 100	+ 100	0.70
II	+ 60	+ 60	0.10
III	+ 40	+ 40	0.20

    The company can sell the machine at the end of Year 1 for £60. At the end of Year 2 the machine will be worthless. Advise the company.
6. Given the following information about a project:

Outlay	£1000
Life	5 years
Net cash flow	+ £280 per year
Discount rate	10%

    How sensitive is the decision advice to changes in the estimate of the life and the annual net cash flow?

Problems

1. The directors of Linnet Oil plc are considering whether to make an immediate payment of £20 million for a licence to drill oil in a particular geographical area. Having acquired the licence, the company would commission a seismic survey to determine whether the area is a suitable prospect, i.e.

whether there are any geological structures present which could contain oil. If the area is a suitable prospect, exploration wells would be drilled to discover if oil is in fact present. If oil is present, appraisal wells would be drilled to ascertain the size and characteristics of the potential field.

The company's development expert has produced the following data about the licence area, based upon the results from adjoining areas. If oil is discovered by the exploration wells, the appraisal wells will indicate one of the three following types of oilfield:

Type	Probability of occurrence	Millions of barrels	Expected life (years)
I	60%	negligible	zero
II	32%	42	4
III	8%	2250	10

The annual oil production will decline over the life of the field. To approximate the decline, the expert argues that a sensible approach would be to assume that the annual production of the field during the first half of its life is twice the annual production during the second half. For example, for a type II field the first two years' annual production rate would be 14 million barrels per annum and the second two years' annual production rate would be 7 million barrels per annum.

During the entire life of the field, a barrel of oil is expected to sell for $26.4 and the $/£ rate is expected to be 1.2$/£. The annual operating cash surplus is expected to be 45% of sales revenue. The combined tax costs for the company are usually 77% of the operating cash surplus and these tax cash flows can be assumed to arise one year after the cash flows relating to sales and other costs. Production of oil would start in one year's time and the first annual net revenues would arise at the end of the first year of production.

The cost of drilling the appraisal well will be £100 million and drilling the exploration well will cost £10 million. Both costs will be paid in one year's time. The seismic survey costs of £2 million will be paid immediately. All three of the costs, together with the cost of the licence to drill oil, will give rise to tax relief equal to 50% of the cost, receivable one year after the cost is paid.

It is expected that there will be a 50% chance that the seismic survey will indicate the prospect of oil and a 30% chance that the exploration drilling will find oil. The company's after-tax cost of capital for this type of project is 15% per annum.

Required:
(a) Calculate the expected net present value of the venture.
(b) Calculate the maximum price the company should pay for an alternative type of seismic survey which will reduce the probability of indicating a positive prospect from 50% to 30% and so increase from 30% to 50% the chance that the exploration drilling will find oil.

2. Southgate Ltd is investigating the introduction of a new alcoholic drink, to be called Mildmay. Extensive market research by an outside agency, at a cost of £10 000, has suggested that a price of £5 per bottle to the retail trade would be acceptable.

Production of Mildmay will require specialized distilling and flavouring equipment which, it is estimated, would cost £200 000. As with most distilling equipment, this installation is likely to have a long production life but, due to its rather specialized nature, when production of Mildmay ceases it will only be able to be sold for scrap for about £2000 (net of dismantling costs). Variable costs of production are estimated at £3 per bottle and overheads are estimated at £25 000 per year, avoidable only if production ceases.

At the proposed selling price, the drink trade is expected to demand 50 000 bottles per year, well within the capacity of the production equipment, but after four years interest is expected to decline and so production will cease. However, the company believes that it may well be able to extend product life for a further two years by either running a small trade advertising campaign at the start of years 5 and 6 at a cost of £10 000 per year, or alternatively by reducing the price per bottle by 40p in these two years. The market research company believes that the two alternatives would achieve similar sales results, but just what these sales would be is uncertain. If the campaign is suc- cessful in year 5 then sales of 35 000 bottles could be expected in that year, with sales of 28 000 or only 9000 bottles being equally likely in year 6, or alternatively the year 5 promotion may be relatively unsuccessful with sales of only 7000 bottles in that year and an equal likelihood of either 12 000 or 5000 bottles in the following year. The market research agency believes that the campaign has only a 60% chance of being successful in year 5.

All expenses and revenues will be paid or received in cash at the end of the year in which they arise, with the exception of the production equipment, for which payment is due at the start of the first year of manufacture and the advertising expenditure which must be paid for at the start of each year in which a campaign is mounted. The company normally uses a 10% discount rate for project evaluation purposes.

Required:
(a) Evaluate the financial feasibility of the proposed new drink, in respect of its normal expected life of four years, including in your presentation details about the sensitivity of the decision advice to changes in all the estimates made, except the scrap value and discount rate.
(b) Briefly, advise management on the results of the sensitivity analysis.
(c) Evaluate which of the two alternative methods (if any) should be used to extend the product life.

3. A small company in the house-building industry has £201 000 cash which is surplus to current requirements. The cash will eventually be used to help finance the construction of a small housing development. The housing devel- opment depends upon obtaining permission to build the houses from the local government planning department. It is believed that this permission will be given in two years' time.

The £201 000 can be invested in the money market to yield a return of 10% per year.

Alternatively an opportunity exits for the funds to be invested on a temporary basis in Goer, a family-owned car hire business which wishes to expand its car hire fleet by thirty cars costing £6700 each. Goer is temporarily short of funds because of recent inheritance tax payments. If the funds are invested with Goer they will produce an annual net cash inflow to the building company, but the size of this cash flow is now known with certainty, and the cash flow at the end of the second year is dependent upon the cash flow at the end of the first year. Estimates of the net cash inflows to the building company are detailed below.

End of Year 1		End of Year 2	
Probability	Cash inflow (£)	Probability	Cash inflow (£)
0.6	80 000	0.6	80 000
		0.4	90 000
0.4	100 000	0.6	100 000
		0.4	110 000

In addition Goer will make a payment to the building company at the end of the first year of £141 000, or at the end of the second year of £81 000. The building company has to choose at the end of the first year whether to receive payment of £141 000 then or £81 000 a year later. If the payment of £141 000 is received by the building company at the end of the first year the investment will be terminated and there will be no further cash flows to the building company from Goer.

18% per year is considered to be an appropriate discount rate for investments in the car hire business.

Required:
(a) Prepare a report recommending whether the building company should invest in the car hire business or in the money market. All relevant calculations must be included in your report.

Ignore taxation. State clearly any assumptions that you make.
(b) Discuss the practical problems of incorporating abandonment opportunities into the capital investment decision-making process.

Suggest possible reasons why a company might decide to abandon an investment project part way through its expected economic life.

4. The management of Haydn Ltd is planning the launch of a new micro-computer, the SQ. The market for micro-computers is very competitive and the anticipated product life of the SQ is only three years. The marketing director of Haydn Ltd has produced the following table showing three different estimates of likely demand for the SQ during each year of its life.

Demand predictions	Probability	Year 1 Units	Year 2 Units	Year 3 Units
Most optimistic	0.2	32 000	16 000	12 000
Best guess	0.5	16 000	8000	6000
Most pessimistic	0.3	4000	2000	1500

The above estimates assume a constant selling price of £500 over the three years. The variable production cost per unit of an SQ is £400.

The production director has indicated that the factory is in a position to produce 32 000, 16 000 or 4000 units per annum, but, once decided, the chosen production level could not be increased until the start of the following year. The total cost of setting up the production line would consist of fixed costs of £1 million, and variable costs of £50 for each unit of production capacity. These costs would be paid at the start of the year's production.

A market research firm has offered, for a fee of £300 000, to carry out a detailed survey which would determine precisely the level of demand for the SQ. The management of Haydn Ltd wishes to know whether the market survey is likely to be worthwhile.

In order to assess whether the survey is worth undertaking, the directors of Haydn Ltd have asked that the following simplifying assumptions be made:

(i) cash flows relating both to sales and variable production costs are to be deemed to arise at the end of the year in which they are incurred;

(ii) demand can be represented by only one of the three sets of probabilities envisaged by the marketing director;

(iii) the level of the demand in the first year will determine the levels demanded in the second and third years;

(iv) the appropriate discount rate for the venture is 10% per annum; and

(v) stock levels will remain unchanged.

Required:

(a) Determine the initial production capacity that Haydn Ltd should choose, and compute the resulting expected net present value of producing and selling at that level.

(b) Calculate whether the market survey should be commissioned, and comment on any reservations you might have relating to the use of expected values as an aid in decision making.

(c) Discuss the advantages to the company of conducting a market survey of this kind.

11 Overseas capital investments

Introduction

Domestic versus foreign projects

The final topic relating to investment decisions that we are going to look at are those concerning overseas operations. Whilst the underlying principles of decision making remain the same, the appraisal of capital investments in foreign countries involves several difficulties not present in domestic project appraisal. Principal among these difficulties are the following:

1. Foreign exchange (FX) rates fluctuate over time in an essentially unpredictable way. Therefore an overseas project's cash flows are exposed to the risk of adverse FX movements.

2. There are a variety of ways in which an overseas government (the 'host' government) might take action which adversely discriminates against an overseas project once the investment has been undertaken. Such actions might range from the imposition of a penal rate of taxation, and/or restrictions on the remittance of project net cash flows back to the parent, to confiscation of the project's assets without compensation. These possibilities are referred to as 'country risk'.

3. There is the problem of correctly evaluating the systematic risk and required expected rate of return on the project within an international, rather than domestic, context.

4. Finally, there is the problem of the correct project appraisal procedure. In particular, should the analysis be undertaken from the viewpoint of the project itself, or from the viewpoint of the parent company? This problem arises because of differences that can occur between a project's net cash flows, and a project's net cash flows which are available for repatriation back to the parent company.

This chapter examines these difficulties and the way in which they might be overcome.

The basic approach

A project in a foreign country generates a stream of net cash flows in the currency of its host country. How is the parent to evaluate those cash flows in an NPV analysis? We can formulate two possible approaches to the problem which should provide exactly the same expected result.

Using as an example a UK company investing in the US, the two alternative approaches are:

1. The project's dollar cash flows are discounted at the dollar discount rate to generate a $NPV. This can then be converted at the $/£ spot rate[1] to give a sterling NPV.
2. The project's dollar cash flows are converted to sterling cash flows. These sterling cash flows are then discounted at the sterling discount rate to generate a sterling NPV.

Notice how each approach starts off at exactly the same point (the project's dollar cash flows), and ends up at exactly the same point (the sterling NPV). Both approaches are illustrated in Example 1.

As both approaches provide exactly the same results, given our estimates, which approach should be used in practice is likely to depend on what information is available, and how difficult it might be to forecast the information that may *not* be available. Generally, it may be assumed that management might be more uneasy about forecasting future foreign exchange (FX) rates than they would be about forecasting the required dollar return. Therefore approach 1 may be the more likely one to be found in practice. There is, however, a lack of empirical evidence on the matter.

Example 1

	Year	$m.
US project's net cash flows:	0	−10
	1	+5
	2	+6
	3	+4

The $/£ spot rate is 1.8050 and the dollar is expected to depreciate by 5% per year. A similar-risk UK-based project would be expected to earn a minimum return of 20%.

Calculations
Given the spot rate and the expected rate of annual depreciation, the future exchange rates can be estimated:

$$1.8050(1.05)^1 = 1.8952 : \text{Year 1}$$
$$1.8050(1.05)^2 = 1.9900 : \text{Year 2}$$
$$1.8050(1.05)^3 = 2.0895 : \text{Year 3}$$

Adapting the IRPT, the dollar discount rate can be estimated:

$$\frac{\text{US discount rate} - \text{UK discount rate}}{1 + \text{UK discount rate}} = \% \text{ change in US\$}$$

$$\frac{\text{US discount rate} - 0.20}{1 + 0.02} = +0.05$$

$$\text{US discount rate} = (0.05 \times 1.20) - 0.20 = 0.26 \text{ or } 26\%$$

Approach 1:

Year	$m		26% discount factors		$ PV c/fs
0	−10		1	=	−10
1	+5		0.7936	=	+3.968
2	+6		0.6299	=	+3.779
3	+4		0.4999	=	+2.000
					$−0.253m NPV

$$-\$0.253m \div 1.8050 = -\pounds0.14m \text{ NPV}$$

Approach 2:

Year	$m		$/£ rate		£m		20% discount factors		£PV c/fs
0	−10	÷	1.8050	=	−5.540	×	1	=	−5.540
1	+5	÷	1.8952	=	+2.638	×	0.8333	=	+2.198
2	+6	÷	1.9900	=	+3.015	×	0.6944	=	+2.094
3	+4	÷	2.0895	=	+1.914	×	0.5787	=	+1.108
									$−0.14m NPV

The project cash flows

Whichever approach to the appraisal of overseas projects is used, both take as their starting point the project's net cash flows denominated in the host country's currency. It is here that some controversy is found.

The point of dispute is whether the project's net cash flows should be viewed from the standpoint of the project itself, or from the standpoint of the parent. In other words should the year-by-year net operating cash flows of the project be evaluated, or should the project's net cash flows *available to be remitted back to the parent be evaluated?*

Example 2

Rush plc is thinking of undertaking a capital investment in an overseas country whose currency is the dollar. The project's net cash flows are:

Year	$m
0	−10
1	+8
2	+4
3	+3.5

At the current $/£ spot rate of 2.50, the project will require an outlay of $4 million. The company intends to finance the whole of this out of retained earnings. Given the systematic risk involved, it is thought that 20% is a suitable required rate of return in dollar terms. The company follows a policy of paying out all of each year's net cash flow as a dividend.

The host country's laws permit foreign projects to remit back to their parents a maximum annual cash flow equal to 10% of the project's cost. Any surplus (or blocked) cash flows have to be placed on special deposit at an interest rate of 5%. All blocked funds can be remitted back to the parent at the end of the project's life. From the viewpoint of the project, it produces a positive NPV and so is acceptable:

Year	$m	×	20% discount		
0	−10	×	1	=	−10
1	+8	×	0.8333	=	+6.67
2	+4	×	0.6944	=	+2.78
3	+3.5	×	0.5787	=	+2.02
					$+1.47m NPV

$$+\$1.47m \div 2.50 = +\pounds0.588m\ NPV$$

However, from the viewpoint of the parent the project is undesirable, as it has a negative NPV:

Year	1	2	3
+ project cash flow	+8	+ 4	+ 3.5
Blocked funds		7	+10.35
interest		+ 0.35	+ 0.52
Total cash flow	+8	+11.35	+14.37
Repatriated c/f	−1	− 1	−14.37
Blocked funds	+7	+10.35	−

Year	$m	×	20% disc.		
0	−10	×	1	=	−10
1	+ 1	×	0.8333	=	+0.83
2	+ 1	×	0.6944	=	+0.69
3	+14.37	×	0.5787	=	+8.32
					$−0.16m NPV

$$-\$0.16m \div 2.50 = -\pounds64\ 000\ NPV$$

With foreign country projects these two cash flows can often be significantly different because of host country restrictions on the repatriation of project net cash flows. Example 2 shows how crucial the difference might be.

Although there has been some controversy over this matter, it is difficult to understand why. It should appear obvious that, as it is the parent which is investing in the project, the project *must* be evaluated from the parent's viewpoint.

That is to say, what is important is the NPV of the project's cash flows that are available to be remitted back to the parent. The fact that the project used in Example 2 has a positive NPV when viewed in its own right must be irrelevant. However good an investment might appear to be, there is little point in undertaking that investment if the investor cannot enjoy its benefits. Thus Rush plc, acting on its shareholders' behalf, are not going to be interested in undertaking the project if it does not represent a positive NPV investment from their point of view.

Overseas currency finance

The conclusion reached above then raises an interesting point as far as financing is concerned. One of the fundamental principles of capital investment appraisal is that the financing decision can be kept separate from the investment decision. This then leads us always to exclude *financing* cash flows in calculating a project's NPV.

The reason for this is *not* that the financing cash flows are being *ignored*, but that their present value is always *equal* to the amount of finance involved. Therefore the outlay on a project at 'Year 0' reflects the present value of the financing cash flows involved with the outlay. Example 3 simply illustrates this point, which has been made in earlier chapters, but which is of particular importance as far as overseas project appraisal is concerned.

Example 3

A company wishes to buy a machine for £1000. It has a net operating cash flow of £450 per year for each of the three years of its life and a zero scrap value. Given the systematic risk of the project, a 15% discount rate is thought suitable for evaluation purposes.

The machine is to be financed by a three-year £1000 term loan at 10% interest. Ignoring tax (which would just be a complication, but which would not change the conclusions drawn), the approach used is to calculate the project's NPV, without *apparently* taking either the loan interest payments or loan repayment into account:

$$(-1000 + 450A_{3-0.15} = +27.44 \text{ NPV})$$

However, the loan cash flows are *not* being ignored. They involve the following cash flows

Year	£
0	
1	− 100
2	− 100
3	−1000

Applying the principle that the discount rate should always reflect the risk of the cash flow, the discount rate that would best reflect the risk of the loan cash flow would be the loan interest rate itself; and so:

Year	£		10% discount		
0					
1	− 100	×	0.9091	=	− 90.91
2	− 100	×	0.8264	=	− 82.64
3	−1000	×	0.7513	=	− 836.43
					PV − 1000^2

Therefore, in entering the project's outlay of £1000 in the NPV analysis we are implicitly entering the *present value* of the financing cash flows involved with the project.

However, problems can arise as far as this principle is concerned when part or all of a foreign project's finance is raised in the foreign country rather than – what has been implicitly assumed so far – via the export of sterling. This is because the foreign financing can affect the amount of the project's cash flows available to be remitted back to the parent. To illustrate this, let us return to Rush plc and the project dealt with in Example 2, but now involve some foreign currency financing. Example 4 gives the details.

Example 4

Rush plc now propose to finance the foreign project (referred to in Example 2) as a joint venture with investors in the host country. Foreign investors will buy $5 million of equity and Rush plc will export £2 million for the remaining 50% of the equity. The company plans to follow its normal policy of paying out each year's entire net cash flow as dividends.

Under these circumstances, from the *project's* viewpoint, its NPV remains at +£0.588 million. However, from the *parent's* viewpoint, the revised financing plans alter their analysis:

Year	1	2	3
+project cash flow	+8	+4	+3.5
−foreign dividends	−4	−2	−1.75
+blocked funds		+3	+4.15
+interest		+0.15	+0.21
Total cash flow	+4	+5.15	+6.11
Repatriated c/f	−1	−1	−6.11
Blocked funds	+3	+4.15	−

Year	$m	×	20% discount		
0	-5^2	×	1	=	−5
1	+1	×	0.8333	=	+0.83
2	+1	×	0.6944	=	+0.69
3	+6.11	×	0.5787	=	+3.54
					$+0.06m

$$+\$0.06m \div 2.50 = +£24\ 000\ NPV$$

As a result the foreign project which formerly produced a negative NPV now produces a positive NPV.

In Example 4 it can be seen that because of the change in the source of the finance (dollars rather than sterling for 50% of the financing requirement) the resulting impact on the cash flows available to the parent now makes this particular project worthwhile.

Example 4 contains a very important conclusion as far as foreign project appraisal is concerned: the cash flows of any finance raised in the host country *must* be included in the NPV evaluation of the project, if there are restrictions imposed on the repatriation of the project's cash flows back to the parent. If there are no restrictions on net cash flow remittance back to the parent, then the project should be appraised on the same as any domestic project – excluding all the financing cash flows.

The project discount rate

The conclusion reached in the above section then leads on to the problem about identifying the correct discount rate to use (whether Approach 1 is applied and a dollar discount rate is required, or Approach 2 is applied and a sterling discount rate is needed). With the Rush plc example used in Examples 2 and 4 the problem was deliberately avoided by using all-equity financing. In such a case the discount rate simply has to reflect the systematic business risk of the project.

The all-equity financing used in the two Rush plc examples also helped avoid having to make a distinction between taxed and no-tax cases. Therefore the analysis to date applies equally to both situations. However, we know from previous chapters that as soon as we start to look seriously at the choice and identification of the discount rate, we *must* distinguish between taxed and no-tax situations. For the moment, we will proceed on the assumption that there are no taxes.

What would happen in the Rush plc example if the company had originally intended to finance the project by exporting £4m, of which £2m would be in the form of retained earnings and the other £2m would be raised via a three-year term loan? In these circumstances, the sterling discount rate would have been the project's weighted average cost of capital.

However, what if Rush then decided to raise the three-year term loan in the US in dollars? In these circumstances, as far as the project appraisal from the parent's viewpoint is concerned, what would be evaluated would be the project's cash flows available for repatriation back to the parent. The point here is that these cash flows would be the ones that were available for equity only (the debt interest having been paid in dollars). As a result, the discount rate to apply to these cash flows would be one which reflected the project's business risk *plus* the financial risk that arises from the gearing – in other words the cost of equity capital. Example 5 illustrates the situation, making use of the Rush plc data.

Example 5

Rush plc had decided to use a 20% discount rate in dollar terms because they had identified the project's asset beta to be 1.6. In the US, the current return on government stocks is 12% and the return on the New York Stock Exchange index is 17%. Therefore, using the CAPM:

$$20\% = 12\% + (17\% - 12\%) \times 1.6$$

The company now propose to finance the $10 million project by exporting sterling to finance half the project and then raise a three-year $5 million term loan in the US for the remainder. The interest rate on the loan would be 12% as it would be viewed in the US as being virtually risk-free.

$$\text{Given the relationship: } \beta_{assets} = \beta_{equity} \times \frac{V_E}{V_0}$$

$$\text{then } \beta_{equity} = \beta_{assets} \times \frac{V_0}{V_E} = 1.6 \times \frac{2}{1} = 3.2$$

and the dollar return required on the project, from the *equity's* viewpoint, can be estimated via the CAPM:

$$28\% = 12\% + (17\% - 12\%) \times 3.2$$

The project appraisal analysis is now as follows:

Year	1	2	3
Project cash flows	+8	+ 4	+3.5
– Interest payments	−0.6	− 0.6	−0.6
– loan			−5.0
+ blocked funds		+ 6.4	+9.12
+ interest		+ 0.32	+0.46
Total cash flow	+7.4	+10.12	+7.48
Repatriated c/f	−1	− 1	−7.48
Blocked funds	+6.4	+ 9.12	–

Year	$m	×	28% discount		
0	−5	×	1	=	−5
1	+1	×	0.7812	=	+0.78
2	+1	×	0.6103	=	+0.61
3	+7.48	× 3	0.4768	=	+3.57
					$−0.04m

$$-\$0.04 \div 2.50 = -16\,000 \text{ NPV}$$

From the parent company's viewpoint, the project is not worthwhile.

Foreign projects in a taxed world

The only really satisfactory approach to use in a taxed world is an adjusted present value (APV) analysis. This approach is covered in Chapter 21 of Lumby and Jones (1999). In the case of an overseas investment decision, it is vital to look at the project's cash flows from the parent's viewpoint, and the analysis requires the decomposition of the various elements. Example 6 illustrates an application of APV.

Example 6

Visa plc is a highly profitable UK conglomerate. It is thinking of undertaking a capital investment in an overseas country whose currency is the dollar. The following information is available:

Project:	Cost: $12m.
	Life: three years
	Scrap value: $3.4m.
	Operating cash flow: $8m year, pre-tax
Finance:	$4m three-year term loan at 15%
	£3m three-year term loan at 9.5%
	£1m retained earnings
	These financing arrangements fully utilize the project's debt capacity.
Risk:	The project is in an area that the company knows well as far as UK investment is concerned and an asset beta of 1.40 is usually applied.
Market data:	In the UK, the risk-free rate of return is 6% and the return on the FTSE market index is 16%.
Tax and other data:	The UK corporate tax rate is 35%, paid twelve months in arrears. The corporate tax rate of the host country is 40%, payable at each year-end without delay. In the host country, straight-line depreciation on cost, and interest charges, are both allowable expenses against tax. Overseas investors are allowed only to remit 50% of each year's pre-tax, but after interest, accounting projects back to the parent. All blocked funds earn 5% tax free in a special government account and can only be repatriated at the end of the project's life.
	The project is not expected to attract any UK tax on the remitted cash flow.
	The current spot exchange rate is $2.00 = £1. The dollar is expected to depreciate against sterling by 5% per year, for the foreseeable future.

Calculations:
The estimated FX rate in twelve months' time is: $2.00\,(1.05)^1 = 2.10$.
The £ base-case discount rate can be found from the CAPM:

$$6\% + (16\% - 6\%)\,1.40 = 20\%$$

Using the IRPT, the dollar base-case discount rate can now be estimated:

$$\$ \text{ required return} = (0.05 \times 1.20) + 0.20 = 0.26 \text{ or } 26\%$$

The project can now be evaluated, as if it were all-equity financed:

	($m)
Annual operating cash flow	+8
less depreciation	−4
Annual accounting profit	+4

Tax charge: $4m × 0.40 = $1.6m/year
Remittable cash flow: $4m × 0.50 = $2m/year

Parent cash flow analysis:

		($m)		
Year		1	2	3
Operating cash flow	:	+8	+ 8	+ 8
Tax charge	:	−1.6	− 1.6	− 1.6
Scrap value	:			+ 3.4
Tax charge on scrap	:			− 1.36
Blocked funds	:		+ 4.4	+ 9.02
Interest at 5%	:		+ 0.22	+ 0.45
Net cash flow		+6.4	+11.02	+17.91
Remittable cash flow	:	−2.0	− 2.0	−17.91
Blocked cash flow	:	+4.4	+ 9.2	−

Base-case PV calculation:

Year	$m		26% discount[3]		
0	−12	×	1	=	−12
1	+ 2	×	0.7936	=	+ 1.59
2	+ 2	×	0.6299	=	+ 1.26
3	+17.91	×	0.4999	=	+ 8.95
					$−0.20m

$$−\$0.2m ÷ 2.00 = −£0.1m \text{ base-case present value}$$

Present value of the financing side-effects:

(i) *Tax relief on $ loan*

$4m × 0.15 = $0.6m/year interest
$06m × 0.40 = $0.24m/year tax relief

None of this tax relief can be remitted back to the parent until Year 3 and will be reinvested up to that time at 5% interest. Thus the PV of the additional Year 3 cash flows is:

$$\left. \begin{array}{l} \$0.24m × S_{3\neg0.05}(1.15)^{-3} \\ \$0.24m × 3.1525 × 0.6575 \end{array} \right\} = + \$0.50m ÷ 2.00 = +£0.25m$$

(ii) *PV of increase in blocked funds:*

The debt interest charges will reduce the company's accounting profit, and so will reduce the level of remittable cash flows:

$0.6m/year interest = reduction in accounting profit
$0.6m × 0.50 = $0.3m/year increase in blocked funds

$$\left. \begin{array}{l} \$0.3m × A_{3\neg0.05}(1.15)^{-3} \\ \$0.3m × 2.2832 \end{array} \right\} = + \$0.68m ÷ 2.00 = +£0.34m$$

(iii) *PV of the increased terminal cash flow to parent*

The additional blocked funds are inveted to yield 5% and are remitted at Year 3:

$$\left. \begin{array}{l} \$0.3m × S_{3\neg0.05}(1.15)^{-3} \\ \$0.3m × 3.1525 × 0.6575 \end{array} \right\} = + \$0.62m ÷ 2.00 = +£0.31m$$

(iv) *Tax relief on £ loan*

£3m × 0.095 = £0.285m/year interest
£0.285m × 0.35 = £0.1m/year tax relief

$$\left.\begin{array}{l} \text{£0.1m} \times A_{3\neg0.095}(1 + 0.095)^{-1} \\ \text{£0.1m} \times 2.5089 \times 0.9132 \end{array}\right\} = +\text{£0.23m}$$

Adjusted present value:

	(£m)
Base-case PV	: −0.10
PV $ loan tax shield	: +0.25
PV of increase in blocked funds	: −0.34
PV of increase in terminal c/f	: +0.31
PV £ loan tax shield	: +0.23
APV	: £+0.35m

The project is worthwhile. From the parent company's viewpoint it is expected to have a positive APV of £350 000 approximately.

This is clearly a complicated exercise but it emphasizes the fact that overseas investment decisions are complex decisions that require a relatively complex analysis if all relevant factors are to be taken into account.

A simpler approach

A simpler approach to that of Example 6 which should still produce an analysis with an acceptable degree of accuracy, can be suggested. This would involve using the approach used in Example 5 to produce a modified base-case present value and then allowing for just the UK-based financing side effects.

In this approach, the base-case cash flows would be the project cash flows remittable to the parent and the base-case discount rate would, effectively, be the cost of equity capital which reflected the combined business and financial risk of this cash flow. Example 7 takes the same Visa plc problem as used in Example 6, but applies this simpler analysis.

Example 7

Accounting profit:

		($m)
Annual operating cash flow	:	+8
less depreciation	:	−4
less interest	:	−0.6
Accounting profit		−3.4

Annual tax charge: $3.4m × 0.40 = $1.36m
Annual remittable cash flow: $3.4m × 0.50 = $1.7m

Projects remittable cash flows to parent:

			($m)	
Year	1		2	3
Operating cash flow	+8		+ 8	+ 8
Tax charge	−1.36		− 1.36	− 1.36
Interest payments	−0.6		− 0.6	− 0.6
Loan repayments				− 4.0
Scrap value				+ 3.4
Scrap tax charge				− 1.36
Blocked funds			+ 4.34	+ 8.9
Interest at 5%			+ 0.22	+ 0.44
Net cash flow	+6.04		+10.6	+13.42
Remittable cash flow	−1.7		− 1.7	−13.42
Blocked funds	+4.34		+8.9	−

Thus the revised 'base-case cash flow' is:

Year	($m)
0	− 8
1	+ 1.7
2	+ 1.7
3	+13.42

The 'base-case discount rate' can be calculated via the equity beta found from the following expression:

$$\beta_{assets} = \beta_{equity} \times \frac{V_E}{V_E + V_B(1-T_C)} + \beta_{debt} \times \frac{V_B(1-T_C)}{V_E + V_B(1-T_C)}$$

Assuming (for convenience) that the debt beta is zero, then:

$$\beta_{equity} = \beta_{assets} \times \frac{V_E + V_B(1-T_C)}{V_E}$$

where β_{assets} = 1.40 (given)
V_E = £4m (exported £: loan plus retained earnings)
V_B = £2m (overseas currency loan)
T_C = overseas corporate tax rate

$$\beta_{equity} \times = \frac{4+2(1-0.40)}{4} = 1.82$$

and using the CAPM, a £ discount rate can be generated:

$$6\% + (16\% - 6\%) \times 1.82 = 24.2\%$$

Using the IRPT, a $ discount rate can then be calculated:

$$(0.05 \times 1.242) + 0.242 = 0.304 \text{ or } 30.4\%$$

'Base-case present value':

Year	$m		30.4% disc		
0	− 8	×	1	=	−8
1	+ 1.7	×	0.7669	=	+1.30
2	+ 1.7	×	0.5881	=	+1.00
3	+13.42	×	0.4510	=	+6.05
					$+0.35m ÷ 2.00
				=	£+0.17m

Present value of the financing side-effects:

£ loan tax shield:

£3m × 0.095 = £0.285m/year interest
£0.285m × 0.35 = £0.1m/year tax relief

$$\left. \begin{array}{l} \$0.1m \times A_{3\neg 0.095}(1 + 0.095)^{-1} \\ \$0.1m \times 2.5089 \times 0.9132 \end{array} \right\} = +£0.23m$$

Adjusted present value:

	($m)
Base-case present value	+0.17
PV of £ loan tax shield	+0.23
	£+0.40m

This analysis also indicates acceptance: the project is expected to have a positive APV of £400 000.

Translation risk

Translation risk can be defined as the risk a company is exposed to through movements in FX rates when it holds medium-to-long term assets and liabilities in an overseas currency. The concept specifically refers to the fact that, with such assets and liabilities, at each year-end their values have to be *translated* into sterling terms for inclusion in the parent company's balance sheet. Example 8 illustrates the problems that might arise.

Example 8

A UK company undertakes a project in the US, costing $10 million. It is financed through the export of sterling via a £5 million loan. The $/£ exchange rate if 2.00.
   The parent company's opening balance sheet will show:

Balance sheet

£ Loan: £5m	$ Assets: £5m

Suppose twelve months go by and the $/£ exchange rate has now moved to 3.00. The company's balance sheet now shows up an FX loss.[4]

Balance sheet

£ Loan: £5m	$ Assets: £3.33m
less FX loss: (£1.67m)	
£3.33m	

The reason for the loss is that the $10 million worth of assets are now only worth £3.33 million in sterling terms because the dollar has depreciated against sterling.[5]

Overcoming the firm's exposure to translation risk is quite simple – if it is possible. The solution is to finance the project through a *dollar* loan rather than a *sterling* loan. In such circumstances, the company is protected against FX risk through the *matching* principle: the foreign currency asset is matched with a foreign currency liability. Therefore a fall in the value of one – through a movement in the FX rate – will be countered (or matched) through a corresponding fall in the other. Example 9 illustrates the situation.

Example 9

Using the data from Example 8, the UK company financed the project with a $10 million loan, then the opening balance sheet would show:

Balance sheet

£ Loan: £5m	$ Assets: £5m

Twelve months later when the FX rate has moved to $3.00, the balance sheet now becomes:

Balance sheet

£ Loan: £3.33m	$ Assets: £3.33m

Although the sterling value of the assets has declined, this decline has been matched by the sterling worth of the dollar loan. As a result there is no net FX loss.

The difficulty with the solution to the problem of translation risk as advocated in Example 9 is that such a financing method is usually unavailable or inadvisable. For example, many governments insist that a minimum proportion of a project's outlay is financed directly by the parent company. Even where such a requirement is not legally stipulated, it is probably not a very good idea, from a public relations viewpoint, for the parent not to put in any of its *own* money into the project.

Indeed, there is a third reason why 100% foreign currency financing might not be possible. Quite simply the host country's capital market may not be sufficiently developed to provide the financing levels required.

Given, therefore, that it is unrealistic to suppose that 100% foreign currency financing is possible, the standard financing advice for overseas projects is:

1. The project's *property fixed assets*: finance with a foreign currency loan;
2. The project's *non-property fixed assets*: finance via the export of sterling;
3. The project's *working capital requirements*: finance with a foreign currency loan.

This advice means that the firm will be protected from FX risk as far as property fixed assets and working capital are concerned, through the matching principle. But what about the non-property fixed assets?

It is with the non-property fixed assets that the Law of One Price comes to the rescue. The Law of One Price (shown here in $/£) states that the pound sterling price of a good multiplied by the exchange rate, equals the dollar price of the same good. For example, suppose a lap-top PC costs £1500 in the UK and the $/£ spot rate is 1.7000 dollars to the pound, the law of one price suggests that the price of the same computer in the USA will be $1500 \times 1.7 = \$2550$.

The reason for this is abitrage. Should the computer be available in the USA for only $2200 then it could be bought at a Sterling equivalent of $2200 \div 1.7000 = £1294$ and exported to the UK to be sold for £1500. The argument goes that increased demand in the USA will push up the price whilst increased supply in the UK will force down the price until an equilibrium position is reached.

Of course, in the real world things don't work out quite like this, as golfers will tell you (the prices of golf equipment in the USA have been consistently and significantly lower than those in the UK for many years). One problem is the transportation cost of goods but far more significant are other market imperfections. It is not too difficult to go to France or Ireland to pick up a new car but until recently, manufacturers have placed significant obstacles in the way of people attempting to do this. In some cases they have refused to supply UK customers wishing to purchase a car abroad. There are also issues such as import tarrifs and quotas where governments impose restrictions. However, there is evidence that purchasing from abroad is becoming easier and more transparent. The internet has provided a vehicle both for identifying overseas prices and for ordering the goods. Similarly, governments within trading zones such as the European Community are working to ensure that inter-country barriers to trade are removed. All of this should mean that the Law of One Price will become more relevant but there will still be problems where the goods are not physically capable of international trade, such as land and buildings.

Returning to our analysis, the idea here is that non-property fixed assets (such as industrial machinery) obey, to some extent, the workings of the Law of One Price because they are capable of being traded internationally. Neither property fixed assets nor working capital (with the possible exception of some categories of stock) are capable of being physically traded internationally, and so do not follow the law and need to be protected against FX risk through matching.

We will use what appears to be a highly specific example to illustrate how the law of one price can give protection against FX risk. However, the example is only as specific as it appears to ease the explanation. It will *tend* to hold generally, whatever the circumstances, given that the assets in question can be traded internationally (and that the transportation costs do not form too significant an element in its total value). Example 10 gives the details.

Example 10

Suppose that the $10 million US project referred to in Example 8 was composed of the following elements:

Property:	$2m
Machinery:	$7m
Working Capital:	$1m

The suggested financing scheme would be a $3 million loan and $7 million worth of exported sterling.

The fall in the $/£ FX rate from 2.00 to 3.00 from one year-end to the next will cause the sterling worth of the US property and working capital to decline, but this will be matched by a corresponding decline in the sterling worth of the dollar loan. But in these circumstances what happens as far as the US machinery is concerned?

Support (for the purpose of easing the explanation) that the machinery in question is manufactured in the UK and is normally sold for £3.5 million. At an opening $/£ FX rate of 2.00, this is why it cost $7 million to purchase it for the US project.

After an elapse of twelve months, the machinery still costs £3.5 million but, because the dollar has depreciated against sterling, the US cost of the machinery now becomes: £3.5m × 3.00 = $10.5m. (What is seen here is the working through of the Law of One Price: the sterling price of a good × $/£ FX rate = dollar price of the good.)

Therefore (ignoring the problem of depreciation which is just a complication and does not change the basis of the argument), we would be justified in valuing the machinery of our US project at the end of the first year at $10.5 million rather than $7 million on a *replacement cost* basis. (And the company's UK auditors are likely to accept such an argument.)

As a result the company's balance sheets would appear as follows:

Opening balance sheet: $/£ = 2.00

$ loan	:	£1.5m	$2m property	:	£1m
£ funding	:	£3.5m	$7m machinery	:	£3.5m
		£5.0m	$1m work. capt.	:	£0.5m
					£5.0m

Balance sheet at Year 1: $/£ = 3.00

$ loan	: £1m	$2m property	: £0.67m
£ funding	: £3.5m	$7m machinery	: £3.5m
		$1m work. capt.	: £0.33m
	£4.5m		
			£4.5m

The company has managed to hedge its exposure to FX translation risk through a combination of the matching principle and the operation of the Law of One Price.

It is not suggested that the Law of One Price will work as *perfectly* in practice as is the case in Example 10. But, given that the dollar depreciates against sterling and given that industrial machinery is traded internationally, then there will be a definite tendency for the dollar worth of the machine to rise as the value of the dollar declines. Thus, at the very least, companies can expect to get *some* protection (if not perfect protection) against FX risk through the workings of the law.

In summary therefore, the general principle behind financing foreign projects is to raise as much finance as possible in the overseas currency so as to get the maximum protection from translation risk through matching. Where 100% foreign currency financing is not possible, then the company should try to ensure that at least those assets which are not going to be responsive to the operation of the Law of One Price are financed in the overseas currency.

However, we should remind you that it is debatable whether or not translation represents a real risk. It really all depends on the significance placed on the numbers used in financial statements.

Economic risk

The previous discussion on translation risk also touches upon another FX risk of foreign investments which could be called *economic* risk. This is the risk of *unexpected* changes in FX rates.

For example, a proper investment appraisal evaluation might have been undertaken which had indicated that a project would bring about an increase in parent shareholders' wealth. The project then performs perfectly to plan but, because of unexpected and adverse FX movements, in hindsight, it leads to a reduction in parent company shareholders' wealth.

The possible presence of this risk causes real difficulties. The first question it raises is whether the risk is systematic or unsystematic. The second is, if it is systematic, how should it be taken into account in the appraisal process? There is, of course, an even more fundamental question here: does this type of risk exist at all? Example 11 illustrates what is behind this latter question. The $/£ FX rates shown in the example are spot rates (which we have seen before) and future rates which, in this case, are estimated using The Purchasing Power Parity Theorem. PPPT is explained in chapter 23 of Lumby and Jones (1999). It is based on the idea that exchange rates will move to maintain purchasing power parity. So if the inflation rate is 4% in the UK but 6% in the USA, crudely speaking, we would expect the $US to depreciate by around 2% against £ Sterling. The Interest Rate Parity Theorem is also used in the example and is covered in the same chapter of Lumby and Jones (1999) This works on the principle that if international financial markets are efficient, it will not be possible to obtain a better real rate of risk free return in one country rather than another. A higher interest rate is linked to a higher expected adverse movement on exchange rates

Example 11

A US project costs $1 million. It has a life of three years and results in an annual production output of 1000 units. The net after-tax cash flow resulting from the production is expected to be $0.5 million in *current* terms. This cash amount is expected to increase in line with the average US inflation rate which is expected to remain constant at 8% per year.

The project will be entirely financed with sterling and there are no restrictions on net cash flow remittance to the UK parent. A similar-risk UK project would be expected to produce a minimum annual return of 16%.

The current $/£ spot exchange rate is 1.9000 and UK general inflation rate is expected to remain constant at 5% per year.

On the basis of this information, the dollar discount rate can be estimated via the IRPT. First though, the $/£ FX rate of change has to be estimated. This can be done through the PPPT:

$$\frac{0.08 - 0.05}{1.05} = +0.0286$$

and so, using the IRPT:

$$\$ \text{ discount rate} = (0.0286 \times 1.16) + 0.16 = 0.193 \text{ or } 19.3\%$$

The project can now be evaluated:

Year	$m		19.3% discount		
0	−1.0	×	1	=	−1.00
1	+0.54	×	0.8382	=	+0.453
2	+0.583	×	0.7026	=	+0.410
3	+0.630	×	0.5889	=	+0.371
					$+0.234m NPV

$$\$+ 0.234m \div 1.90 = £+0.123m \text{ NPV}$$

The project is worthwhile and should be accepted.

If the firm then undertakes the project, the $/£ FX rates that they are expecting over the next three years can be found from the PPPT:

Spot:	1.9000 (given)
Year 1:	1.9000 (1 + 0.0286) = 1.9543
Year 2:	1.9543 (1 + 0.0286) = 2.0102
Year 3:	2.0102 (1 + 0.0286) = 2.0677

Therefore, they are expecting the following sterling cash flow from the project:

Year	$m	÷	$/£	=	£m
0	−1	÷	1.9000	=	−0.526
1	+0.54	÷	1.9543	=	+0.276
2	+0.583	÷	2.0102	=	+0.290
3	+0.630	÷	2.0677	=	+0.305

(And this cash flow will, of course, have a + NPV of £123 000 when discounted at 16% (ignoring rounding errors).)

However, suppose that US inflation turns out to be higher than expected, say 12% rather than 8%. It means that the future exchange rates will also differ.

$$\text{Rate of change in \$:} \quad \frac{0.12 - 0.05}{1.05} = +0.067$$

Year 1:	1.9000 (1 + 0.067) = 2.0273
Year 2:	2.0273 (1 + 0.067) = 2.1631
Year 3:	2.1631 (1 + 0.067) = 2.3081

Will the UK parent suffer as a result of this unexpected, adverse movement in the $/£ FX rates? They should not, if the project performs as expected and produces 1000 units per year; the reason being that the *increased* US inflation rate *should* result in *increased* dollar cash flows from the project which will now inflate up at 12% rather than 8%:

Year	$m	÷	$/£	=	£m
0	−1	÷	1.9000	=	−0.526
1	+0.56	÷	2.0273	=	+0.276
2	+0.627	÷	2.1631	=	+0.290
3	+0.702	÷	2.3081	=	+0.304

Therefore the parent will receive exactly the same sterling cash flow, whose NPV will remain at +£123,000.

The problem with Example 11 is that life does not work quite so perfectly. Whilst the IRPT works quite well the actual workings of the PPPT tend to be more approximate because of the imperfections in the workings of the law of one price. Therefore the FX rates may not turn out as predicted at a 12% inflation level and, indeed, the project's net after-tax cash flow may not respond, in the perfect way illustrated, to the rise in US inflation. Thus it is fairly safe to conclude that, in the real world, the risk of unexpected FX movements *does* exist for firms in investing overseas.

This then brings us back to the first question posed: is this risk wholly systematic or unsystematic or partly both? The answer is highly uncertain, but probably some of it is capable of being diversified away through international diversification.

The uncertainty arises because economists cannot agree whether individual country capital markets are *segmented* (and so largely independent of each other) or *integrated*. But, despite this, there is a relatively simple solution (although this is not always possible to apply and it is far from a perfect answer). That solution is to eliminate the risk of unexpected FX rate movements by using the forward markets to sell forward a project's expected foreign currency net cash flow. Forward markets provide a mechanism for entering into contracts to buy and sell currencies at some date in the future but at a price that is agreed today.

This solution may not be possible to apply in practice because forward markets only extend substantial periods of time forward in the world's major currencies. If the project was in Egypt, for example, we would have difficulties trying to apply this solution. Even when suitably extended forward markets do exist (such as with $/£), forward contracts are for *certain* amounts of currency, while the project's cash flow is only *expected*. Thus a perfect hedge against the FX risk is unlikely to be achieved.

Alternatives to the forward sale of currencies also exist through the matching principle. For example an overseas currency loan extending over the life of the project could be raised. This loan could be converted immediately into sterling and capital and interest could be repaid out of the project's net cash flow. Again, this would not give a perfect hedge, but it would provide a significant degree of protection. A further alternative would be to use the overseas project's net cash flow to purchase exportable goods from the host country; thereby converting the project's FX risk-exposed cash flow into a non-exposed (or, less exposed) goods flow.

Country/Political risk

The final risk attached to foreign projects is country or political risk. There is an academic debate as to whether or not there is a difference between country risk and political risk but we will treat them as though they are one and the same. This is the risk that, once a project has been undertaken, something of a political or serious economic nature will happen to inhibit the ability of the company to remit the cash flows expected from the project. This may be because of war or revolution or it may simply be that the host government adversely changes the 'rules of the game' for either political or economic reasons. Whilst there is evidence that there is little systematic, quantitative analysis by companies of this type of risk, simply because it is so unpredictable, it is fair to say that it is generally possible to judge if a partner country is high or low risk. We hesitate to mention high risk countries on the grounds that this could be taken as an insult but it is safe to suggest that countries such as the USA, Canada, Australia and our European partners would generally be seen as low risk, along with many other politically stable countries. Demirag and Goddard (page 273) provide details of a political risk ranking exercise carried out by *Euromoney* in 1992 and also discuss a number of other ranking systems. Whilst these rankings are better than nothing, they are bound to remain more or less subjective.

It is unusual for governments to seize the assets of overseas companies, if only because it is likely to be counterproductive in the longer term. Multinational companies exercise considerable power in terms of the control of both production and markets. There are also international bodies that might be expected to exert pressure on countries that act in an unreasonable way. Thus whilst assets might be lost or destroyed as the result of war or expropriation, the most likely problems concern changes to the rules on the transfer of cash out of the host country.

As far as the risks of restrictions being imposed unexpectedly on net cash flow repatriation, the simple rule is to try and minimize its possible impact by using as many different remittance channels as are available. Thus a project's net cash flows may be remitted back to the parent in the form of dividend payments or interest payments. If the overseas project undertakes any process for which the parent has royalty rights, then royalty payments may be another possible channel.

Although an overseas project's lower and middle management are drawn from the host country itself, the top management are normally seconded from the parent. The parent might then charge the foreign project for the services of these top management, effectively using the management charge as a further means of remitting back the project's net cash flow.

Finally, if there is any transfer of goods between the parent and the overseas project, then the transfer pricing mechanism can be employed as yet another channel for remitting back the project's net cash flows. This is covered in the next section

Obviously, national governments are aware of all these different possible channels and so if they *really* want to restrict the repatriation of a project's net cash flows to an overseas parent, then they are perfectly capable of doing so. However, sometimes a government might want to be *seen* to be doing something about restricting foreign project cash flows, without wishing to restrict them absolutely. Thus they might enforce restrictions on, for example, dividends as this is seen as a politically sensitive area linked directly to profits. At the same time, however, such things as interest and royalty payments may be seen as much more legitimate business expenses and so remain unrestricted.

As far as the other elements of country risk are concerned there are two main possible courses of action that can be taken to reduce them. The first would be to tie-in host country investors or even the host government, through such things as joint ventures. This sort of arrangement is likely to discourage any host government from taking such adverse action against the project that the overseas parent pulls out, if this would then cause the project to fail. Such action would not only hurt the overseas parent, but would also hurt host country investors.

The second course of action is insurance. It is possible to insure an overseas project against the most extreme forms of country risk such as expropriation. In such circumstances, the cost of the insurance should be included as part of the overall cost of undertaking the project in any financial appraisal.

Management charges and transfer pricing

Management charges and transfer prices are both normal parts of business activity that can be manipulated to circumvent restrictions on the tranfer of funds through dividends.

Management charges are simply a way of charging a division or a subsidiary company for services provided by other parts of the company. This might include the the cost of computer facilities, a share of world wide marketing costs or part of the central managment costs including all kinds of head office costs. Generally speaking these might be expected to reflect the real cost of the services being provided to the subsidiary or division but this is not always the case even when there is no international dimension. Increasing the charge represents one way of transferring profit and (possibly) cash from one country to another. However, it is likely that the authorities of the host country will look closely at really significant management charges if they are serious about controlling overseas remittances.

Transfer prices pose more of a problem in terms of government control. Goods and services will often pass from one group company or division to another. There are a number of ways of deciding on the prices to be charged for transfer (transfer prices) and in general these are designed to achieve overall corporate objectives, in particular (we assume) maximization of shareholder wealth. Thus good transfer prices will encourage divisional and subsidiary managers to act in the best interests of the company. It is beyond the scope of this book to go into the detail of the setting of transfer prices and the interested reader can refer to any good management accounting text such as Drury for an analysis of this. However, the manipulation of transfer prices offers a relatively simple way of moving profit from one country to another. Let us assume that we have a company based in the UK – St George plc, with subsidiary companies in Urbanaland, a country with high taxes and restrictions on dividend payments, and also Alpland, a very stable country with very low corporate taxes and no retriction on dividend payments. St George buys goods from and sell goods to its subsidiary in Urbanaland. It also sells finished goods to a retailing subsidiary in Alpland. By seeting the price for goods sold to Urbanaland artificially high and that for goods bought from Urbanaland artificially low, St George can move its profits out of Urbanaland and into the UK. Furthermore, by setting the transfer price for goods sold from the UK to Alpland artificially low, the profits can be moved again to Alpland with its advantageous tax regime. This type of manipulation has long been recognized and some states in the USA have sought to put a stop to it by passing laws that specify that tax will be paid on the higher of the profit declared in the state or the wordwide profit of the company multiplied by the proportion of worldwide turnover accounted for by the state. The fact that such a crude device is seen as being justifiable is an indication of the difficulties outside bodies might have in assessing the appropriateness or otherwise of the transfer prices being used. One of the most notorious cases of manipulation of transfer prices involved the sale of the drugs Librium and Valium in the late 1960s and early 1970s by the Swiss company Hoffman-La Roche to its UK subsidiary at vastly inflated prices at a time when taxation was high in the UK and low in Switzerland.

Summary

This chapter has provided a fairly brief overview of a highly complex area which contains many still unresolved difficulties. The main points covered were as follows:

- As far as foreign project appraisal is concerned, there are two equivalent approaches: the project's overseas currency cash flows can be converted to sterling cash flows and a sterling discount rate applied; alternatively, the project's overseas currency cash flows can be discounted at the overseas currency discount rate to produce an NPV. This can then be converted at spot into a sterling NPV.

- A major difference between domestic and foreign project evaluation arises when the latter suffers from cash flow remittance restrictions. In such circumstances the project must be evaluated from the viewpoint of the cash flows that are available to be remitted back to the parent. In particular, this means including in the project's cash flows any foreign currency financing cash flows.

- Once taxation is brought into consideration, then an APV analysis becomes appropriate. However, such an approach can be complex and a simplified approach can be utilized by modifying APV.

- Foreign project financing can play a significant role in reducing the parent's exposure to translation risk. Here, the standard advice is to finance the project requirement for property and working capital in the overseas currency, while the non-property fixed assets can be financed via the export of sterling.

- Economic and country/political risk were examined and ways by which exposure to both may be reduced were discussed.

- Finally management charges and transfer prices were considered as a way of moving profits and cash around on an international basis.

Notes

1. The spot rate is the rate for immediate currency conversion on any particular day.

2. The rounding error is just two pence.

3. Notice, the parent only has to contribute $5 million to the project, in terms of sterling.

4. These discount factors are not included in the tables supplied and have been calculated separately.

5. For simplicity, these examples ignore depreciation. The conclusions of the analysis remain unchanged in a more realistic setting.

6. The dollar *could* equally have appreciated, and an FX gain would have been made.

Further reading

1. International aspects of investment appraisal and financing decisions are complex and form the subject matter of specialist books. Buckley, *Multinational Finance*, Prentice Hall 1992, Eiteman Stonehill and Moffet, *Multinational Business Finance*, Addison Wesley 1992 and I. Demirag and S. Goddard *Financial Management for International Business*, McGraw Hill 1994 provide good coverage.

2. Good introductory articles on the subject matter include: A.C. Shapiro, 'Capital Budgeting for the Multinational Corporation', *Financial Management*, Spring 1978, and, by the same author, 'International Capital Budgeting', *Midland Corporate Finance Journal*, Spring 1983; A. Buckley, 'Evaluating Overseas Projects', *Accountancy*, May 1987; J.B. Holland, 'Overseas Capital Investment', in Firth and Keane (eds), *Issues in Finance*, Philip Allen 1986; and M. Wilson, 'Capital Budgeting for Foreign Direct Investment', *Managerial Finance*, Summer 1990.

3. On the use of APV in an international context, see: D.R. Lessard, 'Evaluating Foreign Projects – an Adjusted Present Value Approach', in D. Lessard (ed.), *International Financial Management*, Warren, Gorham and Lamont 1979.
4. On the financing problem see: M.R. Eaher, 'Denomination Decision for Multinational Transactions', *Financial Management*, Autumn 1980 and A. Buckley, 'Financing Overseas Subsidiaries', *Accountancy*, August 1987.
5. On setting transfer prices see: C. Drury, *Management and Cost Accounting*, 5th Edition, Thomson Learning 2000.
6. Other articles of interest include: R.C. Hechman, 'Foreign Exchange Exposure: Accounting Measures and Economic Reality', *Journal of Cash Management*, February–March 1983; S.H. Goodman, 'Foreign Exchange Rate Forecasting Techniques', *Journal of Finance*, May 1979; and D.J. Oblack and R.J. Helm, 'Survey and Analysis of Capital Budgeting Methods Used by Multinationals', *Financial Management*, Winter 1980.

Quickie questions

1. What are the two basic approaches by which a UK company can evaluate a US project?
2. Why should foreign financing flows be included in an overseas project's appraisal?
3. What is the standard advice for financing overseas projects?
4. What possible channels might a company use to remit back a foreign project's cash flows?
5. What is country risk?
6. What is economic risk?

Problems

1. Polycalc plc is an internationally diversified company. It is presently considering undertaking a capital investment in Australia to manufacture agricultural fertilizers. The project would require immediate capital expenditure of A$15 million plus A$5 million of working capital which would be recovered at the end of the project's four-year life. It is estimated that an annual revenue of A$18 million would be generated by the project, with annual operating costs of A$5 million. Straight-line depreciation over the life of the project is an allowable expense against company tax in Australia which is charged at a rate of 50%, payable at each year-end without delay. The project can be assumed to have a zero scrap value.

   Polycalc plans to finance the project with a £5 million four-year loan at 10% from the Euro-sterling market, plus £5 million of retained earnings. The proposed financing scheme reflects the belief that the project would have a debt capacity of two-thirds of *capital* cost. Issue costs on the Euro debt will be $2\frac{1}{2}$% and are tax deductible.

   In the UK the fertilizer industry has an equity beta of 1.40 and an average debt:equity gearing ratio of 1:4. Debt capital can be assumed to be virtually risk-free. The current return on UK government stock is 7.1% and the market return is 17.85%.

   Corporate tax in the UK is at 35% and can be assumed to be payable at each year-end without delay. Because of a double-taxation agreement, Polycalc will not have to pay any UK tax on the project. The company is expected to have a substantial UK tax liability from its other operations for the foreseeable future.

The current A$/£ spot rate is 2.0000 and the A$ is expected to depreciate against the £ at an annual rate of 10%.

Required:
(a) Using the adjusted present value technique, advise the management of Polycalc on the project's desirability.
(b) Comment briefly on the company's intended financing plans for the Australian project. Suggest, with reasons, a more sensible alternative.

2. Scouse plc is a successful manufacturing company based in the north of England. As a result of the changing relationship between the EU and Eastern European countries an opportunity has arisen to invest in Glumrovia. The directors of Scouse plc have decided that because of the risky nature of investments in this part of the world, they will require a return of at least 20% after tax on the project.

The government of Glumrovia is prepared to grant Scouse plc a five-year licence to operate and market research suggests that cash flows from the project will be as follows (in 000s of Glumrovian $):

Year	1	2	3	4	5
	250	400	500	600	700

However much of the increase is because of expected rates of inflation and the G$/sterling exchange rate is expected to be:

Year	1	2	3	4	5
	4	5	6	7	8

as compared with the current rate of 3G$ to the £1.

The project will cost G$600 000 to set up but the present Glumrovian government will pay G$600 000 to Scouse plc for the business (not including working capital) at the end of the five-year period. They will also lend Scouse plc the G$250 000 required for working capital at the advantageous rate of 6% to be repaid at the end of the five-year period. Scouse plc will pay Glumrovian tax on profits after interest at the rate of 20% at the end of each year at which time the balance of profits can be remitted to the UK. There is a tax arrangement between the governments of Glumrovia and the UK so that any Glumrovian tax paid can be offset against UK tax. UK tax is payable at the rate of 30% and you should assume that it is payable at the time that the cash is remitted to the UK. As yet there is no stock exchange in Glumrovia as the Christian Democrats who replaced the Communist regime that ran the country from 1948 to 1993 have not had time to get around to all of the economic reforms required. An article in the *Guardian* dated 28 February 1998 reveals that the people of Glumrovia are disappointed with the pace of reform and that the elections in 2000 might well see a big upswing in Communist influence.

Assume all cash flows take place at the end of periods.

(a) Prepare a report for the management of Scouse plc that analyses the data available and makes argued recommendations as to whether or not the project should be taken on.
(b)Discuss the possible problems that might confront a company making the type of decision facing Scouse plc.

Tables

Compounding and discount tables (including mid-point discount tables)

Table A Compound interest factor $(1 + i)^N$

i		0.04	0.06	0.08	0.10	0.12	0.14	0.16	0.18	0.20
N	1	1.0400	1.0600	1.0800	1.1000	1.1200	1.1400	1.1600	1.1800	1.2000
	2	1.0816	1.1236	1.1664	1.2100	1.2544	1.2996	1.3456	1.3924	1.4400
	3	1.1249	1.1910	1.2597	1.3310	1.4049	1.4815	1.5609	1.6430	1.7280
	4	1.1699	1.2625	1.3605	1.4641	1.5735	1.6890	1.8106	1.9338	2.0736
	5	1.2167	1.3382	1.4693	1.6105	1.7623	1.9254	2.1003	2.2878	2.4883
	6	1.2653	1.4185	1.5869	1.7716	1.9738	2.1950	2.4364	2.6996	2.9860
	7	1.3159	1.5036	1.7138	1.9487	2.2107	2.5023	2.8262	3.1855	3.5832
	8	1.3686	1.5939	1.8509	2.1436	2.4760	2.8526	3.2784	3.7589	4.2998
	9	1.4233	1.6895	1.9990	2.3580	2.7731	3.2519	3.8030	4.4335	5.1598
	10	1.4802	1.7909	2.1589	2.5937	3.1058	3.7072	4.4114	5.2338	6.1917
	11	1.5395	1.8983	2.3316	2.8531	3.4785	4.2262	5.1173	6.1759	7.4301
	12	1.6010	2.0122	2.5182	3.1384	3.8960	4.8179	5.9360	7.2876	8.9161
	13	1.6651	2.1329	2.7196	3.4523	4.3635	5.4924	6.8858	8.5994	10.6993
	14	1.7317	2.2609	2.9372	3.7975	4.8871	6.2613	7.9875	10.1472	12.8392
	15	1.8009	2.3966	3.1722	4.1773	5.4736	7.1379	9.2655	11.9737	15.4070

Table B Present value factor $(1 + i)^{-N}$

i		0.04	0.06	0.08	0.10	0.12	0.14	0.16	0.18	0.20
N	1	0.9615	0.9434	0.9259	0.9091	0.8929	0.8772	0.8621	0.8475	0.8333
	2	0.9246	0.8900	0.8573	0.8264	0.7972	0.7695	0.7432	0.7182	0.6944
	3	0.8890	0.8396	0.7938	0.7513	0.7118	0.6750	0.6407	0.6086	0.5787
	4	0.8548	0.7921	0.7350	0.6830	0.6355	0.5921	0.5523	0.5158	0.4823
	5	0.8219	0.7473	0.6806	0.6209	0.5674	0.5194	0.4761	0.4371	0.4019
	6	0.7903	0.7050	0.6302	0.5645	0.5066	0.4556	0.4014	0.3704	0.3349
	7	0.7599	0.6651	0.5835	0.5132	0.4532	0.3996	0.3538	0.3139	0.2791
	8	0.7307	0.6274	0.5403	0.4665	0.4039	0.3506	0.3050	0.2660	0.2326
	9	0.7026	0.5919	0.5002	0.4241	0.3606	0.3075	0.2630	0.2255	0.1938
	10	0.6756	0.5584	0.4632	0.3855	0.3220	0.2697	0.2267	0.1911	0.1615
	11	0.6496	0.5268	0.4289	0.3505	0.2875	0.2366	0.1954	0.1619	0.1346
	12	0.6246	0.4970	0.3971	0.3186	0.2567	0.2076	0.1685	0.1372	0.1122
	13	0.6006	0.4686	0.3677	0.2897	0.2292	0.1821	0.1452	0.1163	0.0935
	14	0.5775	0.4423	0.3405	0.2633	0.2046	0.1597	0.1252	0.0985	0.0779
	15	0.5553	0.4173	0.3152	0.2394	0.1827	0.1401	0.1079	0.0835	0.0649

Table C Present value of an annuity $A_{N\neg i}$

i	0.04	0.06	0.08	0.10	0.12	0.14	0.16	0.18	0.20
N 1	0.9615	0.9434	0.9259	0.9091	0.8929	0.8772	0.8621	0.8475	0.8333
2	1.8861	1.8334	1.7833	1.7355	1.6901	1.6467	1.6052	1.5656	1.5278
3	2.7751	2.6730	2.5771	2.4869	2.4018	2.3216	2.2459	2.1743	2.1065
4	3.6299	3.,4651	3.3121	3.1699	3.0373	2.9137	2.7982	2.6901	2.5887
5	4.4518	4.2124	3.9927	3.7908	3.6048	3.4331	3.2743	3.1272	2.9906
6	5.2421	4.9173	4.6229	4.3553	4.1114	3.8887	3.6847	3.4976	3.3255
7	6.0021	5.5824	5.2064	4.8684	4.5638	4.2883	4.0386	3.8115	3.6046
8	6.7327	6.2098	5.7466	5.3349	4.9676	4.6389	4.3436	4.0776	3.8372
9	7.4353	6.8017	6.2469	5.7590	5.3282	4.9464	4.6065	4.3030	4.0310
10	8.1109	7.3601	6.7101	6.1446	5.6502	5.2161	4.8332	4.4941	4.1925
11	8.7605	7.8869	7.1390	6.4951	5.9377	5.4527	5.0286	4.6560	4.3271
12	9.3851	8.3838	7.5361	6.8137	6.1944	5.6603	5.1971	4.7932	4.4392
13	9.9856	8.8527	7.9038	7.1034	6.4235	5.8424	5.3423	4.9095	4.5327
14	10.5631	9.2950	8.2442	7.3667	6.6282	6.0021	5.4675	5.0081	4.6106
15	11.1184	9.7122	8.5595	7.6061	6.8109	6.1422	5.5755	5.0916	4.6755

Table D Terminal value of an annuity $S_{N\neg i}$

i	0.04	0.06	0.08	0.10	0.12	0.14	0.16	0.18	0.20
N 1	1.0000	1.0000	1.0000	1.0000	1.0000	1.0000	1.0000	1.0000	1.0000
2	2.0400	2.0600	2.0800	2.1000	2.1200	2.1400	2.1600	2.1800	2.2000
3	3.1216	3.1836	3.2464	3.3100	3.3744	3.4396	3.5056	3.5724	3.6400
4	4.2465	4.3746	4.5061	4.6410	4.7793	4.9211	5.0665	5.2154	5.3680
5	5.4163	5.6371	5.8666	6.1051	6.3528	6.6101	6.8771	7.1542	7.4416
6	6.6330	6.9753	7.3359	7.7156	8.1152	8.5355	8.9775	9.4420	9.9299
7	7.8983	8.3938	8.9228	9.4872	10.0890	10.7305	11.4139	12.1415	12.9159
8	9.2142	9.8975	10.6366	11.4359	12.2997	13.2328	14.2401	15.3270	16.4991
9	10.5828	11.4913	12.4876	13.5795	14.7757	16.0853	17.5185	19.0859	20.7989
10	12.0061	13.1808	14.4866	15.9374	17.5487	19.3373	21.3215	23.5213	25.9587
11	13.4864	14.9716	16.6455	18.5312	20.6546	23.0445	25.7329	28.7551	32.1504
12	15.0258	16.8699	18.9771	21.3843	24.1331	27.2707	30.8502	34.9311	39.5805
13	16.6268	18.8821	21.4953	24.5227	28.0291	32.0887	36.7862	42.2187	48.4966
14	18.2919	21.0151	24.2149	27.9750	32.3926	37.5811	43.6720	50.8180	59.1959
15	20.0236	23.2760	27.1521	31.7725	37.2797	43.8424	51.6595	60.9653	72.0351

Table E Annual equivalent factor $A^{-1}_{N \neg i}$

i	0.04	0.06	0.08	0.10	0.12	0.14	0.16	0.18	0.20
N 1	1.0400	1.0600	1.0800	1.1000	1.1200	1.1400	1.1600	1.1800	1.2000
2	0.5302	0.5454	0.5608	0.5762	0.5917	0.6073	0.6230	0.6387	0.6545
3	0.3603	0.3741	0.3880	0.4021	0.4163	0.4307	0.4453	0.4599	0.4747
4	0.2755	0.2886	0.3019	0.3155	0.3292	0.3432	0.3574	0.3717	0.3863
5	0.2446	0.2374	0.2505	0.2638	0.2774	0.2913	0.3054	0.3198	0.3344
6	0.1908	0.2034	0.2163	0.2296	0.2432	0.2572	0.2714	0.2859	0.3007
7	0.1666	0.1791	0.1921	0.2054	0.2191	0.2332	0.2476	0.2624	0.2774
8	0.1485	0.1610	0.1740	0.1874	0.2013	0.2156	0.2302	0.2452	0.2606
9	0.1345	0.1470	0.1601	0.1736	0.1877	0.2022	0.2171	0.2324	0.2481
10	0.1233	0.1359	0.1490	0.1627	0.1770	0.1917	0.2069	0.2225	0.2385
11	0.1141	0.1268	0.1401	0.1540	0.1684	0.1834	0.1989	0.2148	0.2311
12	0.1066	0.1193	0.1327	0.1468	0.1614	0.1767	0.1924	0.2086	0.2253
13	0.1001	0.1130	0.1265	0.1408	0.1557	0.1712	0.1872	0.2037	0.2206
14	0.0947	0.1076	0.1213	0.1357	0.1509	0.1666	0.1829	0.1997	0.2169
15	0.0899	0.1030	0.1168	0.1315	0.1468	0.1628	0.1794	0.1964	0.2139

Table F Sinking fund factor $S^{-1}_{N \neg i}$

i	0.04	0.06	0.08	0.10	0.12	0.14	0.16	0.18	0.20
N 1	1.0000	1.0000	1.0000	1.0000	1.0000	1.0000	1.0000	1.0000	1.0000
2	0.4902	0.4854	0.4808	0.4762	0.4717	0.4673	0.4630	0.4587	0.4545
3	0.3203	0.3141	0.3080	0.3021	0.2963	0.2907	0.2853	0.2799	0.2747
4	0.2355	0.2286	0.2219	0.2155	0.2092	0.2032	0.1974	0.1917	0.1863
5	0.1846	0.1774	0.1705	0.1638	0.1574	0.1513	0.1454	0.1398	0.1344
6	0.1508	0.1343	0.1363	0.1296	0.1232	0.1172	0.1114	0.1059	0.1007
7	0.1266	0.1191	0.1121	0.1054	0.0991	0.0932	0.0876	0.0824	0.0774
8	0.1085	0.1010	0.0940	0.0874	0.0813	0.0756	0.0702	0.0652	0.0606
9	0.0945	0.0870	0.0801	0.0736	0.0677	0.0622	0.0571	0.0524	0.0481
10	0.0833	0.0759	0.0690	0.0627	0.0570	0.0517	0.0469	0.0425	0.0385
11	0.0741	0.0668	0.0601	0.0540	0.0484	0.0434	0.0389	0.0348	0.0311
12	0.0666	0.0593	0.0527	0.0468	0.0414	0.0367	0.0324	0.0286	0.0253
13	0.0601	0.0530	0.0465	0.0408	0.0357	0.0312	0.0272	0.0237	0.0206
14	0.0547	0.0476	0.0413	0.0357	0.0309	0.0266	0.0229	0.0197	0.0169
15	0.0499	0.0430	0.0368	0.0315	0.0268	0.0228	0.0194	0.0164	0.0139

Table G Compound interest factor $(1 + i)^{N-0.5}$

Present value of £1 received evenly through year

i	0.04	0.06	0.08	0.10	0.12	0.14	0.16	0.18	0.20
N 1	0.9806	0.9713	0.9623	0.9535	0.9449	0.9366	0.9285	0.9206	0.9129
2	0.9429	0.9163	0.8910	0.8668	0.8437	0.8216	0.8004	0.7801	0.7607
3	0.9066	0.8644	0.8250	0.7880	0.7533	0.7207	0.6900	0.6611	0.6339
4	0.8717	0.8155	0.7639	0.7164	0.6726	0.6322	0.5948	0.5603	0.5283
5	0.8382	0.7693	0.7073	0.6512	0.6005	0.5545	0.5128	0.4748	0.4402
6	0.8060	0.7258	0.6549	0.5920	0.5362	0.4864	0.4421	0.4024	0.3669
7	0.7750	0.6847	0.6064	0.5382	0.4787	0.4267	0.3811	0.3410	0.3057
8	0.7452	0.6460	0.5615	0.4893	0.4274	0.3743	0.3285	0.2890	0.2548
9	0.7165	0.6094	0.5199	0.4448	0.3816	0.3283	0.2832	0.2449	0.2123
10	0.6889	0.5749	0.4814	0.4044	0.3407	0.2880	0.2441	0.2075	0.1769
11	0.6624	0.5424	0.4457	0.3676	0.3042	0.2526	0.2105	0.1759	0.1474
12	0.6370	0.5117	0.4127	0.3342	0.2716	0.2216	0.1814	0.1491	0.1229
13	0.6125	0.4827	0.3821	0.3038	0.2425	0.1944	0.1564	0.1263	0.1024
14	0.5889	0.4554	0.3538	0.2762	0.2165	0.1705	0.1348	0.1071	0.0853
15	0.5663	0.4296	0.3276	0.2511	0.1933	0.1496	0.1162	0.0907	0.0711

Using this discount factor actually assumes that the cash flows take place in the middle of the year. However this is a very good approximation for cash flows that are spread evenly during the year.

Table H Present value of an annuity $A_{N-.05\,-i}$

Present value of £1 received each year evenly throughout the year

i	2%	4%	6%	8%	10%	12%	14%	16%	18%	20%
N 1	0.9901	0.9806	0.9713	0.9623	0.9535	0.9449	0.9366	0.9285	0.9206	0.9129
2	1.9609	1.9234	1.8876	1.8532	1.8202	1.7886	1.7582	1.7289	1.7007	1.6736
3	2.9126	2.8300	2.7520	2.6782	2.6082	2.5419	2.4788	2.4189	2.3619	2.3075
4	3.8456	3.7018	3.5675	3.4421	3.3246	3.2144	3.1110	3.0137	2.9222	2.8358
5	4.7604	4.5400	4.3369	4.1493	3.9758	3.8149	3.6655	3.5265	3.3970	3.2761
6	5.6572	5.3460	5.0627	4.8042	4.5678	4.3511	4.1520	3.9686	3.7994	3.6429
7	6.5364	6.1209	5.7474	5.4106	5.1060	4.8298	4.5787	4.3497	4.1404	3.9486
8	7.3984	6.8661	6.3934	5.9721	5.5953	5.2573	4.9530	4.6782	4.4294	4.2034
9	8.2435	7.5826	7.0028	6.4920	6.0401	5.6389	5.2813	4.9614	4.6743	4.4157
10	9.0720	8.2715	7.5777	6.9733	6.4445	5.9796	5.5693	5.2055	4.8818	4.5926
11	9.8842	8.9340	8.1200	7.4190	6.8121	6.2839	5.8219	5.4160	5.0577	4.7401
12	10.6806	9.5709	8.6317	7.8317	7.1463	6.5555	6.0435	5.5975	5.2068	4.8629
13	11.4613	10.1834	9.1144	8.2138	7.4501	6.7980	6.2379	5.7539	5.3331	4.9653
14	12.2267	10.7723	9.5698	8.5677	7.7262	7.0146	6.4085	5.8887	5.4401	5.0506
15	12.9771	11.3386	9.9994	8.8953	7.9773	7.2079	6.5580	6.0050	5.5309	5.1217

Using this discount factor actually assumes that the cash flows take place in the middle of each year. However this is a very good approximation for cash flows that are spread evenly during each year. It will be noticed that at 10% over 10 years, the annuity factor is 6.4445 whilst using the year end cash flow assumption (table C) produces a factor of 6.1446. It is a matter of judgement as to whether or not this difference (of 5%) is seen as being significant.

Area under the normal curve

Table I Areas under the normal distribution

z	0.00	0.01	0.02	0.03	0.04	0.05	0.06	0.07	0.08	0.09
0.0	.0000	.0040	.0080	.0120	.0160	.0199	.0239	.0279	.0319	.0359
0.1	.0398	.0438	.0478	.0517	.0557	.0596	.0636	.0675	.0714	.0753
0.2	.0793	.0832	.0871	.0910	.0948	.0987	.1026	.1064	.1103	.1141
0.3	.1179	.1217	.1255	.1293	.1331	.1368	.1406	.1443	.1480	.1517
0.4	.1554	.1591	.1628	.1664	.1700	.1736	.1772	.1808	.1844	.1879
0.5	.1915	.1950	.1985	.2019	.2054	.2088	.2123	.2157	.2190	.2224
0.6	.2257	.2291	.2324	.2357	.2389	.2422	.2454	.2486	.2517	.2549
0.7	.2580	.2611	.2642	.2673	.2704	.2734	.2764	.2794	.2823	.2852
0.8	.2881	.2910	.2939	.2967	.2995	.3023	.3051	.3078	.3106	.3133
0.9	.3159	.3186	.3212	.3238	.3264	.3289	.3315	.3340	.3365	.3389
1.0	.3413	.3438	.3461	.3485	.3508	.3531	.3554	.3577	.3599	.3621
1.1	.3643	.3665	.3686	.3708	.3729	.3749	.3770	.3790	.3810	.3830
1.2	.3849	.3869	.3888	.3907	.3925	.3944	.3962	.3980	.3997	.4015
1.3	.4032	.4049	.4066	.4082	.4099	.4115	.4131	.4147	.4162	.4177
1.4	.4192	.4207	.4222	.4236	.4251	.4265	.4279	.4292	.4306	.4319
1.5	.4332	.4345	.4357	.4370	.4382	.4394	.4406	.4418	.4429	.4441
1.6	.4452	.4463	.4474	.4484	.4495	.4505	.4515	.4525	.4535	.4545
1.7	.4554	.4564	.4573	.4582	.4591	.4599	.4608	.4616	.4625	.4633
1.8	.4641	.4649	.4656	.4664	.4671	.4678	.4686	.4693	.4699	.4706
1.9	.4713	.4719	.4726	.4732	.4738	.4744	.4750	.4756	.4761	.4767
2.0	.4773	.4778	.4783	.4788	.4793	.4798	.4803	.4808	.4812	.4817
2.1	.4821	.4826	.4830	.4834	.4838	.4842	.4846	.4850	.4854	.4857
2.2	.4861	.4864	.4868	.4871	.4875	.4878	.4881	.4884	.4887	.4890
2.3	.4893	.4896	.4898	.4901	.4904	.4906	.4909	.4911	.4913	.4916
2.4	.4918	.4920	.4922	.4925	.4927	.4929	.4931	.4932	.4934	.4936
2.5	.4938	.4940	.4941	.4943	.4945	.4946	.4948	.4949	.4951	.4952
2.6	.4953	.4955	.4956	.4957	.4959	.4960	.4961	.4962	.4963	.4964
2.7	.4965	.4966	.4967	.4968	.4969	.4970	.4971	.4972	.4973	.4974
2.8	.4974	.4975	.4976	.4977	.4977	.4978	.4979	.4979	.4980	.4981
2.9	.4981	.4982	.4982	.4982	.4984	.4984	.4985	.4985	.4986	.4986
3.0	.4987	.4987	.4987	.4988	.4988	.4989	.4989	.4989	.4990	.4990

Natural logarithms

Table J

N	0	1	2	3	4	5	6	7	8	9
1.0	0.0000	.0099	.0198	.0295	.0392	.0487	.0582	.0676	.0769	.0861
.1	.0953	.1043	.1133	.1222	.1310	.1397	.1484	.1570	.1655	.1739
.2	.1823	.1906	.1988	.2070	.2151	.2231	.2311	.2390	.2468	.2546
.3	.2623	.2700	.2776	.2851	.2926	.3001	.3074	.3148	.3220	.3293
.4	.3364	.3435	.3506	.3576	.3646	.3715	.3784	.3852	.3920	.3987
.5	.4054	.4121	.4187	.4252	.4317	.4382	.4446	.4510	.4574	.4637
.6	.4700	.4762	.4824	.4885	.4947	.5007	.5068	.5128	.5187	.5247
.7	.5306	.5364	.5423	.5481	.5538	.5596	.5653	.5709	.5766	.5822
.8	.5877	.5933	.5988	.6043	.6097	.6151	.6205	.6259	.6312	.6365
.9	.6418	.6471	.6523	.6575	.6626	.6678	.6729	.6780	.6831	.6881
2.0	0.6931	.6981	.7031	.7080	.7129	.7178	.7227	.7275	.7323	.7371
.1	.7419	.7466	.7514	.7561	.7608	.7654	.7701	.7747	.7793	.7839
.2	.7884	.7929	.7975	.8020	.8064	.8109	.8153	.8197	.8241	.8285
.3	.8329	.8372	.8415	.8458	.8501	.8542	.8586	.8628	.8671	.8712
.4	.8754	.8796	.8837	.8878	.8920	.8960	.9001	.9042	.9082	.9122
.5	.9162	.9202	.9242	.9282	.9321	.9360	.9400	.0439	.9477	.9516
.6	.9555	.9593	.9631	.9669	.9707	.9745	.9783	.9820	.9858	.9895
.7	.9932	.9969	.0006[a]	.0043[a]	.0079[a]	.0116[a]	.0152[a]	.0188[a]	.0224[a]	.0260[a]
.8	1.0296	.0331[a]	.0367	.0402	.0438	.0473	.0508	.0543	.0577	.0612
.9	.0647	.0681	.0715	.0750	.0784	.0818	.0851	.0885	.0919	.0952
3.0	1.0986	.1019	.1052	.1085	.1118	.1151	.1184	.1216	.1249	.1281
.1	.1314	.1346	.1378	.1410	.1442	.1474	.1505	.1537	.1568	.1600
.2	.1631	.1662	.1693	.1724	.1755	.1786	.1817	.1847	.1878	.1908
.3	.1939	.1969	.1999	.2029	.2059	.2089	.2119	.2149	.2178	.2208
.4	.2237	.2267	.2296	.2325	.2354	.2383	.2412	.2441	.2470	.2499
.5	.2527	.2556	.2584	.2613	.2641	.2669	.2697	.2725	.2753	.2781
.6	.2809	.2837	.2864	.2892	.2919	.2947	.2974	.3001	.3029	.3056
.7	.3083	.3110	.3137	.3164	.3190	.3217	.3244	.3270	.3297	.3323
.8	.3350	.3376	.3402	.3428	.3454	.3480	.3506	.3532	.3558	.3584
.9	.3609	.3635	.3660	.3686	.3711	.3737	.3762	.3787	.3812	.3837
4.0	1.3862	.3887	.3912	.3937	.3962	.3987	.4011	.4036	.4061	.4085
.1	.4109	.4134	.4158	.4182	.4207	.4231	.4255	.4279	.4303	.4327
.2	.4350	.4374	.4398	.4422	.4445	.4469	.4492	.4516	.4539	.4562
.3	.4586	.4609	.4632	.4655	.4678	.4701	.4724	.4747	.4770	.4793
.4	.4816	.4838	.4861	.4884	.4906	.4929	.4951	.4973	.4996	.5018
.5	.5040	.5063	.5085	.5107	.5129	.5151	.5173	.5195	.5217	.5238
.6	.5260	.5282	.5303	.5325	.5347	.5368	.5390	.5411	.5433	.5454
.7	.5475	.5496	.5518	.5539	.5560	.5581	.5602	.5623	.5644	.5665
.8	.5686	.5707	.5727	.5748	.5769	.5789	.5810	.5830	.5851	.5871
.9	.5892	.5912	.5933	.5953	.5973	.5993	.6014	.6034	.6054	.6074

a. Add 1.0 to indicated figure.

Answers to quickie questions

Introduction

1. The process by which the company seeks out alternative courses of action, alternative projects, etc.

2. The assumed objective of financial decision making is maximization of shareholder wealth. Whilst recognizing that this is a simplification of the real world, it is reasonable to accept that this should be the main objective, other things being equal.

3. It is a *reporting* concept, not a decision-making concept. Its use is to report on the success or failure of decisions taken. It has only a secondary role in the decision-making process itself. Accounting profit is also based on historic cost whereas financial management is concerned with value. The two things are very different. Finally, profit as reported is subject to the judgement of the accountant and cannot be regarded as entirely reliable.

4. On the basis of the expected flow of dividends they will generate in the future.

Chapter 1

1. The problem is one of control. How does the principal control the agent to ensure that the agent acts in the principal's best interests?

2. Fiduciary responsibilities; independent external audit; Stock Exchange Yellow Book listing rules; Stock Exchange's 'model code' for directors' share dealings; Companies Act regulations on directors' transaction and Cadbury Committee 'code of best practice'.

3. Reward managerial ability, not luck; rewards should have a significant impact on managerial remuneration; reward system should work two ways; concept of risk should be taken into account; the shareholder's time horizon should be taken into account; scheme should be simple, inexpensive and difficult to manipulate.

Chapter 2

1. (a) Where are we now?
   (b) Where do we want to be?
   (c) How are we going to get there?

2. SWOT analysis helps to answer the question: where are we now? SWOT stands for: S = strengths; W = weaknesses; O = opportunities and T = threats.

3. The 'Boston Box' is a form of matrix analysis used to try to identify answers to the second question: where does the firm want to go in the future?

4. The idea of 'value drivers' arises out of Porter's work. Value drivers are: buyer power, supplier power, entry opportunities, substitute possibilities and competitor rivalry.

5. This again arises out of Porter's ideas on competitive strategy. There are four alternative strategic approaches that companies can follow:

   (a) broad product differentiation;
   (b) narrow product differentiation;
   (c) broad-based cost leadership;
   (d) narrow-based cost leadership.

6. In order to achieve the objective of maximizing shareholder wealth, management need to devise a strategy as to how this objective is to be achieved. Thus a strategy – based on an understanding of the business 'value drivers' – is a vital first stage in the achievement of the company's objective.

7. The responsibilities of the chief accountant would include:

   (a) preparation of internal and external financial reports;
   (b) responsibility for all aspects of the company's management information system;
   (c) all budgetary control procedures;
   (d) pricing policies;
   (e) capital investment appraisal and working capital management.

8. See Fig. 2.4 in the text.

9. It allows highly *illiquid* securities (e.g. shares) that are issued by companies to be held as highly *liquid* investments by investors, as it provides a market-place where such investments can be easily bought and sold.

10. Investors are generally assumed to be risk-averse. The idea of an individual being anything other than risk-averse is somewhat illogical and it is difficult to imagine why anybody would actively seek risk without reward. This dislike of risk does not mean that investors will not take on risky investments, but that they have to be rewarded for doing so. The reward is given in terms of a higher expected return on the investment: the higher the risk, the higher must be its expected return.

Chapter 3

1. Stage one: The best of the alternative projects has the shortest pay-back.
   Stage two: Accept the best project as long as its payback period satisfies the decision criterion.

2. Working capital is excluded from the analysis. Net cash flow:

0	−11 000	
1	+ 4000	Payback = 2.75 years
2	+ 4000	
3	+ 4000	
4	+ 3000	
5	+ 3000	

3. (a) Quick and simple to calculate.
   (b) Thought to automatically select less-risky projects in mutually exclusive decision situations.
   (c) Saves management the trouble of having to estimate project cash flows beyond the maximum payback time-period.
   (d) Convenient method to use in capital rationing.

4. The payback criterion is reduced until total capital expenditure equates with the amount of finance available.

5. (a) Management's experience of successful projects within the firm.
   (b) Industry practice.
   (c) Reflects the limit of management's forecasting skills.

   However, none of these can be seen as being really objective.

6. The payback decision rule, adjusted to take account of the time value of money.

7. Ignores cash flows outside the payback time period. (The fact that 'normal' payback ignores the time value of money is equally important but this criticism can, of course, be easily overcome through the use of discounted payback.)

8. Money has a time value because it can earn a rate of interest/a rate of return. This has nothing to do with inflation although that might have an effect on the levels of return expected.

9. The question does not specify which ARR/ROCE to calculate, so *both* are given:

Annual depreciation: $(\pounds 11\ 000 - \pounds 1000) \div 5 = \pounds 2000$.

Profit:				
£4000	—	£2000	=	£2000 Yr 1
4000	—	2000	=	2000 Yr 2
4000	—	2000	=	2000 Yr 3
3000	—	2000	=	1000 Yr 4
2000	—	2000	=	0 Yr 5
Total profit			=	£7000 ÷ 5 = £1400
			=	Av. ann. profit

Average capital employed:

$$\frac{\pounds 11\ 000 - \pounds 1000}{2} + \pounds 1000 + \pounds 4000 = \pounds 10\ 000$$

Return on initial capital employed $= \pounds 1400 \div \pounds 15\ 000 = 9\frac{1}{3}\%$
Return on average capital employed $= \pounds 1400 \div \pounds 10\ 000 = 14\%$

10. (a) Evaluates via a percentage rate of return.
    (b) Evaluates on the basis of profitability.
    (c) Appears logical to evaluate projects on the same basis as management have their own performance evaluated by shareholders.

11. (a) Ignores the time value of money.
    (b) Evaluates on the basis of profit, not cash, flow.

Chapter 4

1. This is an example of the economic concept of diminishing marginal utility. Each additional £1 of t_0 consumption forgone, through investment, is likely to be of increasing value in terms of consumption benefits forgone. Each additional £1 of future consumption gained is likely to be of decreasing value. Hence, the time value of money rises.

2. The complete range of maximum consumption combinations that the firm owner can obtain at t_0 and t_1.

3. The marginal return on the investment opportunity at any particular point.

4. A curve of constant utility. All combinations of consumption at t_0 and t_1 that lie along a single indifference curve would provide the same level of utility or satisfaction.

5. It invests until the return on the marginal investment equates with the owner's marginal time value of money.

6. Lending at t_0 would reduce the amount of money available for consumption at t_0 and increase the amount available at t_1, hence the move would be *up* the financial investment line.

7. The firm should continue to invest in projects as long as the marginal rate of return is not less than the market rate of interest. This rule is, of course, obvious. There would be little point in investing money in a project which gave a lower return than what could be obtained by lending the money on the capital market.

The cash (dividend) distribution to shareholders in t_0 and t_1 that arises out of the firm's investment decision can then be redistributed by shareholders, using the capital markets, to suit their own set of indifference curves.

8. A risky investment is one where the outcome is uncertain.

9. Ensure that any project earns at least the capital market rate of return that is available for investments of equivalent risk to the project.

10. (a) Single time horizon.
    (b) Infinitely divisible projects.
    (c) All independent projects.
    (d) Rational investors.

11. Investors dislike risk: they are said to be risk-averse. Hence they require a reward for taking on a risk, which is the expectation (but, of course, not the certainty) of a higher return.

12. In these circumstances, the market rate of return offers you greater compensation than you require to forgo current consumption. Therefore you would want to lend money.

Chapter 5

1.
0	-1000	×	1	=	$-$	1000
1	$+ \; 500$	×	0.8772	=	$+$	438.60
2	$+ \; 600$	×	0.7695	=	$+$	461.70
3	$+ \; 400$	×	0.6750	=	$+$	270
					$+$	170.30 NPV

2. There are several interpretations:

   (a) It produces a return > 10%.
   (b) It produces £120 more (in t_0 terms) than a £1000 capital market investment of similar risk.
   (c) The project would produce a sufficient cash flow to repay its outlay, pay its financing charges *and* provide an additional £120 in t_0 terms.
   (d) If accepted, shareholder wealth would increase by £120.

3. At 4% discount rate: NPV = +147.48
   At 20% discount rate: NPV = -9.28

$$\text{Therefore IRR} = 4\% + \left[\frac{147.48}{147.48 - (-9.28)} \times (20\% - 4\%) \right]$$

$$= 19.05\% \text{ approx.}$$

With any problem like this it is a good idea to use a computer to arrive at an answer. In this case the solution, using the IRR function of a spreadsheet is 18.825%.

4.

Year	Cash flow		Discount factor		
0	−500	×	1	=	−500
1	+200	×	0.9091	=	+181.82
2	+300	×	0.8264	=	+247.92
3	+200	×	0.7513	=	+150.26

$500 - 181.82 - 247.92 = 70.26 \div 150.26 = 0.47$

$\therefore$ payback is 2.47 years approx.

5. The return available elsewhere on the capital market on a similar risk investment.

6. For the same project they should be identical. In both cases they are the opportunity cost return referred to in the answer above to question five.

7. $+350\,A_{4-0.10} = 350 \times 3.1699 = +1109.47$.

8. (a) Annuity due.
   (b) Immediate annuity.
   (c) Deferred annuity.

9. Given the PV of a perpetuity is: $\dfrac{\text{Annual amount}}{\text{Discount rate}}$, then:

$$\text{IRR} = \frac{£100}{£1000} = 0.10 \text{ or } 10\%$$

$$\text{because: } -£1000 + \frac{£100}{0.10} = 0 \text{ NPV}$$

10. $-1000 + 200\,A_{2-0.16} + 500\,A_{3-0.16}\,(1 + 0.16)^{-2} = \text{NPV}$
    $-1000 + (200 \times 1.6052) + (500 \times 2.2459 \times 0.7432) = +£155.62$

Chapter 6

1. The NPV rule is to accept whichever project has the largest positive NPV. Differences in magnitude, duration and risk can be ignored. Hence project A should be accepted.

2. The assumptions made are:

   (a) There is a perfect capital market so that the firm can finance the large project just as easily as it can finance the small project.
   (b) The projects represent independent decisions in that they are not part of a continuous replacement chain.
   (c) The discount rates used do correctly reflect the risk of each project.

3. NPV and IRR both make assumptions about the rate of return at which project-generated cash flows are reinvested. NPV assumes that the rate is the market discount rate, while IRR assumes that it is equal to the IRP of the project generating those cash flows. Given a perfect capital market, the NPV method is making the correct assumption.

4. Non-conventional cash flows, where there is more than one change in sign. The problem can be avoided by using the 'extended yield technique' or the 'modified IRR'.

5. Using the extended yield technique:

$$\text{Year 3: } -20(1 + 0.10)^{-3} = -15.02 \text{ at Year 0}$$

Therefore the revised cash flow is:
$$\begin{array}{rr} 0 & -115.02 \\ 1 & +60 \\ 2 & +80 \end{array}$$

At a 4% discount rate: +16.64 NPV
At a 20% discount rate: −9.46 NPV

$$\therefore \text{IRR} = 4\% + \left[\frac{16.64}{16.64 - (-9.46)} \times (20\% - 4\%) \right] = 14.2\%.$$

6.

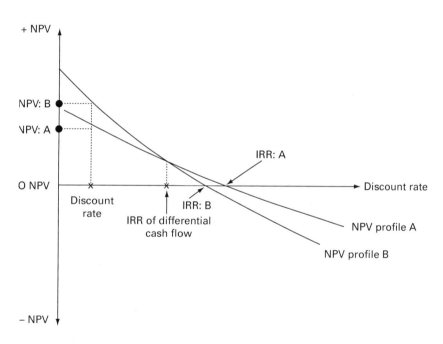

7. If IRR diff. c/f > hurdle rate: accept project smallest IRR.
   If IRR diff. c/f < hurdle rate: accept project largest IRR.

8.
$$\begin{array}{lll} & & (£) \\ 1 & +40(1.10)^2 & = & +60.5 \\ 2 & +80(1.10)^1 & = & +88 \\ 3 & -30 & = & -30 \\ \end{array}$$
Year 3 Terminal value   +118.50

	Year	(£)
Modified cash flow of the project:	0	− 80
	3	+118.50

Estimating the IRR using linear interpolation:

NPV at 5% = +22.36

NPV at 20% = −11.42

$$\text{IRR} = 5\% + \left[\frac{22.36}{22.36 - (-11.42)} \times (20\% - 5\%) \right] = 14.9\%.$$

Chapter 7

1. $\dfrac{(1.13)}{(1.04)} - 1 = 0.086$ or 8.6%

2. Either: Project money cash flows discounted at the market discount rate to NPV.

   or: Project money cash flows discounted at the general rate of inflation and then at the real discount rate to NPV.

3. The money cash flow, deflated (discounted) by the general rate of inflation.

4. $\dfrac{1.155}{1.05} - 1 = 0.10 = $ real discount rate

   (a) £10 000 $(1.05)^2 = $ £11 025
   (b) £10 000
   (a) £11 025 $(1.155)^{-2} = $ £11 025 $(1.10)^{-2}$ $(1.05)^{-2} = $ £8263.73
   (b) £10 000 $(1.155)^{-2} = $ £10 000 $(1.10)^{-2}$ $(1.05)^{-2} = $ £7495.45

5.

		WDA					Tax relief	Timing
500	×	0.25	=	+125	×	0.35	= +43.75	Year 2
$\dfrac{125}{375}$	×	0.25	=	+ 93.75	×	0.35	= +32.81	Year 3
$\dfrac{93.75}{281.25}$	−	0	=	+281.25	×	0.35	= +98.44	Year 4

6. Historic cost: £60 000 – irrelevant, sunk cost.
   Written-down book value: £10 000 – irrelevant non-economic figure.
   Scrap now: £3000
   Rent and then scrap: £2500 + £800 = £3300.

   Therefore, if the machine is used to undertake the project, the best opportunity forgone is the 'rent and then scrap' alternative. So this is the opportunity cost of using the machine on the project: −£3300.

7. Discount the after-tax cash flows by the after-tax discount rate.

8. They are non-incremental.

9. Market price of factory space: £2 per m^2 (external opportunity cost)
   Contribution £15 per m^2 (internal opportunity cost)
   Cost to project: $150 \times (£15 + £2) = $ £2550.

Chapter 8

1. Hard and soft capital rationing.

2. The firm cannot necessarily accept a project just because it has a positive NPV, nor can it necessarily reject a project just because it has a negative NPV. Hence the standard NPV decision rule breaks down. In theory capital rationing should not exist because we assume that cash will be available for investments at an appropriate rate of return. In another sense it causes no problem for NPV because we could assume that the appropriate discount rate is the return on the alternative investments (i.e. opportunity cost of capital).

3. The benefit–cost ratios are:

$$
\begin{aligned}
&\text{A: } +60 \div 100 = +0.60 \quad (1)\\
&\text{B: } +90 \div 200 = +0.45 \quad (3)\\
&\text{C: } +20 \div 40 = +0.50 \quad (2)\\
&\text{D: } -10 \div 100 = -0.10 \quad (-)
\end{aligned}
$$

200	available	
−100	invest in A, producing	: + 60 NPV
100		
− 40	invest in C, producing	: + 20 NPV
60		
− 60	invest in 30% B, producing	: + 27 NPV
−		+107 Total NPV

4. The benefit–cost ratios are:

$$
\begin{aligned}
&\text{A: } +60 \div 50 = +1.20 \quad (1)\\
&\text{B: } +90 \div 200 = +0.45 \quad (2)\\
&\text{C: } +20 \div 150 = +0.133 \quad (3)\\
&\text{D: } -10 \div - = -
\end{aligned}
$$

240	available	
−50	invest in A, producing	: + 60 NPV
190		
−190	invest in 95% of B, producing:	+ 85.5 NPV
0		+145.5 Total NPV

As D has a *cost–benefit* ratio of: $-10 \div 20 = -0.50$
and B, the marginal project, has a benefit–cost ratio of 0.45, further investment is not worthwhile.

5. Benefit–cost ratios:

$$
\begin{aligned}
&\text{A: } 40 \div 100 = 0.40 \quad (1)\\
&\text{*B: } 30 \div 100 = 0.30 \quad (2)\\
&\text{*C: } 50 \div 200 = 0.25 \quad (3)\\
&\text{D: } 10 \div 100 = 0.10 \quad (4)\\
&\text{E: } 4 \div 50 = 0.08 \quad (5)
\end{aligned}
$$

$$\begin{array}{ll} 300 & \text{available} \\ \underline{-100} & \text{invest in A, producing} \\ 200 & \\ \underline{-100} & \text{invest in B, producing} \\ 100 & \\ \underline{-100} & \text{invest in D, producing} \\ \underline{0} & \end{array} \qquad \begin{array}{l} : \ +40 \text{ NPV} \\ \\ : \ +30 \text{ NPV} \\ \\ : \ +10 \text{ NPV} \\ \overline{+80} \text{ Total NPV} \end{array}$$

alternatively:

$$\begin{array}{ll} 300 & \text{available} \\ \underline{-100} & \text{invest in A, producing} \\ 200 & \\ \underline{-200} & \text{invest in C, producing} \\ \underline{0} & \end{array} \qquad \begin{array}{l} : \ +40 \text{ NPV} \\ \\ : \ +50 \text{ NPV} \\ \overline{+90} \text{ Total NPV} \end{array}$$

Therefore, the best alternative is to undertake projects A and C.

6. $\begin{aligned} 40a \ - \ 20b \ + \ 50c & \qquad \text{Max.} \\ 100a \ + \ 150b \ + \ 200c & \leqslant \ 190 \\ 200a \ + \ 120c & \leqslant \ 110 \ + \ 70b \\ 30c & \leqslant \ 50a \ + \ 70b \\ a, b, c & \leqslant \ 1 \\ a, b, c & \geqslant \ 0 \end{aligned}$

7. *Dual values + 10% discount factor = Total opportunity cost of cash*

1.86	+	1	=	2.86	t_0
0.73	+	0.9091	=	1.6391	t_1
0.64	+	0.8264	=	1.4664	t_2
1.21	+	0.7513	=	1.9613	t_3

    Gain from an extra £1 at t_1:

    $$£1 \times 1.6391 = £1.6391$$

    Loss from repayment of £1, plus interest (i) at t_2

    $$£(1 + i) \times 1.4664 = £1.4664 + 1.4664i$$

    The maximum interest rate would occur at the point where the gain equals the loss:

    $$\begin{aligned} 1.6391 &= 1.4664 + 1.4664i \\ 1.6391 - 1.4664 &= 1.4664i \\ \frac{1.6391 - 1.4664}{1.4664} &= i = 0.118 \text{ or } 11.8\% \text{ max.} \end{aligned}$$

8. NPV:

    $$\begin{array}{rcl} -100 \ \times \ 1 & = & -100 \\ + \ 40 \ \times \ 0.9091 & = & + \ 36.36 \\ + \ 90 \ \times \ 0.8264 & = & + \ 74.38 \\ & & \overline{+ \ 10.74} \text{ NPV} \end{array}$$

    Internal opportunity cost:

$$
\begin{array}{rclcr}
-100 & \times & 1.86 & = & -186 \\
+ 40 & \times & 0.73 & = & + 29.2 \\
+ 90 & \times & 0.64 & = & + 57.6 \\
\hline
& & & & -99.2 \\
\end{array}
$$

Total opportunity cost:

+10.74	NPV
−99.20	Internal opportunity cost
−88.46	Net total opportunity cost

As this net figure is negative, the additional project will not be a worthwhile investment, reject.

Chapter 9

1   It is likely that investors will be risk averse simply because if I have a particular amount of wealth and have an evens chance to gain or lose a sum of money, the amount I stand to lose will be relatively more than the amount I stand to gain. So, for example, I have £1000 and an even chance of winning or losing £100. We measure from the bottom up, the difference between £900 and £1000 is 11% but the difference between £1000 and £1100 is only 10%. So, what I stand to lose is worth more to me than what I might gain *in relative terms.*

2.   Diversification reduces risk because some of the risks associated with investing in general and investing in companies in particular are peculiar to the individual investment. Say that a court finds that a major software company is abusing its market power. This will result in the share price of that company going down but it is unlikely to result in the fall in the share price of other companies. Indeed it might well result in other share prices going up. If investment is spread, it effectively reduces exposure to this company specific (unsystematic or unique) risk.

3.   Systematic (market) risk is related to the economy as a whole but unsystematic (unique) risk is related to a particular company. Unsystematic risk can be diversified away but all portfolios will be exposed to systematic risk. There is no reward for taking on unsystematic risk but the greater the exposure to systematic risk, the greater will be the expected level of return.

4.   There are three things that contribute to the general level of economic activity in the economy and other macro-economic factors.

   1. The sensitivity of the company's revenues to the general level of economic activity in the economy and other macro-economic factors.
   2. The proportion of fixed to variable costs (i.e. the degree of cost sensitivity).
   3. The level of financial gearing or leverage (i.e. the amount of interest bearing debt compared to shareholder equity).

The first of these is a function of the company's type of business but a management can have some influence over the second and third factors.

5. $E(r_x) = r_F + [E(r_M) - r_F] b_x$

6. Expected return $= 6\% + (13\% - 6\%) \times 1.3 = 15.1\%$

7. WACC $= (.8 \times 20\%) + (.2 \times 8\% \times (100\% - 25\%)) = 17.2\%$

8. The use of WACC is really only appropriate where the project in question is of exactly the same risk class as the average project already undertaken by the company. Whilst we could argue that beta (CAPM) is only appropriate where the risk class has been identified, the process is more transparent and also more practical.

Chapter 10

1. Success: $- 1000 + 500 A_{3 - 0.10} = + 243$ NPV
    Failure: $- 1000 + 350 A_{3 - 0.10} = -130$ NPV

State	Prob.		NPV		
I	0.45	$\times$	+243	=	+109
II	0.55	$\times$	-130	=	-72
					+ 37 ENPV

2. Survey indicates

	Action	Prob.		Outcome		
State I	Accept	0.45	$\times$	+243 NPV	=	+109
State II	Reject	0.55	$\times$	0 NPV	=	0
						+109 ENPV

ENPV with survey	:	+109
ENPV without survey	:	+37
Max. worth of survey	:	+72

3. Survey indicates

	Probability			State
State I correctly	0.45×0.75	=	0.3375	A
State I incorrectly	0.45×0.25	=	0.1125	B
State II correctly	0.55×0.75	=	0.4125	C
State II incorrectly	0.55×0.25	=	0.1375	D

State	Action	Prob.		Outcome		
A	Accept	0.3375	$\times$	+ 243 NPV	=	+82
B	Accept	0.1125	$\times$	- 72 NPV	=	- 8
C	Reject	0.4125	$\times$	0 NPV	=	0
D	Reject	0.1375	$\times$	-243 NPV	=	-33
				ENPV		+41

ENPV with survey	:	+41
ENPV without survey	:	+37
Max. worth of survey	:	+ 4

4.

State	Prob.		NPV		
I	0.3	×	+ 100	=	+ 30
II	0.5	×	+ 50	=	+ 25
III	0.2	×	− 300	=	− 60
			ENPV		− 5

Therefore, without the survey we would *not* accept the project and so incur a zero NPV.

Survey indicates	Action	Prob.		Outcome		
I	Accept	0.3	×	+100	=	+30
II	Accept	0.5	×	+ 50	=	+25
III	Reject	0.2	×	0	=	0
				ENPV		+55

ENPV with survey	:	+55
ENPV without survey	:	0
Max. worth of survey	:	+55

5. If the machine is bought and, at the end of Yr 1, the decision is taken *not* to abandon the project, then the outcome will be:

State	Yr 1	Yr 2	NPV	Decision
I	−60	+100	+ 23.43	Don't abandon
II	−60	+ 60	− 6.81	Abandon
III	−60	+ 40	−21.93	Abandon

The investment decision is therefore:

State	Yr 0	Yr 1	Yr 2	NPV		Prob.	
I	− 140	+100	+100	+22.57	×	0.70	= + 15.80
II	− 140	+ 60 ⎫ + 60 ⎭		−35.65	×	0.10	= −3.56
III	− 140	+ 40 ⎫ + 60 ⎭		−53.04	×	0.20	= −10.61
				ENPV			+ 1.63

The complete decision is that the company should purchase the machine but, if either states II or III occur, then the machine should be sold off at the end of the first year.

6. $-1000 + 280\, A_{5-0.10} = +61.42$ NPV

Life = x   At 5 year life: +61.42 NPV
At 4 year life:
$-1,000 + 280\, A_{4-0.10} = -112.40$ NPV

Using linear interpolation:

$$x = 4 + \left[\frac{112.40}{61.42 + 112.40} \times (5 - 4) \right] = 4.65 \text{ yrs.}$$

Thus the life of the project can be reduced by up to 0.35 of a year (approx $4\frac{1}{4}$ months) before the original decision advice is incorrect. This represents a maximum change of $0.35 \div 5 = 7\%$.

Net cash flow = *x*

$$-1000 + x\,A_{5-0.10} = 0\ NPV$$

$$x = 1000 \div A_{5-0.10} = 264$$

Thus the annual net cash flow can fall by up to 16 per year, or $16 \div 280 = 5.7\%$ before the original decision advice is incorrect.

Chapter 11

1. (a) Project's dollar cash flows are discounted by dollar discount rate to give a dollar NPV which is then converted at spot to a sterling NPV; or
   (b) Project's dollar cash flows are converted into sterling cash flows and then discounted at the sterling discount rate to give a sterling NPV.

2. Because they may well affect the cash flow available to be remitted back to the parent.

3. Property fixed assets and working capital, finance in the overseas currency. Non-property fixed assets, finance via the export of sterling.

4. (a) Dividends;
   (b) interest;
   (c) management charges;
   (d) royalty payments;
   (e) transfer prices.

5. The risk that the host government might adversely change the 'rules of the game' after the company have undertaken the investment.

6. Economic risk describes the risk that a company is exposed to from unexpected FX rate movements and their resulting impact on the sterling worth of a foreign project's cash flows.

Index